07/21

POLITICS BY
OTHER MEANS

POLITICS BY
OTHER MEANS

*Higher Education
and Group Thinking*

DAVID BROMWICH

Yale University Press
New Haven and London

Published with assistance from the foundation established in memory of Amasa Stone Mather, of the Class of 1907, Yale College.

Designed by Jill Breitbarth and set in Palatino type by DEKR Corporation, Woburn, Massachusetts.
Printed in the United States of America by Vail-Ballou Press, Binghamton, New York.

Library of Congress Cataloging-in-Publication Data

Bromwich, David, 1951–
    Politics by other means : higher education and group thinking / David Bromwich.
        p.   cm.
    Includes bibliographical references (p.   ) and index.
    ISBN 0–300–05702–4 (alk. paper)
    1. Politics and education—United States.   2. Education, Higher—United States—Philosophy.   3. United States—Intellectual life—20th century.   I. Title.
LC89.B745   1992
378′.01′0973—dc20   92-7914
                                CIP

A catalogue record for this book is available from the British Library.

The paper in this book meets the guidelines for permanence and durability of the Committee on Production Guidelines for Book Longevity of the Council on Library Resources.

10 9 8 7 6 5 4 3 2 1

To Peter Connolly

CONTENTS

This book has a critical aim which requires a measure of historical analysis. It defends a liberal idea of tradition. At the same time, it tells of the collision of ideologies in higher education, starting in the Reagan years. The two subjects look distinct, and each is sufficiently intricate. They are brought together in an account of the current dispute about innovations in the teaching of the arts and letters. "War," wrote Clausewitz, "is the continuation of politics by other means"; and the thought seemed right for a book that asks how far the dispute in education is itself an extension of politics by other means. I believe there is such a thing as politics by ordinary means: a field of action with virtues of its own, largely distinct from those of education. Yet politics and education turn out to be identical if one accepts the ethic of group thinking, which looks on all learning as a form of social adjustment. This remains the common premise today, whether one has in view groups as large as "the West" or groups on any smaller scale. The results are always the same. Conceits and dogmas of conformity, some of them cruel, all of them timid, cling to the group when they cannot survive in a less settled company. Thoughts, in turn, come into a mind alone, which could never pass through the sorting medium of the group.

Politics is not education; the means make a difference to the end. And for the same reason, group thinking is not thinking. The conduct of both sides in the present controversy, as I see it, has everything to do with a disparity between the self-contained (mostly left-wing) culture of the academy and the static (and right-wing) political culture that dominates America today. I write as an admirer of neither culture. On the theory of tradition that I defend, useful reform implies a sense of continuity between past and present. Any new practice appealing enough to gain wide acceptance, and to be incorporated in a familiar way of life, is likely to have some points in common with older habits of thought and feeling. This holds true in politics, and no less in education. So far, it may sound like a traditional view. It is liberal as well because it tries to account for the reasons one can give in advocating a *change*.

A reader alert to this theoretical concern will notice its appearance in chapter 4. For the rest, the book has a polemical motive which I make no effort to conceal. In fall 1986 I published in *Dissent* an attack on the notion of a "core tradition" of moral and political thought, then being advanced by William J. Bennett and George F. Will. As the first battle of the pamphlet wars that show no sign of ending, the exchange can claim a certain chronological interest. Both men proposed to remedy the decay of American society by a stiffer curriculum of great books in high school and in college. They might be correct, I said, about the condition of our society and about the best books to read; but in supposing that a social climate of all-out modernization could be reversed by an anti-modern syllabus, they committed a double fallacy. They assumed that social and intellectual life were wholly separate spheres. And they assumed that the spheres could nevertheless be joined for special purposes, with a reactionary reform of thought assisting a reactionary reform of society. This vitamin-injection theory of culture and society grows out of a shallow understanding of tradition.

In fall 1989, I published in the same journal an attack on the culture of the academic left. The elite of "theory"—in departments of literature, politics, the law schools, and elsewhere—proposed a rejection of traditional learning on principle. Inherited ways of thought and feeling are in this view a mask for power and domination. To live without illusions, to be capable of subverting any cultural practice, one needs to be fortified by nothing but the right weapons of analysis. Here, it seemed to me, were the fallacies of Bennett and Will, but now with a different end in view. The raw materials of social life are again taken to be infinitely remediable by a therapy of the mind. But whereas, in the conservative argument, social life is repaired by the discarded virtues of old thought, in the radical argument it is repaired by the still-to-be-invented virtues of new thought. It does not occur to either party in this debate that the function of criticism might be to start with virtues that are at once old and available.

Public opinion has been invited to cast its lot with one or the other of these simplifying creeds. For in the academy, the radical position goes almost undisputed, even if it is hardly identified with a majority. Outside the academy only the conservative position makes a pretense of argument. I have been told often by members of both camps that my reactions are too negative. Calm reflection has made them more so. Both cultures are deeply sick, and it would be a good thing to rid ourselves of both. When I wrote the articles, this stand seemed to me eccentric, or at least untested. I have since come to feel that the articles represented a point of view many people hold in an inchoate way and are waiting to see developed. The result is that chapters 2 and 3 (on the antiquarian-reactionary and the academic-radical ideas of tradition) and chapter 4 (my attempt at a corrective) have been augmented by two others, written last, which complete the argument by placing it in context. Chapter 1 surveys some typical recent episodes in the clash of the rival cultures. Chapter 5 offers a history and an analysis of the crisis of literary study: a pragmatic test of the general theme of continuity and innovation.

My conclusions will seem less romantic than the speculation (ventured by Roger Kimball in *Tenured Radicals*) that an organized movement of left-wing professors, rising slowly in the ranks of our institutions, has now achieved a power with which it hopes to defraud the American people of their cultural inheritance. Nor can I claim the sweep of the theory (sketched by Allan Bloom in *The Closing of the American Mind*) that a combination of scientific empiricism, philosophical relativism, and a popular morality of the will, have cast a shadow of unbelief over the common faith in established power. Many radicals, of course, share with Kimball the belief that they have come a long way on the slow march through institutions; as they share with Bloom the belief that a tacit connection with power will support a class of powerless theorists, who alone are wise and good. If my account looks narrow beside these grand explanations from the right, I hope it is not so contemptuous of public scrutiny as most replies from the left. I would claim a single fresh emphasis for the perspective of this book. It has grown out of an experience of teaching, and it may recall, for others, certain truths familiar from teaching and from learning.

The conservative pamphleteers start from a premise that only the ignorant or forgetful would deny. With the American academy, as with American society in general, the sixties mark a great divide. It was then that the universities began to think of themselves as separate communities. The truth is that since then they have never stopped. And yet, once the upheavals of 1964–71 had settled, the American public took little note of goings-on in the academy. There should be nothing surprising in this: the broad suffrage of American opinion remains as indifferent as ever to intellectual matters. Meanwhile, through the late seventies and the eighties, the academy itself showed a curious indifference to the likely effect of changes then agitating in disciplines like literature and history. By the mid-eighties, the vanguard of scholars were aware that they had traveled far from an answerable concern with merit, judgment, and the knowledge of the past, as these things are generally understood. But they were busy evolving a self-image that drew the limits of their answerability from within. In the field of literary study, the words *sense*, *judgment*, *accuracy*, *taste*, and *common* (common *anything*), began to be subject to a delicate prohibition. This followed from the usual protective instinct of an ascetic priesthood. What was unusual in this case was the rapidity with which the priests consolidated their hold. In achieving control of journals, departments, and professional organizations, a new consensus seemed to ignite suddenly in the years 1985–90, from the modest tinderpile of the late seventies. By 1990, it was possible for a senior editor of an established journal of literary history to admonish a young scholar who had submitted an article for publication: "You stick too close to the text."

Ironic insiders say that all this happened because nobody was minding the shop. It would be just as fair to say that nobody cared much about the goods that were sold. Until recently, we had in America a class of intellectual journalists who showed an unintimidated interest in works of scholarship. That class has vanished—a fact so perplexing that, though the membership of the class was widely recognized twenty years ago, many scholars now want to deny that such persons *could* have existed. The decline of a public intellectual style meant the loss of a practical wisdom that could challenge academic pieties without an edge of philistinism. In our time, the reliable motive for public criticism has come to be the scandal: the scandal about a politician's mistress, the scandal of senators bribed by bankers, the scandal of the collaborationist professor, the scandal about "political correctness." This, then, is how a story brewing for a decade came to be known in less than a year. The exchange of views has now manifestly become a contest for power. The high-minded priests have decided that they meant to be politicians all along. The grubbing politicians have determined that they never wanted to give up being priests. It is a contest for the control of intellectual life between two groups that have fallen equally out of the practice of giving intellectual value to the objects they praise or blame.

Both groups are addicted to the word *culture*, yet they use it at cross-purposes. The politicians mean by culture an affair of museums and monuments (the older and more hackneyed the better). The priests mean by culture an affair of genetics and environment (the newer and more opaque the better). The uniformity of the contrast may help to establish how far my view is from being a middle way between these two. The adepts of monumental culture are right-wing in politics and conservative in education. The adepts of environmental culture are left-wing in politics and communitarian in education. Both groups on religious grounds show an enormous deference toward institutions: they believe in the power of institutions to shape the thoughts of an individual mind; they think this power is irresistible, and the great question therefore becomes how to give it the correct bias. By contrast, I defend a traditional idea of liberal education, but my politics are democratic, my deeper beliefs are anti-institutional, and I try to rouse the sentiment of fellow believers that these after all are a possible combination.

Because I speak here of a right-wing culture outside the universities, and a left-wing culture inside, it is fair to announce a qualification that extends throughout the book. The entities are real, and they are useful to name. But in speaking of them thus, I have in mind only the most visible parties to emerge in a debate that is still going on. American academic culture is complex and heterogeneous, and vastly more than its left wing. American political culture is still more complex and heterogeneous, and vastly more than its right wing. The story I tell with a few selected characters is far from the whole story. Nor does it aim to free itself from a moral that may hold interest in wider circles than these. The book is a defense of tradition as a social and a personal fact—but personal first and last and most. In education, the knowledge of a tradition matters because it can be part of self-knowledge. Indeed, I have written partly to suggest the worth to liberalism of not giving up the ideals associated with the individual mind. These may be rationalizations of many social practices that one deplores, but they are also a constitutive good of most reforms that one might praise.

The reader is well warned concerning my prejudices, for, in the course of the book, they oblige me to use in a pejorative sense certain words that need not be pejorative. *Culture* is one of these. A great confusion now prevails between culture as social identity and culture as a tacit knowledge acquired by choice and affinity. If I could use the word and be sure that people would understand the second meaning, it would appear in the following chapters frequently and without blame. At present, however, most people have in view the first meaning of culture; they use the word in the hope of borrowing a reflected prestige from the second. I want to starve them of this credit. I therefore write against the idea of culture and speak of it, in its likely current meaning, as an institutional lie.

Another word liable to the same kind of distortion is *community*. As it has usually been understood, a community is a group of people bound by practices whose general utility everyone, some-how, recognizes, but whose justification few could easily explain. A community shares a way of life because it has to. Eric Hobsbawm says with beautiful accuracy of the German word *Heimat* (homeland) that we love it because "it doesn't need us. It goes on quite well without us." But in the past few decades, a meaning of community has developed which claims for it the intimate and binding power of the German *Heim* (home): we love it because it needs us; and it wants all of us. A community on this model is bound not by practices but by the resolve to attitudinize together as often as possible. Thus the reasons for rejecting community are the same as the reasons for rejecting culture.

Finally, a similar stricture applies, with greater force, in the treatment here of what it means to be professional, or to exhibit the virtue of *professionalism*. Both words used to be a compliment—earned by someone who gracefully performed a task that required a particular skill. In this sense, professionalism is connected with ideas of honor and not merely with commercial success or parochial conformity. But in the current usage of the academy (a usage that is growing elsewhere, too), a professional is someone who is proud of belonging to an opinion-community, and professionalism is a deliberate refinement of the attitudes which make for mutual sub-jection within that community. Common speech may still recognize a difference between attitudes and competence: the very idea of a qualified judge is founded on some such distinction. But the dif-ference has lost much of its credit in the academy and the words *professional* and *professionalism* are code for the ineffable something that has been gained in return.

The professional communitarian of culture will reply that in stint-ing all praise of culture, community, and profession in their inno-vative senses, I must lean on archaic sources of authority, on "dil-ettantish amateurism," for example, or "old-fashioned belles-lettrism." These are not in fact plausible names for a position that anyone can defend today; and I do not take them to be salvageable as useful criteria even in literary study. But if one looks at the key words—*old, belle, lettres, dilettante, amateur*—in their literal senses, I think that something is revealed by the choice of these as dismissive epithets. The professionalists are trying to scour our minds of every ameliorative idea of age, beauty, elegance, delight, and love. I cannot agree to despise these things, however shop-worn they appear when translated into French and then translated back into English clichés to supply the impressible material for a slating assessment by thoroughbred professionals.

By a professional scholar, I would like to mean a qualified judge who takes into account the interests of people as formed by some-thing besides their knowable background and projectible likings and resentments. The aim would be to perform a separable function in society—as free as that of a free artist; as distinct as that of an honest judge at law. I am not sure how far such a class of persons has ever existed in the academy. I am sure that we are no closer now to sponsoring them than we were thirty years ago. But to give up even the hope of attaining such an ideal only assures that we shall pass continually farther from it. If a number of persons ever arise who associate themselves with this function, and who want to call themselves professional, whatever my preferred word might be I will gladly declare that by affinity and loyalty I belong to them.

For encouragement and advice, and to check my impressions, I have relied on Thomas Crow, Maria DiBattista, Amy Gutmann, Edward Mendelson, Barbara Packer, Yopie Prins, and Richard Rorty. John Hollander kept many topics vivid in conversation and helped me to believe in the worth of saying the things I wanted to say. George Kateb, Ross Borden, and Georgann Witte made com-ments on the manuscript that improved the book; and I owe to Kateb the concept of group narcissism, which is explored under various names throughout these pages. Jeffrey Stout offered a num-ber of suggestions I have followed in revising chapters 4 and 5. Irving Howe published early versions of chapters 2 and 3 in *Dissent* (Fall 1986 and Fall 1989): I am indebted to his example, his care as a reader, and his sense of balance, which often corrected mine. I am grateful to the other editors, as well as to many readers of *Dissent*, for their depth of interest and their responsiveness. Ellen

Graham, of Yale University Press, saw a book in some essays and ideas: they have come together thanks to her support. Jonathan Brent made acute observations at a later stage which led to several adjustments of emphasis.

A version of chapter 4 was read at the conference on "The Use and Abuse of Tradition," at the University of North Carolina, Greensboro, April 1990, organized by Mary Ellis Gibson. Some paragraphs of chapter 1 adapt a response that was read at the Lionel Trilling Seminar, Columbia University, November 1990, and published as "Higher Education and Group Thinking" in *Raritan* (Summer 1991). Portions of chapter 5 draw on "The Cost of Professionalism in the Humanities," from *Learned Societies and the Evolution of the Disciplines* (American Council of Learned Societies, Occasional Paper no. 5, 1988); and on reviews for the *New Republic* of two books: *Contingencies of Value*, by Barbara Herrnstein Smith (December 12, 1988), and *Giants and Dwarfs*, by Allan Bloom (January 28, 1991). The timely references of chapter 2 are altered here only by an occasional shift of tense. Throughout, I have cropped and thinned the more obvious repetitions, conscious that, in a work of this kind, a degree of insistence is unavoidable. The reader will easily follow my use of sources in the text. The notes give references for the longer quotations, with afterthoughts, corroborating instances, and additional materials that appeared to me useful and interesting without being central to the argument.

The intelligence is defeated as soon as the expression of one's thoughts is preceded, explicitly or implicitly, by the little word "we."

—Simone Weil, *The Need for Roots*

I

PART ONE

1

THE NEW
FUNDAMENTALISTS

I am concerned in these pages with two environments, a conservative political culture outside the academy and a radical political culture inside. Both, in the past decade, have isolated themselves from criticism, and both to an unprecedented degree have disciplined and stereotyped their products beyond the hope of self-criticism. Whatever may be good or useful about either of them is now far on the way to ruin. Both cultures have grown provincial rather than cosmopolitan: their members talk to the same people, receive the same narrow and defensive advice, from one occasion of judgment to the next. But they are provincial in another sense as well. They make such sparing use of our traditions that they are wrecking the chances of continuity with the moral ideals of liberalism—the very ideals of free expression and personal autonomy which have long been what the world rightly admires about America: more than our songs, sports, and movies; more than our cars and drugs; more than our wars; much more than the servile culture of crisis-dependent "experts" which many academics are hungry to join.

In later chapters I argue that the shamelessness of our national culture in politics has contributed to produce, by reaction, a new rigor of conformity in the academic culture. The second culture thinks of itself as an antidote to the first, but it is not. It is part of the same disease. For illustration—and the present chapter is one long illustration—one need hardly search further than today's paper. Accordingly, the citizen's notes that follow are derived from no more exalted source than a few of the stories, anecdotes, and editorial columns that have lately appeared in some of our better known newspapers and magazines. Many of my readers will have kept a similar file over the last few years, wondering as I have what to make of such materials.

The *New York Times*, on March 17, 1991, reported that Graham Firestone, a student at the State University of New York at Binghamton, had been charged by the school's administration with "lewd and indecent behavior." Firestone had displayed on the door to his room several centerfold photographs from *Penthouse;* according to the charge, the pictures were intended to give and did in fact give offense: the dormitory supervisor, with her husband, made the official complaint that started the proceedings. In response, Firestone invoked the first amendment, and as of March 17 the case was under administrative review, with a final decision pending. Of the testimony heard against him, some came from the university's Affirmative Action office, which called the centerfolds "degrading and abusive to women." The article does not say what precedent exists at the school for trespasses of a similar sort, or under what code previous offenders in the same category had been punished.

The accused in this case fought hard; he came to believe that it was "a free-speech issue," and said: "The fact that I'm being punished at all is crazy." He had been struck by the paternalism of the dormitory supervisor, Denise Nelson, who, in delivering the accusation along with her husband, cited "fellow students" as objectors to the display. Yet not one student came forward to support the complaint. Steven Nelson for his part defended the irregularity: "With some university rules, we don't always have victims coming forward to respond. . . . I was acting in the best interests of the community." The students, the supposed victims in the case, were too dull or too complacent, were incompetent to express or, perhaps, even to discover by introspection, their imputed detestation of the display. The Nelsons were therefore helping them—"acting in the best interests of the community." What community was this? And who were Mr. and Mrs. Nelson to act on its behalf?

Plainly, not the community that allows *Penthouse* to be sold on magazine stands nationwide—in suburban malls, in supermarkets, in railway stations and airports and at first-floor kiosks in great office buildings. Not the same community, either, in which an auto mechanic, an owner of a copy shop, or a freelance artisan or merchant of any kind, may display the same pictures—may, that is, at the risk of turning away all who are offended. The displayer of *Penthouse* is subject to no preemptive action from the sensitive feelings of the patron or even the boycott-organizer.

Graham Firestone, by displaying the pictures, himself risked turning away in disgust some persons who might possibly have become his friends, or who might have taken a different interest in him than they could with this as his advertisement. In putting the photographs up and keeping them posted, he established that he was a vulgar young man. The character brings with it, among other penalties, that of attracting vulgar company. Firestone by his gesture was giving memorable insult to persons for whom delicacy of taste might be one element of their refinement. He also of course risked injury (possibly unintended) to his parents, by seeming the sort of person about whom people can say, "He was badly brought up." And he invited being told to his face that he is a lout, a boor, a creep, with the probability that people might say worse behind his back. Still, by the usual standard of moral surveillance enforceable today in America, these acts of censure exhaust our stock of punishments.

Here, then, is the question such a case raises in acute form. Is the standard of the universities looser than that of society at large, or is it tighter? And, whatever it is, *ought* it be either looser or tighter? As soon as the question is asked, one realizes that on this whole subject an appalling confusion has descended.

To judge by the circumstances of the dispute, at SUNY Binghamton the university standard aims to be tighter than the usual social standard. To display the photographs is accordingly taken to be a cause for something more than routine censure. And yet, assuming that Binghamton resembles the comparable institutions known to me, in certain respects the university standard is also looser than the social standard. Had Firestone been rumored to possess a hoard of marijuana, he would likely have been given a

severe warning by a dean before the campus police were sent to
make a serious search. This *benevolent* paternalism has long been
an understood feature of life on campus. What then explains the
sudden binding fast of the inside standard—as if to assure that it
shall differ from the outside standard in being selectively prose-
cutorial as well as selectively custodial? What anxious irony must
prevail toward society at large, to justify the deployment of ad hoc
strictures developed by a dormitory guardian, approved by the
Affirmative Action office, and sanctioned by the university? These
pages try to answer that question. Or rather they try, by a multi-
plication of instances, to measure the depth of the anxiety from
which it has become possible for the question to be asked.

One can observe in most of the following examples a pattern I
have to notice in concluding with Firestone. I will call it, in the
familiar slang of poker, *rhetorically upping the ante*. But it may be
more simply considered an aspect of Lifemanship among the Perfect Ones—Mr. and Mrs. Nelson and their unsleeping allies. It is
remarkable how quickly one party in the Firestone episode, the
Affirmative Action office, upped the ante by exploiting the unconscious prevalence of a double standard. For that office called the
display of the pictures *degrading* and *abusive*. Degrading such pictures undoubtedly are, for pornography like this has a restless
appetite to destroy all self-respect. Of the personal virtues, self-
respect is impossible to achieve without a fixed boundary between
private and public things, and it is this boundary that the invasive
pictures want to cross and recross, until the memory of it begins
to be erased. But on no ordinary understanding of the word could
a mere display of pictures be described as abusive. To use that
word charges the atmosphere, morally, in a way as spectacular as
it is unwarranted.

Abuse always carries a suggestion of the direct, the palpable and
physical threat. In exploiting such a suggestion for all its moralizing
weight, the Affirmative Action office behaved with reckless opportunism. If it is indeed possible to believe that the display of Firestone's pictures was abusive, then the annual budget of the office

should be donated in full to a campaign of unstinting legal reforms, to assure that no copy of *Penthouse* is sold within a hundred-mile radius of campus. At SUNY Binghamton, however, in a pattern we shall see repeated elsewhere, the symbolic inside gesture is really a substitute for external action that is not taken.

As an exercise in what Freud calls "reality testing," let us remind ourselves of the sort of thing that does happen in the society outside the universities—in the moral culture that the universities have begun to rival by their self-policing ambitions. In the *New York Times* for March 23, 1991—soon after the Gulf war—there appeared a curious anecdote about the practice of law in New York State. Justice John G. Dier of the state supreme court had ruled that a county district attorney, William Montgomery III, was permitted to wear an American flag pinned to his lapel while addressing a jury. By this decision the judge reversed a lower court decision which had forbidden Montgomery from the same heartfelt, patriotic, and (for a district attorney) competitively valuable display of a national symbol. The initial complaint against his innovation had been made by a defense lawyer, Kurt Mausert, on the ground that at a time of feverish patriotism, the flag, when worn by a prosecutor, might send an extracurricular message of intimidation to members of the jury: *vote against the prosecution and you vote against the flag.* Mausert, had he chosen to be a mere lawyer, and not a tiresome man of principle, could have worn an identical flag pin on his own lapel and taken some of the sting out of the contest. But the lower court saw the point of his objection. Pretty plainly, the spirit of the Constitution—relentless as it is in forbidding tests of loyalty or belief, or anything remotely suggestive of such tests—cherishes an objection like his and justifies the lower court.

Judge Dier, however, the state supreme court justice who overturned this common-sense libertarian ruling, had his mind on larger matters. "I find it very difficult to understand that anyone who is a citizen of this country could object to another citizen of this country wearing an American flag pin. *And especially today with the situation as it exists in the Middle East*" (emphasis added). The situation ought of course to have as little bearing as possible on the finding in a case like this. The "situation as it exists" can have some very bad days, and that is when the law ought most to reflect a judgment taken in a cool hour. But Judge Dier saw himself as an affirmative action officer for the Gulf war. So eager was he to foster a general assent to the wartime mood that he failed to grasp the logic of illicit influence, on which the defense lawyer Mausert and the lower court judge had founded their objections. His excitement, indeed, led him to extend the same logic on a broader front. He was anxious to see if he could close up even the loopholes by which anyone with a patriotism as unresponsive as Mausert's was allowed to practice law "with the situation as it exists"—though, as he must have known if he stopped to think, his ruling would last far beyond the situation of March 1991. Obedient to his enthusiasm, Judge Dier ordered that Mausert's name be stricken from the ranks of lawyers permitted to defend indigent clients in Warren County, New York.

Pause now, briefly, to work out the parallel of the Firestone and Mausert stories to its discouraging conclusion. In school, you are punished for displaying signs that send the wrong message (about women). Out of school, you are punished for not displaying signs that send the right message (about the American flag). The more one deplores the hysterical paternalism of Judge Dier, the more one ought to deplore the hysterical paternalism of Denise and Steven Nelson and the local authorities whom they mobilized.

Thus far, we may seem to have been occupied in the realm of manners: such debates go on in any culture, over what people think it is proper to advertise or to restrict, to endorse or to reprobate. But when the stakes for approval are high enough, the subject matter of such a debate can incite the energy necessary for devising explicit codes of conduct: prescriptive, and not merely general and negative, guidelines that aim to control what can and cannot be said. Along with these, on many campuses, have come a host of new criteria—unconnected with merit, but otherwise so various as to elude a general description—to control the selection of people who are allowed to speak with educational authority, and with other kinds of authority.

The *Wall Street Journal* for January 4, 1991, carried an editorial, with relevant facts, concerning an unprecedented attempt then being sustained by the administration at Hampshire College in Amherst, Massachusetts, to stop the reappointment of two junior professors of literature. The first thing to note about this incident is that it was not a tenure decision, not, that is, the appointment of someone to the status of permanent faculty, where consideration must be given to the candidate's ultimate appropriateness, and where published work is often scrutinized by outside referees. In the latter sort of candidacy, a negative vote may occur for a number of reasons, though it must be scrupulously justified by reference to the character and quality of the candidate's work. But the present was not a question of this sort. It was a matter of simply renewing the contracts of two junior professors.

At Hampshire, Jeffrey Wallen, assistant professor of comparative literature, and Norman Holland, assistant professor of Hispanic literature, were supported for renewal of contract by the relevant committees in their academic fields, with votes of 20 to 7, and 23 to 4, respectively. In these circumstances the college president's approval would normally be taken for granted. But here, the president, Gregory S. Prince, chose to resubmit the cases to the control of a "college committee on faculty appointments, which, Professor Wallen notes, included some of his most vocal political antagonists, advocates of the Third World Studies agenda." The committee voted to reverse the original votes for renewal, at which point Wallen requested that the negative decision be reconsidered by a college committee on academic freedom. It was found by this, the third but not the last of the committees we shall encounter, that both Wallen's and Holland's freedom had been infringed. At the time of the article, the president had taken the unheard-of step of referring the case to still another adjudicating body, to see if he could get a second negative decision to nullify the second positive one.

What were the offenses of the two assistant professors at Hampshire? That they taught poorly, or lacked the necessary intimate knowledge of their subjects? Nothing of the sort. Holland is described in the article as "Panamanian-American," which is as much as to say that, by definition, he met at least one nonacademic criterion of intimacy. So much the more extraordinary must his transgression have been to warrant the opprobrium. "They wanted me," he said, "to be either Cesar Chavez or Juan Valdez"—either a political organizer, who could stand from week to week as a paragon of agitation, or a victim of colonial oppression whose case might become a spur to compassion and to shared resentment by others. Instead, Holland chose to teach certain works of European literature as part of the curriculum—this, in a field that owes one of its present academic names, "colonial and postcolonial," to the extent of the European influence on the whole culture of the region. But in making his pedagogic choice, Holland had opened himself to the charge of *Eurocentrism*. Wallen for his part was accused of a "failure to mount a 'Third World challenge' to 'the canon.'" Then, too—in this resembling Holland—he did not characterize European literature as a virus, against which students were to be inoculated in suitably small doses and with elaborate warnings. Those who clamored for the dismissal of both teachers were vehement against their "lack of independence"—a term of art here, as it has been in earlier times, for a refusal to think and talk as others wanted them to think and talk.

That right thinking must issue in conformity of opinion is the central mass-culture idea of our time. A recognition of this fact, near the start of the McCarthy era, prompted Harold Rosenberg to nickname the groups who lived by such beliefs "the herd of independent minds." Rosenberg was, and remains, exceptional in the acuteness with which he saw that the mass in question could come in all sizes, the small being no less insidious than the large; for a mass of fifty persons well enough placed are capable of a thoughtlessness equal to the aggregate efforts of five million. "Mass culture," he wrote, "whether of the flat plain of the One Big Mass or of the pyramid of the Many Small Masses, must deny the validity of the single human being's effort to arrive at a consciousness of himself and of his situation. The insight of the 'particular man' must be crushed by the 'substantial doctrine.'" By means like these, an image or cliché comes to be fixed which can turn even a Cesar Chavez into a Juan Valdez. In 1948, when Rosenberg made his observations, the leading mass-culture superstition was "that there exists a kind of human dead center in which everyone is identical with everyone else"—with the superstitious hope that if the culture maker "can hit that psychic bull's eye he can make all of mankind twitch at once."[1] At that time it could still seem that the one big mass outweighed the many small ones. But today, the same promotional idea about mass identity has been transferred to the small, the ethnically or racially or sexually or religiously defined, masses. Within these, it is flatteringly supposed that every specimen, member, or replicant can be made to twitch at once. The president of Hampshire College, so willing to conciliate the first faculty members who took offense at a rival member's want of the right sort of independence, was, in fact, only following a practice now widely accepted in American culture.

Consider the intense controversy over the Broadway casting for the London play *Miss Saigon*. An English actor of great power, Jonathan Pryce, had created the role and was expected to bring it to America—as, in the event, he has. But for a time it looked as if the play would never be launched here. The Committee on Racial Equality, of Actors' Equity, voted to bar Pryce from performing the role on the ground that a special search had not been conducted for Asian-American actors who might act the leading role of a Vietnamese pimp. The producer of the play, Cameron Mackintosh, as producers will, had simply chosen the man he wanted. Against this uncooperative way of proceeding a spokeswoman for the Pan Asian Repertory Theater, Tisa Chang, protested as a licensed guardian of the human dead center of Broadway: "While we respect every artist's right to artistic expression, it cannot come at the expense of other cultures. The insensitivity and arrogance of Cameron Mackintosh in this matter is inexcusable" (*New York Times,* August 16, 1990). Note, in this statement, a conjunction we will see again and again: art and culture are in tension with each other, and when an issue forces a choice it is art that must give way. Indeed, by "culture" seems to be meant the product of some routine exchanges between genetics and environment. An actor who *is* such a product is the natural choice to *express* such a product. To question the idea that a work of art is a product at all is to demand an impossible sacrifice from culture. It also, of course, betokens insensitivity. Whereas the poisonous beliefs that race experience *can be gauged,* and that it *has authority over personal experience,* are in this context a mark of superior sensitivity.

As I shall argue throughout, it seems to me that art, like thinking, does exist in tension with culture thus defined. You cannot serve both at once—cannot even pretend to when, as often happens, the two come into open conflict. "In an ideal world," Chang's statement continues, "any artist can play any role for which he or she is suited. Until that time arrives, artists of color must fight to retain access to the few roles which are culturally and racially specific to them." The last sentence is a sophistry. After all, the only index of having truly obtained access on this scheme is to obtain the role. But there are many other confusions here—all stemming from a determination to respect art only within the ground rules of culture, and from a prior definition of culture that ties it to the social or anthropological group, rather than to individual taste or judgment. Art is—not perhaps guileless—but more trustful than Tisa Chang and Actors' Equity. It actually aspires to show us the ideal world that her statement puts off to an unrealizable millennium.

It follows that in art, the suitability of person to role is a matter of strength of imagination—only that. And in this sense, no role ever written by a true artist has ever been culturally or racially specific. It has been humanly specific, and humanly general and translatable, or it never was art. Shylock and Othello are not racially specific parts; the mind that created them did not imagine the first to be played by a Jew, or the second by a black—these were not even likely resources among the actors of the day. He may, in a certain sense, hardly have imagined the parts being played at all, except in the mind of the reader. But the test of reading may be evoked more largely here, for it reveals much about the shallowness of our hold on ideas of racial specificity.

What would it be for a reader of, say, *The Merchant of Venice,* to imagine Shylock being "played" (all the while one was reading) by a racially specific Jew? What is it then to imagine the same part being played (less authentically? more subtly, but illicitly? all, anyway, still in the privacy of one's mind) by a racially translated non-Jew. These are curious experiments. They twist the mind in knots, and they offer no edification whatever. One thing, however, does emerge: the sort of mind that would engage in these exercises for long, that would take them solemnly as proving something about art, or about human life, is an *idolatrous* mind. The name of the idol is cultural identity, and for those who bow down to it, and on its behalf extort the belief that sympathy comes in the exact coinage of a given group, cultural identity has replaced the imagination of humanity. With a work of genius, there is no central casting. Yet in the absence of specifiable guidelines, the struggle for "representation" by groups would come to a simple struggle for better conditions of work. Very well; the way to achieve such conditions on the terms offered by art is to strive for an uncontrolled representation: an Asian-American for Shylock, a Jew for Miss Saigon, and both for anything else they can possibly do. The other way lies a vice more inexpungible than self-conceit—namely, the self-idolatry of a group. Those who indulge it are under an enchantment which makes them forget that a corporate body has no soul.

Lately, the self-idolatry of groups has been praised as an innovative virtue. In a *New York Times* op-ed of September 26, 1990, August Wilson brought before the public his case for finding a black director to make a film of his play *Fences.* He spoke of two criteria that seemed significant to him in enforcing the selection, with evident anguish when faced by their possible incompatibility: for, first, Wilson did not want to pick a director *merely* because he or she was black; but second, he wanted assurance against the director's being someone who was not black—it would, he believed, do his play an injustice to accept a non-black director merely on the ground of talent. "At the time of my last meeting with Paramount, in January 1990, a well-known, highly respected white director wanted very much to direct the film. I don't know his work, but he is universally praised for sensitive and intelligent direction. I accept that he is a very fine film director. But he is not black. He is not a product of black American culture—a culture that was honed out of the black experience and fired in the kiln of slavery and survival—and he does not share the sensibilities of black Americans." Here we have an interesting argument, and symptomatic in a number of ways.

The choice of the word *sensibilities* brings out a main source of the confusion. It is a difficult word, which, in an older sense now seldom used, could imply "consciousness of injury; susceptibility to the thought of one's own wounds." In the more modern sense that was likely to have been in the front of Wilson's mind, sensibility denotes an acquired tact for judging aesthetic sensations. A short generalization may catch the distinction here. The sensibility (old meaning), or experiential sensitivity of a black person, is, by definition, incommunicable. By contrast, the sensibility (new meaning), which makes a work of art about black experience appreciable to others, is brought into being by the act of communication. That is to say, a secret comes to be known by many who were not originally "in it"; known, even, in aspects that have eluded some who were in it; and the identity of those others who come to know is not projectable by race. Something changes, respecting the very character of what is to be understood, as one passes from a call for life-experience to a call for art-experience. It is for this reason that works of art have sometimes been praised for their sympathy—a capability of feeling unexpectedly for others and the fate of others. Sympathy is a better thing, and a higher thing, than empathy. It is not even to be compared with the licensed empathy of X for Y, where all the world agree in advance that Y is only another X.

As appears from his argument, Wilson is uncertain whether he wants to claim for his work the self-sympathies of experience or the communicable sympathies of art. To the extent that he finds himself prey to this doubt, he is unhappy about the choice between an accredited experience that is entirely his and the always challengeable status of a work of art. He is, to put it another way, uncertain whether his work aspires to the authenticity of something suffered or the authenticity of something made. But the confusion goes much further. Contending, as he does, in the shadow-region where cultural sensitivity and artistic sympathy compete for authority (with the cover-term *sensibility* splitting the difference between them), to avoid the appearance of a double standard Wilson is driven to impose his self-image on the history of American culture as a whole. We have always been divided, he says, according to the feelings of members of groups, which precisely correspond to the mass experience of groups. "As Americans of various races," he concedes, "we share a broad cultural ground." But then, "within these commonalities are specifics: specific ideas and attitudes that are not shared." White Americans, for example, are subdivided into "various European *ethnic* groups which share a common history and sensibility." However, "Black Americans are a *racial* group which do not share the same sensibilities." It is unclear from this account whether the white ethnic groups are properly to be conceived as divided from each other, or whether in fact, though separate, they still somehow share a single sensibility. Clearly, however, the message is that blacks differ more from all the whites together than any group of whites can possibly differ from another.

How true is this? A white Protestant who grew up in a southern town where blacks lived, too, who had learned something of their customs and their ways of talking, might feel rather less cut off from them psychologically than from city-dwelling Jews or Italians, not one specimen of whom he had ever met. A black in the same situation might feel similarly about the sort of white people with whom he had long been familiar, as distinct from the sort of black people with whom he was wholly unfamiliar. Such are the intuitions of common sense—supported, in this case, by a good deal of autobiographical testimony. But Wilson is sure that the intuitions are false. (It must follow that the personal accounts arise from false consciousness, a massive fraud imposed by the liberal mind upon the experience of whites and blacks.) For blacks have "a different way of responding to the world," "different ideas," and—more to the point for Wilson's dealings with Paramount—"different aesthetics." In the light of these divisions, "Someone who does not share the specifics of a culture remains an outsider, no matter how astute a student or how well-meaning their intentions. . . . The job [of director of *Fences*] requires someone who shares the specifics of the culture of black Americans."

Wilson is aware that his separatism, if it allowed special exemptions with aesthetic group-identity permitted on only one side, could easily be exposed as racist. He therefore decides at last to offer a broad, quite vague, gesture of cultural and racial tolerance; though the question now arises, What can tolerance come to on these principles? His answer is as bold as it is consistent: "What to do? Let's make a rule. Blacks don't direct Italian films. Italians don't direct Jewish films. Jews don't direct black American films. That might account for about 3 percent of the films that are made in this country. The other 97 percent—the action-adventure, horror, comedy, romance, suspense, western, or any combination thereof, that the Hollywood and independent mills grind out—let it be every man for himself."[2] This may have been half intended as a parody of a view that Wilson recognizes as bankrupt. Even if it were a parody, it would betray the desperateness of the frame of mind that entertains the thought (for the length of an op-ed piece, or several years of talks with Paramount). But the uneasiness of Wilson's tone makes it clear that the passage started by being meant in earnest—in cynical earnest. For what but cynicism could prompt an artist to revolve in his mind so corrupt a bargain? The corruption of mind is patent at the end, when Wilson, without even the sham of an improving wish for the general culture, pleads that he only wants a small piece of the action.

He neglects the metaphysical dimension of the problem which would have interested a serious parodist. How can one know when a work that appears to fit the genre of, say, "suspense," is Italian suspense or Jewish suspense or black suspense? Will it not fall plainly into one of these categories, depending on the sensibility of the people hired to write and act and direct it? Again, who will be permitted to make the occasional "romance" film about inter-racial romance? And finally, in all such cases, if the film obeys a sufficiently trite formula, does that buy it an exemption from the racial and ethnic settlement?—on the ground that it thereby ceases to be of interest to the "specifics" contracting for the 3 percent bargain? Or should it not, if trite, and designed to make a lot of easy money, accordingly be of *more* interest to the parties in charge of the settlement, as being likely to inspire new investment for the serious, ethnically and racially pure, films that come from the kiln of group survival?

The puzzling distinction anyway is between genre films based on race and genre films based on types of plot. Why should we assume that only the latter are majoritarian trash? Both presume the solemn acceptance of a stereotype, and in this fact consists the defection of mind which makes a work of art impossible. Given, then, that the racially perfect films *aim at a digestible stereotype*, why should they not be asked to pay their way? They might well end by picking up more than 3 percent of the business and in time compete as equals with the thriller, horror, western, or, as Wilson says with unearned condescension, "any combination thereof."

With *Fences*, as with *Miss Saigon*, we see a principled bigotry at work forging a connection between the identity of artists and the subject matter of works of art. ("Paint me an apple! How will I know it's a real painting? Well, it's a real apple, isn't it?") In both cases, the same controlling assumptions may be detected: a distrust of unincorporated talent, which is always liable to appear strange and versatile, and a proportionate respect for things hardened in the kiln of group suffering. (Is there such a thing as group suffer-ing? The terrible fact about group persecutions seems to be that, by the visible index of generic stigmata, they smooth the way for the infliction of individual sufferings. Is it right, then, to argue that the same uniform stigmata are reproduced in the mental ex-perience of the victims themselves? Nothing could so surely grant their torturers in life a profound posthumous satisfaction.) A simple

expression captures the position of those who preach the uniformity of group suffering and its opacity to all who have not suffered
as members of the group. *It takes one to know one.*

This is a sick way of feeling. It confers not just consolation, or
compassion, but merit on victims from the sheer fact of their having
suffered—a compensatory device that is not likely to inhibit the
taste for inflicting new sufferings, any more than it can create the
strength to endure them. The healthy teaching on this subject is
not: those who suffer have a special authority in consequence. It
is rather: suffering oppresses. The worst poison of suffering must
be to drag down the best of one's hopes with the lowest of one's
humiliations. The beginning of a change (if we could make one)
would be to exhibit plainly the poor thing that suffering must be
even in the best (for something besides the having been a victim
does survive in the best and luckiest). But this would have to be
done not by hoarding misery as the property of a group but by
bringing it into the imaginative life of others as part of their shared
humanity. Slavery for American blacks, and the Holocaust for
American Jews, have been made into sacred subjects. The result is
that, as experiences, they have come to sanctify the dignity of pain,
and to create a pride from the unrelievable possession of pain. It
is a pride that is close to fear, close to contempt, liable to stagger
hope and to stun feeling most of all in those who hug it to themselves most fiercely.[3]

It may be said that a view like August Wilson's is merely cruel,
or vexing. His statement nevertheless embodies a grotesque consistency on the subject which has, in a short time, achieved respectability. For this way of conceiving of human experience now
is taught in the schools. An article called "Stepford Writers," in
Lingua Franca (December 1990) by an author using the pseudonym
Chris Altacruise, speaks of a new family of short-story formulas
that have become the blight of graduate writing seminars. The
prevailing canon of faith now being taught in the Masters of Fine
Arts programs—a maxim taught most of all, it appears, by intimi-
dated students to one another—is: write about what you can be
expected to know. And there is this corollary: the outermost limit

of what you know is drawn by the circumstances of your birth and your social or ethnic or racial or religious circumstances. A corresponding feature of MFA practice according to Altacruise has become: never pretend to judge what other people can claim to know from their own experience. The code for punishing a story that stretches the imagination of the writer—a story that tries to pass beyond certain traceable genetic and cultural experiences—now requires the advanced reader to say that he or she *has been offended*. Altacruise cites the following examples verbatim: "I was deeply offended by the language. It smacks of white male elitist oppression." "I was really offended because this story is about people from Kentucky, and I'm from Kentucky, and I'm not like that at all, so I was really insulted."

The article goes on to recount the flattening therapy to which one MFA candidate was subjected, for placing an episode of a story at a Metro stop in Washington, D.C., and then describing a boy hawking papers as "black": "For forty-five minutes the group tore into the writer as a racist, a closet Klansman, based on that one word. The professor wound up lecturing the other writers on their responsibility to write about America's class society as it is rather than present a delusional utopia." The workshop, however, reassembled afterward and, says Altacruise, the members then agreed among themselves that the professor, to have said these things, must himself be "another racist"; so that, "after that attack on the Washington scene . . . not one black character appeared in another story for the rest of the year. The message was clear: Segregation is wrong except in fiction. And because lines of race are also those of class, America's classes vanish as well, or appear one at a time. Homogeneity is preferable to the often ugly and always complex social truths in this country." The upshot from August Wilson's 3 percent bargain appears on this testimony to exceed any effect the argument can have anticipated. Or maybe this is in fact the desired result: a self-imposed segregation that makes its reentry on the national agenda by means of the arts.

Something like the same division of labor has been enforced in the unwritten MFA protocol governing representation of the sexes.

A male writing student made the mistake of composing a scene
where a woman goes to an abortion clinic; as Altacruise summarizes
the scene: "She registered, sat down, read a magazine, then went
through with it. The attack that scene prompted went on for over
an hour and was so savage and personal that the visiting writer,
J. M. Coetzee, whose liberal credentials couldn't be questioned,
had to ask, 'What has he done? I have never seen anything like
this. As far as I can tell the scene does nothing and should be cut.
But what is all this about?'" At which several women in the group
explained that the writer, a man, "had co-opted their subject matter." Here, once again, subject matter dictates the terms of treatment to imagination; indeed, it is not clear that imagination has
any real work to do in the transactions of art. It takes one to know
one. And if you are one already, you know what you need to
know.

Speaking now as a teacher of English literature, I read Altacruise's account with a strong sense of recognition. In the past few
years, in discussions of literary theory, I have grown unhappily
conversant with the prohibitions against "stealing the discourse of
the Other." These form a direct counterpart to the creative-writing
idea of co-opting someone else's subject. It looks as if disputations
like the foregoing, enacted again and again in the tribunals of
ethno-aesthetic criticism, may turn out to be the first dividends of
a demographic approach to art. Sensitivity training, schemes for
the reeducation of delinquent spectators, the passage from mere
criticism to the more probing ministrations of a gently compelled
self-criticism, follow next in the programming of a reliable group
image for the many groups who promote some such achievement
as a moral end.

To say that a new movement in culture has thoughtless advocates
is not yet to discredit it. But too willing an acceptance of the
understandable errors of the thoughtless can contribute to the systematic undervaluing of persons who are thoughtful, unincorporated, and themselves potentially interesting advocates for a group.
In the *New Republic* (February 18, 1991), an article by Stephen R.

Barnett on race consciousness at the University of California campuses told the predicament of an assistant professor, Margo Hendricks, who teaches Renaissance literature at U.C. Santa Cruz.
Hendricks does not care to be counted as "a black woman professor
of English": she is confronted constantly by the brute presumption
of those who treat her as if this were the only description she could
aspire to fit. I am, she told Barnett, "continually being asked, 'How
did you end up in Renaissance studies?'"; a white student once
felt justified in "bluntly demanding to know why I wasn't special-
izing in African American literature." At a conference another
scholar asked her, with the same deferential bigotry, what she
thought of a prominent scholar of black American discourse; on
her saying that she had no opinion, this good-natured white man
of the August Wilson school went on to ask her opinion of *Othello*.
Hendricks, who formerly taught at San Jose State University, re-
called the parallel fate of a student there who, being black, "felt
obligated to do African American"; and another who was made to
feel guilty for not doing African American, and "had a hard time
dealing with the guilt"; and still a third, a Latin-American student
working on African-American literature, who was made to feel that
she ought to do Latin American writers after all.

In the same way, it is a commonplace of our moment that a
woman starting off a career in literary scholarship has better
chances of employment than a man of comparable gifts; but with
the widening of the opportunity may come a narrowing of the
freedom to choose one's subject: the man, if he has the fortune to
find a good position, will be asked to teach what he has chosen,
that is, what he has studied for a good many years; the woman
may well be expected to teach, in addition, a course on "women
in literature" or "gender studies," or otherwise conspicuously to
incorporate a "feminist perspective" in as much of her intellectual
work as possible. In a typical recent case, a Miltonist was told
frankly at a three-year contract renewal that she had disappointed
the expectations with which she was hired; her teaching had been
so little involved with women in literature that, if it continued in
the same pattern, her prospects for tenure would be extremely

poor a few years hence. When she retorted that the expectation of teaching feminist topics had never been broached, either in her interview for the position or later on, the chair replied that in the circumstances so explicit a directive scarcely seemed necessary.

Such despotism of opinion has its proper antidote in Emerson's essay "Self-Reliance"—a great and liberating work with a wrong title. For it is nothing but a series of aphorisms against conformity. The author was a white Protestant male who came to know, in nineteenth-century America, what a sickness group thinking could be for those who were in power. The truths of the essay apply no less to groups that conceive of themselves as out of power and that seek a correspondingly surer control over their membership. Writes Emerson:

> Great works of art . . . teach us to abide by our spontaneous impression with good-humored inflexibility then most when the whole cry of voices is on the other side. Else tomorrow a stranger will say with masterly good sense precisely what we have thought and felt all the time, and we shall be forced to take with shame our own opinion from another.

> The eye was placed where one ray should fall, that it might testify of that particular ray.

> Few and mean as my gifts may be, I actually am, and do not need for my own assurance or the assurance of my fellows any secondary testimony.

> The objection to conforming to usages that have become dead to you is that it scatters your force. It loses your time and blurs the impression of your character. . . . A man must consider what a blind-man's-buff is this game of conformity. If I know your sect I anticipate your argument. . . . Most men have bound their eyes with one or another handkerchief, and attached themselves to some one of these communities of opinion. This conformity makes them not false in a few particulars, authors of a few lies, but false in all particulars. Their every truth is not quite true.

Your genuine action will explain itself and will explain your other genuine actions. Your conformity explains nothing.[4]

These aphorisms stand at an extreme of indifference to public opinion, to the need for common action, or even for occasional collaboration with other persons. But as a counter-statement to the communitarian pieties of our day, it is a good extreme. The same essay also makes in passing the celebrated remark that *imitation is suicide:* a sentiment that used to strike me as exaggerated.

I now know what Emerson meant. The people who believe that it takes one to know one, who know exactly who and what they are, to whom and to what they belong, want no single person ever to survive as singular. They aim at complete possession. One may be tempted to cooperate out of fellow feeling or from weakness of will—two things that are sometimes hard to tell apart. But in moods like these it is useful to recall two further sentences from "Self-Reliance": "Your goodness must have some edge to it,—else it is none. The doctrine of hatred must be preached, as the counteraction of the doctrine of love, when that pules and whines." Against the bureaucrats of sexual, racial, ethnic, and religious purity, who invoke with such misleading intent the language of community, a resistance that amounts to hatred may be the sanest feeling to cherish. It gives, at least, some edge to whatever integral humanity one must call upon, and serves as a reminder that the caring groups are really hard as nails: they want to destroy us, each of us, and always for the sake of all.

The smaller, the tighter, the more disciplined and bigoted the group, the stricter its claims of conformity are likely to be. The consequence for education is frequently that a given way of teaching a group-affiliated subject gains enough coercive prestige to drive out alternative ways of teaching the subject. This would be rotten even if it were new talent driving out old. It is by no means always that. A story in the *New York Times* of January 2, 1991, reported the fate of Robert C. Smith, a professor of political science at San Francisco State University, who for many years has taught a course in Black Politics. He faced competition in the academic year 1990–91 from an apparently similar course by Oba T'Shaka, professor and chairman of Black Studies. Both scholars are black— a point whose relevance will become clear in a moment. Once the conflict emerged, the Black Studies department refused to cross-list Smith's course. It then instigated or condoned—the article does not make clear which—a harassing attempt to discourage students from taking his course at all. The first day of class, Smith found himself confronted by a well-organized contingent of black students, who stood up in a mass, jeered and shouted over his lecture, placed banners at the front of the room, and urged other students to continue the protest and intimidation by assembling at the teacher's home. Of forty-five who showed up on the first day, five remained to take the class for credit; on the last day, Smith toasted the survivors with a bottle of champagne. The most disheartening single detail of the story is that *all* thirty-five of the black students who had started the course were "persuaded" to drop it. The five who stayed were white political science majors.

Intellectually, what can have been at stake between the two courses in conflict, to prompt the black-studies sectarians to use their power so jealously? Smith, the political science professor, taught a version of black politics that stressed the history of American communities in the post–Civil War period. T'Shaka, the black studies professor, taught a version that stressed Afro-American roots and the uniqueness of black experience. One must do a little translating here, as usual with the *New York Times.* Smith evidently seeks to establish how some members of American society, who have long been oppressed and whose politics range from reformist to dissident, still share with others a political order in which they may want to claim the rights of participants. T'Shaka, by contrast, to judge by the extracurricular statements that are quoted, has an interest in showing that a complete difference from American life is inscribed in the very origins of black experience. Where origins are understood to govern destiny, this means that the imperative of black culture is to constitute itself as wholly separate from Eurocentric America.[5]

These differences help to explain the tactics adopted by one side.

The success of the campaign against Smith owed less to its cogency than to the presence, in command in the second course, of a chairman whose department claimed moral authority over the subject matter of both courses. Still, in a quarrel like this over issues of intellectual substance, reasons must be given, and it is interesting to see what the reasons were. "There was no control," complained Professor T'Shaka of Professor Smith, "over the quality" of the teaching of black politics by a professor of political science. Smith's course, the article went on to paraphrase T'Shaka's verdict, "might have too much of what he called a traditional perspective and might not sufficiently represent the Afro-American point of view." Very noticeable here is the assumption that there is just one Afro-American point of view. But what is a "traditional perspective"? I think the phrase means: Smith was likely to be too well in touch with current scholarship on American politics by scholars outside the controlling framework of black studies. From the point of view of mere knowledge, this may seem an uncomplicated virtue. From the point of view of a department whose interests are taken to coincide with the interests of a community, it is an unpardonable crime against the community.

Smith received support to continue his course from administrators at San Francisco State—a move that will seem unusual to anyone who has surveyed comparable incidents elsewhere. They gave no vibrant signals of rhetorical commiseration to the offended "community," and did not try to talk the besieged scholar out of taking his stand. His own judgment of the case afterwards was simply that "it is very difficult to oppose black people without being called racist." This is an alarming judgment to come from a black professor, a pioneer of his subject, who had fought hard to get black politics accepted as a topic within the study of political science. Very different, but as instructive in its way, was T'Shaka's defense of confining such studies in the future to departments specially designated according to race. Asked for his rationale, he compared the study of different races, "Afro-American, native American, and La Raza Studies," to the accepted separation of such discrete branches of science as biology, chemistry, and physics.

That the varieties of human beings named by T'Shaka ought to be seen as presenting objects of study as different as genes, molecules, and the laws of thermodynamics presents an interesting problem for the university curriculum. It also marks an important pragmatic test for the anti-Enlightenment slogan now current in the academic left. For the slogan says: "There is no such thing as Man. We study the different kinds of men and women." The firm line that T'Shaka draws is an outcome that adherents of the slogan generally find acceptable.

The last several examples have dealt with scholars who, because of their color or sex, are assumed to be mouthpieces for others of their color and sex. The crassness of such a belief is disgusting. Why then does it embarrass so few who strive to perpetuate the assumption? Would any of us who feels capable of speaking at all ever consent to be spoken for by an unappointed representative? We would want to say, I think, that the contexts for such an appointment are few, and in every case to be carefully scrutinized by ourselves. And yet the universities have got into the business of promoting and legitimating persons who take on this role unembarrassably; with the result that the universities themselves feel obliged to advance the interests of a class of salaried demagogues: a group who may have far more in common with one another than with the people they are supposed to represent. Awkward moments can still arise when, in a given field of study, the genetic makeup of those who do the teaching makes them ineligible for the role of demagogue, or when the few who are thus qualified refuse to play the role. What then? My next example follows up just such a contingency, and the old administrative instrument that has been revived to meet it: the faculty loyalty oath.

By means of the new oath, faculty members who teach "traditional" subjects avow their docility by agreeing to incorporate such nontraditional "perspectives" as gender, race, and class. A story about a recent oath, too decorous to call it by that name, appeared in the *New York Times* on November 18, 1990. It concerned a dispute then agitating at Clark University, from the refusal to suscribe to such a pledge by an associate professor of philosophy, Christina Hoff Sommers. The language of the oath was that of bureaucratic prompting; on a course proposal form, which the teacher was required to sign, the question was asked: "Insofar as it might be relevant to the content of the course, please explain how pluralistic views are explored and integrated in this course." The same form had been used since 1988, but Sommers detected a note of advance admonition in the phrasing, and she was right. Only at aberrant moments of crisis, in a shameful collapse to political pressure, have professors in the modern secular university been asked to account for the views they incorporate in their teaching. That the "views" here in question were another name for "attitudes" was sufficiently established by the 1990 revision of the form, to which Sommers likewise objected. In its revised version the rhetorical question became a quiet imperative—an offer it would be foolish to refuse. Professors now were *encouraged* to "integrate pluralistic concerns" into their teaching.

Clark University, like Hampshire College and SUNY Binghamton, appears from this incident to be another place where an activist administration has asserted control over curricular reform, as well as over questions of elementary manners that once had been protected by faculty autonomy. Sommers brought a number of suggestions before the faculty, as summarized in the *Times:* "that course proposals be neutral on political and moral character; that speakers representing a cross-section of opinion be invited to campus; and that a faculty committee be created to define diversity and pluralism and their effect on the curriculum." Of course, the issue of equal representation of outside speakers is in no way connected to faculty control over teaching. The inclusion of this point in a list with the others, however, does reveal the frame of mind of a dissident professor who feels trapped on all sides by the artificial consensus her institution has backed. Sommers anyway denies being an opponent of multiculturalism; she describes her teaching as "quite open: I don't use my classroom to promote one thing or another." And a colleague in the Department of Classics is cited as having a reservation like hers: "I don't feel that I need a watchdog paying close attention to my moral purity." The professors who object to the oath, in short, are dismayed by the paternalism of a new morally suasive protocol that does not call itself a code, that insists it is only asking questions and giving plausible advice to grown-ups.

How do things get to this point at a university? In the case of Clark, the legislating body was the Undergraduate Academic Board, composed of six members of the faculty, three students, and the dean of the university. The dean, Douglas Astolfi, who sat for these deliberations, still endorses the mild and helpful corrective sentiment to which professors on their course proposals were asked to subscribe their names. "I do not feel," he said, "that politely reminding the faculty to consider the issues they will include or exclude is in any way an attack on academic freedom. I find it an attack on academic freedom to suggest that they somehow be barred from thinking about these issues." Here is as fine an instance as one could pluck from volumes of faculty minutes to capture the soft-peddled authoritarianism, the exquisite and unconscious tri-ple-think, that gives a daily energy to the life of the academic promoter of community. Note that, in the case described, which the dean knew well in all its stages, the administration was not just "politely reminding" the faculty to "consider the issues" they dealt with in teaching. The administration had begun by *asking*, and gone on to *encouraging*. Politely reminding is a further step down the same path—actually, a step that had not yet been taken—since it assumes an existing agreement about the propriety of the encouragement. This mutual accord between faculty and administration was exactly what was now in question. Politely to remind those who have not approved of the content of the reminder, and who do have some rights in the matter, is indeed an attack on the freedom of action of the persons who are so addressed. In an academic setting, it is an attack on academic freedom.[6]

These are mere issues of principle—about which a dean might be expected to show some clarity of mind. What is disturbing is that the idea of issuing a polite reminder about obligations in teaching should have occurred to anyone. Who, after all, is better qualified to know the obligations that come with a given subject than the professor who has chosen to spend a career in that subject? Who, from a higher perspective than that, is to offer the reminder in the first place; and with what motives; and from the stimulus of what new information? But the machine of administrative self-esteem does not stop here. Astolfi's statement ends with a rhetorical effort to turn the tables on his accusers. They themselves, he says, make the real threat to academic freedom, for their resistance will be taken to discourage others who do want to "explore and integrate pluralistic views." Logically, this is absurd. To say, "I do not want to be told to perform action A," is in no way equivalent to my telling others, "Do not perform action A." Yet as a stroke of lifemanship in the comico-pathetic executive sport whose innings never stop—the game of having more good intentions and being more misunderstood than anyone—Astolfi's move is something finer than a logical blunder. Administratively speaking, it is a magnificent one-and-a-half gainer with a twist from a layout position, ending, against incredible odds, in a perfect belly-flop. The twist comes in the supposition that *those who do not want to be told to do a thing must therefore disapprove of the thing.* The truth is that they may feel themselves to be great approvers and abettors, in their own time, at their own choosing. But for every topic or emphasis one addresses in class, there is some other that drops away, or that must be allowed for the moment a smaller claim. It remains part of the creed of the liberal tradition in education (a tradition so advanced we are still catching up with it), that choices like these are never more wisely made than by someone like Professor Sommers, who has the good fortune to teach the things she cares about.

The suspicion that teaching must now be used to build up a sense of community is strengthened by well-earned anxiety regarding the status of the larger community of America. We live in a political culture where examples of devotion to the common good appear rarely even at the highest levels of government. It follows that devotion to the parochial interests of many small communities must be inculcated in the schools—as in every other turret or trench

the society has left vacant—for the hope is that a common good
will evolve tomorrow from all the unharmonizing ambitions we
foment today. This seems to be our predicament, but it is dismal,
and not in fact the name of a possibility anyone wants to realize.
It is an expediency that banks on a distant reward from the mere
show of an indulgent good nature. But the cherishing of this vague
hope has served to establish more deeply than before the division
between the two cultures I spoke of at the start of this chapter. The
guiding concern and solicitude of the academic system are felt to
be obligatory in exact proportion to the absence of such helps in
the organized system outside.[7] In Rousseau's ideal republic, men
were forced to be free. In the severe republicanism that academic
life has begun to embrace, men and women are forced to be decent,
generous, compassionate, as full as possible of remedial guilt and
well-attested pity—at least, they are required to be like this *in all
their outward signs*. The universities, that is to say, have gone some
way toward acknowledging as an essential function the creation of
citizens. This was always a long-term good they embraced; but the
close work of perfecting the means involves a fresh commitment;
it brings in its train the necessity of searching out all delinquents,
with a rigor proper to a community whose performance must not
only satisfy its own needs but balance the imperfect satisfaction of
those needs outside. All this is new, untried, and exists in a very
uneasy tension with the liberal habits of American democracy.

A celebrated version of the "two moralities" line of thinking—
the academic morality being required in this case to offset the slack
morals and even the manners countenanced by the general community—was employed by Vartan Gregorian, president of Brown
University, in giving grounds for the expulsion in 1991 of an undergraduate, Doug Hann. Doubtless the case warranted serious
censure: Hann went on a reckless drunken spree of imprecations
against Jews, blacks, and gays. His words must be given here,
though they contain no variation on the low-as-dirt formulas of
loathsome rant and bigotry, to permit the reader to judge the
extraordinary way in which his words were construed. He shouted:

"Fuck you, niggers!" "What are you, a faggot?" "What are you, a Jew? Fucking Jew!" Now Gregorian believes himself to be a defender of free speech; he had, in consequence, the difficult task of so defining these words that they would seem an instance of something other than speech; and, in fact, the charge that got Hann expelled was a charge of impermissible *behavior*—specifically, of harassment. Imagine a young man, with all the traits of a mean drunk, naturally coarse of temperament, or with the twisted ugliness that only resentment can cause, turned loose on a bad night in college (the night of his twenty-first birthday), throwing out his string of insults to all who would listen. He is gross, and stupid, a nuisance to others and to himself. But expulsion? On what moral scale can any proportion be discovered between this offense and that punishment?

Here is where harassment comes in. Doug Hann, the argument must try to show, in himself and by his words constituted a violent threat to the self-esteem of the students who heard or overheard him: above all, to those who took personally the things he said. But as the executive director of the Rhode Island American Civil Liberties Union, Steven Brown, scrupulously observed in a letter to Gregorian, "we have not seen any allegation of harassment in the normal sense of the word, i.e., that Mr. Hann *singled out any particular student or students for repeated intimidation*" (emphasis added). What Hann was really doing by his words that night was changing the atmosphere, on one part of the campus, perceptibly for the worse—at least for the moments during which his words were fixed in people's minds. It was much the same offense that a person may commit in civil life by sending a sudden raucous howl through a quiet street—say, a street that contains a library. A public nuisance whose offense is *noise* cannot go unabated, and if the noise continues the neighbors will work to restrain it forcibly, somehow. This, on a common reading, was Hann's situation. By upholding the extraordinary measure of expulsion, President Gregorian showed that some kinds of noise, some brief or protracted changes in the atmosphere, were unthinkable: the *possible* effects were so terrible that the cause must not be tolerated; and new meanings were, in consequence, read into English words to assure that such effects would be discouraged in the future.

I have taken the data reported here from an article by Nat Hentoff in the *Village Voice* ("The Two Vartan Gregorians," March 26, 1991). Hentoff also notes a tacit belief underlying the mode of punishment: that certain undirected words, hurtled into the night air, could fracture the sensibilities of the young. To believe this is to assume an infinite and unutterable fragility in today's students— an idea so patronizing that it is remarkable so few of the students themselves have protested against it. Their silence may have more than one source: actual approval, or, more often, a conniving, half-hearted approval of the punishment; but also a failure (itself the fault of education) to recognize in the demands of expedient paternalism a violation of principle. In the absence of such protests, the sense of the fragility of young communities-in-training could be invoked by Gregorian in a statement of February 12, 1991, where he sought to justify the expulsion. "The university's most compelling challenge," he wrote, "is to achieve a fruitful balance between respecting the rights of its individual members to operate and speak freely in pursuit of the truth, and fostering a climate of mutual respect and adherence to accepted community values and standards of conduct." The first part of the challenge is well described, though perhaps a nuance is missed: the university's function is not to *respect* the rights of its members—that much ought to go without saying—but merely to bring them together, as people whose speech is unfettered. Where such rights are established, the university itself is nothing but the speech, and the unspoken thoughts, that follow from the wide exercise of the rights.

The second part of Gregorian's challenge touches a statesmanlike sonority but is, in fact, nonsense. The university does not have the task of "fostering" anything except the people who can use it. Besides, what could it mean to foster "mutual respect and adherence to accepted community values." The whole meaning of the last clause hangs on a question that is begged. And it is the same question that arose with the dormitory supervisors at SUNY Binghamton: *Which community does Gregorian have in mind?* If it be the community defined by American manners, morals, and laws, then any defection from standards is punishable by disapproval, censure, and an existing body of laws. When faced by grave threats to its standards and its whole code of conduct, society will respond with a vigor appropriate to the occasion. There remains a troubling possibility: we may be close to a national mood in which manners are not trusted to accomplish anything. If this becomes a pattern, it will soon reach the point where, for solutions to the commonest wrangle, we fall back on the lawyers' help of a written code backed by explicit sanctions. But the word *foster* in Gregorian's statement, so close to the word *community*, gives the game away: in the community at large, not enough caring goes on, not enough shepherding, fostering, sensitive testing and establishing of the right climate for moral conduct. The mission of the university on this view is to make up the difference between true public need and the poor satisfaction of that need in civil life. The university thus embodies, in effect, another community. It must aim higher, distribute its rewards and punishments differently—sometimes by a softer, sometimes by a harsher law—in keeping with a single-minded pursuit of its mission. In this way alone, it may hope to counteract the want of decent fostering in the ordinary community.

We have now traveled far on the academic terrain of "sensitivity" and the recent idea that comes with it: that higher education ought to be, in significant measure, a kind of sensitivity training. The putting of this idea into practice reached its furthest point, to date, in a series of events at Yale Law School. I rely here chiefly on a report published by a law student, Jeff Rosen ("Hate Mail," *New Republic*, February 18, 1991). In fall 1990, a white woman enrolled at the law school was raped by two black men in New Haven; soon after, ten black law students found in their mailboxes an inflammatory note about the incident which ended with the sentence: "Now do you know why we call you NIGGERS?" As I write, almost a year later, the author or authors of the letter have not been found, and any decent institution would have done what the faculty of the law school did when the letter was made public. They gave expression to their sympathy for the students who had received copies of the letter, their unqualified condemnation of its sentiments and of the motive from which it must have been written, and their intention of punishing the culprit once he, she, or they were found. But the dean of the law school, Guido Calabresi, went a great deal further than this. He said in a public memorandum that the letters brought out the racism of institutions in which the students and faculty together were implicated. The letters had wounded the students to whom they were addressed: there was now a feeling of hurt that members of the law school community ought to share and try to heal together. By the satisfying transition from an unknown individual to a knowable collective guilt, Calabresi also implied that one might well have formed a conclusion concerning the identity of the author, and that it was very likely a student at the law school.

In the mood that followed this manifesto, a one-day boycott of classes was called by a newly formed ad hoc Committee for Diversity; the same committee also decided, on behalf of their peers, that the best use of the chosen day would be for persons of good faith to attend race-sensitivity workshops run by a New York outfit called Project Reach, which specializes in such events. Most of the faculty and many students were outraged by this development. Without officially endorsing the boycott, Dean Calabresi responded by urging members of the faculty to participate in the therapy sessions, and a sincere mass exchange of feelings was conducted between black and white law students under laboratory conditions. Black students accused and white students confessed to unprosecutable crimes of the heart. The assumption seems to have grown that, to authenticate the collective experience, it must come to be known that a white law student committed the crime.

Here again, Calabresi offered a therapeutic hand. To the question, *What ought to be done to the letter writer?* he answered: "For myself, I am convinced that there is no place in this school for such vicious cowards." The unfound author was thus, by a distinguished representative of the spirit of the American law, tried, convicted, and expelled in advance. As reported by Rosen, three hundred students signed a petition to the same effect. Some margin of principled dissent came into the proceedings with the intervention of the president of Yale, Benno C. Schmidt. Taking account of a last proviso by the dean of the Law School—who had added that expulsion would be justified on the ground that "lawyers shouldn't be cowards"—Schmidt pointed out that "freedom of speech protects cowards, too." So indeed it does. One will not assent to an ad hoc code, devised for the sole purpose of punishing cowardly lawyers, unless one has already developed a strong stomach for the communitarian double standard. But some such standard, as we have seen, is pervasive enough to support the style of paternalist intervention sponsored by Brown University and reduced to a practice by Yale Law School—according to which speech, when sufficiently vile and when directed against victims who fall into a legally ambiguous class of the vulnerable, may, without ceasing to be speech, turn into the moral equivalent of physical harassment.

So ended a representative episode in the history of sensitivity. It was a defeat for anyone who would in public avow racist sentiments. A victory then for what, or whom? Two points are important to my analysis. The professional insulation of the academy, and the consequent weakening of good sense, alone lent plausibility to certain developments in the law school case. First, it became a brooding obsession of many on the scene that the writer or writers of the letter were necessarily white, and very probably law students, or at least persons with direct accomplices in the law school. (The last, in fact, was circumstantially probable given the author's evident knowledge of the names on the mailboxes of black law students.) From the tenor of the collective discussion, nothing was clearer than the hope that the guilty person should be identified as "one of us." Yet events of a similar kind, where unexpected culprits finally emerged—the fire-bombing of the Black Student Union at Wesleyan University, for example—ought to have proved the dubiousness of hunches like this.

A second point about the events is more significant, and by now so commonplace as to elude attention. To boycott classes for a day was felt by the law students to be *the* appropriate signal of their wish to cure American society of a racism that had lately appeared in their own precincts. They therefore submitted with docility to the sensitive ministrations of the community engineers of Project Reach. Yet all this occurred at a time when David Duke and other racists of an admitted virulence were inching closer to power in contests for state or national office. In the early sixties, law students like these, both black and white, would have seized any occasion to throw their weight on the liberal side of struggles in real communities, where people spend more than three years, where they are compelled to live and to die. But for such students now, the struggle they know what to do with takes place in a community exactly the size of a law school.

What has come into the climate of the schools that makes them now able to erase or, more strangely, to simulate a vivid impression of worldly politics? For an explanation here, one has to go back to another climate, that of the late fifties and early sixties, when the first signs began to appear that the universities might satisfy their inmates with all the rewards of an alternative culture. This feeling has one plausible motive in a circumstance I discuss in chapter 3: the universities do contain (in theater, music, the housing and licensing of other arts, the publication of works of scholarship and appreciation) a great deal of what we think of as culture proper. The fact began to be conspicuous, and was often acknowledged with some bewilderment, shortly after the Second World War.[8] But the sense of a separate culture derives from a conscious refinement of manners, and perhaps, also, a hope of moral perfection, which the universities alone stand for with a plausible strength and before a measurable public. Many observers of American culture in the late sixties noticed this tendency then. No view of the predicament is as adequate in its irony, and in its understanding of the moral relations engendered by the new division in culture, as Lionel Trilling's essay of 1965 "The Two Environments."

The way of life Trilling described as belonging to the second, or university, environment was at that time centered on modernist literature and aesthetic experience. It is no longer centered there: what has come to be called "discourse"—a style of mixed aesthetic and analytic claims, which subordinates literature and the arts to culture (in the genetic and environmental sense of culture)—now suggests the image in which the advanced mind of the day recognizes itself. And yet, much of Trilling's analysis is simple and accurate prophecy. Universities, he remarks, were once a place to which one went to mature, and perhaps to conduct one's life, in a setting very different from that of one's rearing and early education. The university of the late nineteenth and early twentieth centuries, however, was never in danger of taking itself for an alternative community. It made its impression by a special consciousness (one marked by irony and at times by opposition), in relation to the worldly community it might aim to criticize but not to rival. But the university environment, Trilling continued, in the late twentieth century itself took on a coherence, a cumulative power from the number and publicity of its outposts, and a secure worldly appeal that made full-time membership far from the act of separating nonconformity that it once had seemed.

In going to work at a university now, as distinct from the situation in the 1860s or even the 1920s, the student "is not being sent into the wilderness, alone, a banished man; we can scarcely fail to know that there stands ready to receive him another 'environment' in which he is pretty sure to be tolerably comfortable, an environment that is organized and that has its own roots in the general economy."[9] Trilling goes on to characterize the first environment, the organized system of our day, as still recognizably similar to the middle-class culture described by Matthew Arnold and Henry Sidgwick—"Philistine and dull, satisfied with its unexamined, unpromising beliefs"; whereas the second environment "defines itself by its difference from and its antagonism to the first," its "concern with moralized taste and with the styles which indicate that one has successfully gained control of the sources of life or which are themselves a means of gaining that control."

The last phrases feel so oddly dated that a little more needs to be said about the change in the academic milieu since Trilling recorded his observations. One might characterize the change by saying that the academic vanguard, in 1965, still could seem to promote above all an aesthetic environment—aesthetic for better or worse, of course; but Trilling's reference to "the sources of life" suggests how much this self-image was apt to imply. None of the cleverer participants in the environment today would ever use such a phrase: they would not begin, even in an ironic perspective, to describe their quest in those words. One can mark the contrast further by saying that the second environment now is less appreciative and enthusiastic than it was. It is critical and speculative. It has gone from a monumental culture with heroes in the recent past to a late culture skeptical of the very idea of heroes. The citizen of the second environment would claim to be attached not to life or the sources of life, whatever they may be, but rather to ideas of thinking as behavior, to the trends of "interpretive communities," to all the speculative dividends of intellectual action free of personal agency.

Trilling thought the second environment would "seem to be the more appealing of the two." One fact about the eighties is that in that decade it ceased to carry its appeal to quite so steady a preponderance of the best students.[10] With this reservation, his summary judgment applies with added force today:

As we watch the development of the second cultural environment, we become less and less certain that it is entirely free of the traits that we reprobate in the first, which may have led us to wish to unfit our students for it. This second environment must always have *some* ethical or spiritual advantage over the first, if only because, even though its influence and its personnel do indeed grow apace, it will never have the actual rule of the world; if its personnel sometimes dreams of rule, it yet knows that it would become bored by the dreary routine that rulers must submit to: the blame for the ugly actualities of rule will therefore always rest on Philistine shoulders. But as our students find it ever easier to take their places in the second cultural environment, as they are ever surer of finding comfort and companions in it, we have to see that it shows the essential traits of any cultural environment: firm presuppositions, received ideas, approved attitudes, and a system of rewards and punishments. The student who decides to enter this second environment, if he considers it from the distance of some provincial city or town, or of a family strong in whatever class feelings it may have, may understandably take his steps toward it in a dramatic mood, in the belief that he ventures into the uncharted fearsome territory of freedom. In point of fact, as his teachers must know if they have any right sense of our life at the present time, he is joining one of the two established cultural parties. If the one he has chosen is in the minority, the party of opposition, this has its recognized advantages.[11]

I have mentioned a change since 1965 in the temperament of many who set the tone of the second environment. There is a change that is perhaps more important, in the relations between the second and the first.

The first environment, that of American public life, is no longer, in its surface traits, conscious of a great difference separating it from the second. This may be in part because the philistinism that defined it has been glossed over by the culture of the image (which now strongly affects education as well). In consequence, the first environment does not see itself as an upholder of the solid virtues— of temperance, and prudence, and a responsible use of power—in anything like the way it used to do. Meanwhile the second environment remains conscious, at times rather artificially so, of its difference from the first. Yet it has grown so large that its very awareness of the first environment can disappear over long intervals; for it has come to be a good deal more of a "total environment" than it used to be. (Many professors, when asked, will confess that it has been years since they talked about politics in a company less than wholly composed of academics.) Now this weakening of the distinction of style between the two environments, and the sharpening of the distinction in politics, have led to an anxious alternation in the minds of educators.

In some moods, they believe, apparently, that universities ought to reflect the interests of the outside world. The strength of the corporate connections between the universities and big business are a constant reminder of the justification for this.[12] In other moods, it seems plausible that they try, or present themselves as trying, to remedy the defects of a society that cannot do this for itself. The number of sidelined political reformers, or of aspiring revolutionists, is huge at a university compared to any other institution. How does this combination of worries affect the thinking of an administrator? A clue may be found in the title, the conciliatory message, and a good deal of the incidental rhetoric of Henry Rosovsky's book *The University: An Owner's Manual*. Rosovsky was for many years dean of faculty at Harvard. His approach is that of a genial technocrat, one who can get along with every kind of person the university offers. He means to speak for the center, if there is a center, at the universities today. And his conclusion is on the whole cheerful: in one variation or another, he likes to repeat that "American universities are the envy of the world." So many of us believe this that it must be true. But what can a man so placed, and so generously disposed, make of the inward-turning and overheated politics that seem a leading fact of the universities today?

I heard the start of an answer when Rosovsky lectured at Columbia University on "recent discontents" in higher education.[13] His main tactic there was to assert that the problem was illusory. The discontents with which he chose to concern himself were some recent reviews of his book which had denounced it as complacent. He also used the occasion to answer complaints about the teacher-student ratio at Harvard and the cost of a Harvard education. It was a simple matter to show that the ratio was variable across different subjects, as appeared only appropriate to the different needs of students in those subjects, and that about as many faculty devoted themselves to as small a number of students as had ever been the case at Harvard. As for the price of an Ivy League education, it had remained pretty constant—over the past several decades, it had cost very nearly what a new Pontiac costs—and in reliability the commodities thus obtained were, Rosovsky implied, thoroughly comparable. Political discontents, he added, did not exist in the modern university in the way critics had suggested. He did not see that they pressed on him where he worked. To the extent that people were unhappy with the situation today, it was because they were put off by new populations in the universities and all the necessary accompaniments that go with a university ceasing to be the preserve of a tiny elite.

It is a thesis of the present book that many recent phenomena of the universities are far from necessary accompaniments of the widening suffrage of students admitted to study. As a democrat I am gladdened by the change; it ought to enlarge the experience of learning and teaching; but a common impression has been that at the same time education itself is narrowing its scope. How can that be? One response to the new demographics of universities is to pay constant attention to the different beginnings of the new students and use the university as a place for diversified social reinforcement. What it says the students are, on their race-class-gender chart, they will now learn themselves to be—but more proudly and resourcefully than before. A different response would be to treat the students as equally enlisting in an intellectual life and varying unpredictably in what they make of that life: they are taken to be equals in this above all. To raise the second view is I think to bring out the strangeness of the first: how socially oriented it is—always to a social result and a sociable feeling—and by the same token how anti-intellectual.

When I accepted an invitation to reply to Rosovsky, my interest was to learn how he judged these distinct approaches to education. Yet both in his lecture and afterwards, he appeared to deny that criticism of education could be anything but a pose, unless it offered a point by point administrable solution to the need for adjudication among constituencies. Having described his reaction this way, however, I am brought up short. For the author of *The University: An Owner's Manual* did not say, or imply, that he was opposed to criticism. Rather, he was opposed to intellectual criticism: the kind of analysis that appeals too severely from habits to principles, and does not take into account the diversity of interests a great institution has to represent. Nor did he say that one ought to refuse to listen to the critics. One ought to be tolerant and hear what they had to say, only take every word with a strong dose of irony. But, to judge by his reactions on this occasion, there is another kind of criticism Rosovsky is prepared to attend to more warmly. This is the directive a society offers to its educators simply by being a society—an apparent tautology which I will explain as well as I can.

If I follow his drift, the proposals that come from a society's being what it is are not, exactly, arguments. They are instead a given and deducible outcome, a machine, as it were, operated by the brute fact of demographics. "Today," an eminent dean announced in 1990, "we face not only justified demands for places in our institutions, but also the desire for cultural survival, multicultural appreciation, and sometimes varying degrees of ethnic separation. The ethnic politics of the extra-mural world will surely be reflected in our midst." When, in the public setting mentioned above, I quoted this statement to Rosovsky, he was careful not to dissociate himself from its guiding impulse. The willingness of education technocrats to put into practice sentiments like these— as urged by a few students and fewer faculty, and sometimes anticipating anything said by those few—has played a fateful part in recent decisions about the curriculum on many campuses. Let us therefore inquire a little into the meaning of the words.

Notice that the statement speaks of "justified demands for places in our institutions," and indeed the demands are justified. But the statement then associates these demands with a "desire for cultural survival" by the insertion of proportional places in a course of study. Rather illicitly, the reasonableness of the second demand is clinched by its being offered as a demand for survival. And here the statement goes far beyond the language of the people whose cause it means to advocate. Usually, they speak of representation rather than survival. They know after all that universities do not have make-or-break power over a whole culture. But these are details. Let us stand back and regard as a whole the argument that a university must *reflect* the composition, the demands, the shifting trends and tendencies of the society it serves by educating.

The criticism of a university that comes from a society's being what it is earns more than a fair hearing from the timely administrator. So great is the credence in what society seems to compel— the big society out there, or the little society in here—so reticent the wish to ascribe to education any separable place in the world, that the administrator is prepared to listen to the curricular readout from the latest demographics; to foster, subsidize, and legitimate the belief that the mind of the student deserves to *survive* only so far as it can prove its descent from one of the socially constructed group minds now on the charts. If I were a student today, I would find this assumption frightening. It is, in truth, more than a license for conformity, it is a four-year sentence to conformity. For there is not one of us who could not, if the will were there, be identified and exhaustively understood as the member of some group. Anyway, from the perspective of teaching this concession to imputed group demand is anti-intellectual.

Yet the demand idea like the core idea has an instructive history. The first glimpse of it came in the sixties when some people, who did not want to be bothered to take a bus out of town for a protest march, started to give an interesting rationale for staying at home. "The university," they said, "is a microcosm of society." A very pleasant thing, if true. If you worked to change the university (it stood to reason), you were doing everything necessary to change society at large. At the time this greatly lowered the stock of extra-curricular politics. It was well known that staying at home, getting good grades, occasionally demanding a new class, program, major, or subsidized meeting place were activities compatible with the deepest human agenda. Now the present mood in higher education has something but not everything to do with the sixties; it is in some ways, in its conscious professionalism and passivity, the very antithesis of the sixties. But the present mood has inherited from that time and from earlier times a reflection theory of education. The function of a university is to reflect a given society. To the extent that the society is inert, the university will be inert; when the society is changing rapidly, the university must register that change in precise measure. And when a society is warped by prejudice and bigotry, heated beyond a prayer of reason to the most vicious proscriptions and persecutions, what then? Should not the university reflect society then too? And if not, why not?

It is at this point that many advocates of the reflection theory quietly give up some part of that theory. They often adopt instead a remedy theory of education. The task of a university now becomes to improve society by the active promotion of views which do not rely on support from any visible outside constituency. This theory is more arrogant than the other though not so anti-intellectual. But in the discourse of higher education today, one commonly finds an uneasy blend of reflection and remedy theories, where the first is invoked to persuade large outside groups, and the second to reassure small inside groups. The position-taking dean who committed himself to the sentences quoted above was treating his audience as at once outsiders and insiders. *We should not expect,* he added in a concluding sentence, *more harmony than exists in the real world.* That is, it would be useless to expect more, but also wrong to expect more, given the justified demands we face. Reduce the demographics to a practice, and what it means is: people want to study that which they are by birth, or have come to be by custom or habit. And so: women's studies for women; Judaic studies for Jews; Afro-American studies for Afro-Americans; Asian-American studies for Asian-Americans. The list is crudely intelligible in principle even though there is no clear place for it to stop. But the contents of the list all point in one direction; this is a genetic code for intellectual identity. It says, I am what I came from (what my parents or their parents were). And to the extent that my background does not absolutely define me, the objects of my culture absolutely do.

What we are dealing with in short is a new fundamentalism. In the absence of articulate resistance, education will place us under the charge of the communitarians of the day, with their many small communities, and their controlling belief that we can only be real if we represent others like ourselves. I had a question for Rosovsky, and I repeat it here for the many others who, without quite giving credence to this mood, have acquiesced in its demands and aided the advance of its projects. Do you believe in the change you are helping to accomplish? Do you go along with the aims of all the separate small communities—disparate, and at times mutually exclusive, as they often are? Do you believe in any of their aims *for education*? I cannot say that I do. And I wonder whether a less than personal consideration can produce an honest answer. It is in any case just this mood of evasion and concession that makes some observers suppose we are living in a period of academic conformity as inexplicable as any the world has seen.

The mood is rendered the more perplexing by the fact that it occurs without the threat of repression. Still, there is no mistaking the signs. The idea of personal thought, of making one's own experiment in life, often the very belief in intellectual liberty is scorned. I am to be judged not by what I say, think, feel, or believe but by where I come from and by what and how much I am willing to do in a group whose moral soundness has already been judged acceptable. Agreeing to membership in such a group, anyone may be proof against any argument, so long as he or she has first resolved to interpret the argument as an attack, and then to resent the attack. The more independent students complain of this from time to time, in private. They say what they are seeing, and wonder if it can be what they think it is, and ask if there is any escape. The message they are hearing—that they can only count as members of a class or type, only really exist by virtue of adopting someone else's thoughts or someone else's practices—they have received from childhood in the slogans and imagery of the mass culture of advertising. Now they are getting it from their teachers as well.[14] If one wants to serve the impulse of autonomy in students like these, what function ought one to perform?

One can pay them the respect at least of giving a report from personal experience. When I hear someone address me as a member of a group—a group from which all one's relevant supposed interests and opinions can be projected—I assume that the person who is taking so much for granted wants to impose on me. This way of addressing me is presumptuous. The person in question, a pollster, say, or an advertising agent, cannot know how hard I have striven to escape from my parents, or for that matter how loyal I remain to some things about them: things not directly traceable to their class, race, gender, or religious or political beliefs. Of course, the strength from which one ventures such an answer is not a constant strength. It is, however, a strength that has much to do with the reflective mood that education seeks to encourage or recover in all of us. If we, as educators, do not believe in the value of this activity, do we believe in the value of anything that could not just as well be carried on somewhere else—at a club, or a neighborhood party, or a meeting of a church group?

The question leads to another which receives a less and less certain answer from educators today. Is it our job to turn students back to their parents safe and sound, intellectually and demographically much as we found them but, if anything, more confident than before that they ought only to be what they already were? Is it the aim of education to assure students that they need not change, need suffer none of the pains of distance that go with the liberation of intellectual life? Or are we a superior social adjustment agency, in the business of granting degrees that mean: "Your son or daughter has turned out correct. Politically, morally, socially correct, at least by this year's standards." An institution going forward on these principles would deserve to be called many things. A laboratory that knows how to monitor everything, and how to create nothing. A church, held together by the hunt for heresies, but without a single ritual, credo, prayer, or prayer book in common. Maybe it would resemble most of all an industrial park, with a perpetual supply of interns and apprentices, but with enough refinement not to want to call itself an industrial park. It does not much matter what we call it, for once the reflection or the remedy theory of education has been accepted, new demographics will always dictate a new name. Whatever the place we work in turns out to be, it will not be a place for thought.

Administrators are not by nature radical reformers. If anything, they are likely to be negotiators, temporizers, followers of the path of least resistance. But they see more of the possible tensions in a university than anyone else, and they are well suited to express, by an array of conciliatory tactics, the first formulation of a tension-reducing synthesis. Maybe it is natural for them to register a morbid sensitivity to the new fundamentalists—those who in one breath want to foster community, and in the next assure us that the effect of taking their advice will be to get "no more harmony than exists in the real world." Yet theirs, to repeat, is a real world of persuasion-communities that are fractious in the maximum possible degree. Given the unattractiveness of the prospect, one may wonder why the dispersal of the *sens commun* should have been reflected so keenly in the dividing up of the curriculum.

The truth is that the debate about the curriculum has become the accidental focus in which a good many tensions of American society are dramatized. Since the lapse of political argument in the mid-seventies, *the universities have existed in a compensatory relationship to the political culture outside them.* Absurdities are therefore countenanced in school—I catalogue a few in chapters 3 and 5, but they have become familiar in journalistic accounts—which would scarcely be allowed except for a belief that they somehow "balance" absurdities of an opposite sort in the political culture outside school. As a basis for common discussion, this state of things is unhealthy enough. But it has led to an expectation among many students and scholars that they should find, in the university itself, the community of like-minded and like-behaving persons whom they have been denied elsewhere—because such people are dispersed, or inarticulate, or persecuted, or simply because not many of them exist outside universities. The bohemian element in society has dwindled to a hardly visible edge. On campus meanwhile it has expanded and has partly merged with the fundamentalisms.

Where each "marginal" group becomes established to the point of stereotype, the tone of the second environment produces a confusion, in the habits of study, between the mood of asking questions and the mood of soliciting grievances. As a teacher I do something new, and something that may be expansive for *learning*, when I ask how far homosexual men and women have experiences different from those of heterosexual men and women, and experiences as well worth studying without sanctimony. The question may grow out of, or may eventually lead to, teaching a new course or writing a new book or just thinking. The move from this to the more censorious kind of inquiry—"How many Chicano authors will you assign if we hire you to teach modern fiction?"—suggests the typical passage to the mood of soliciting grievances. Where the intellectual standard has once shaded into a social standard, elementary truths are forgotten efficiently and imperceptibly. (One such truth is that an artist, of any race or sex or ethnic identity, has more in common with other artists however remote, than with other members of the same "cultural" group.) But a more systematic effect of the curricular franchise has been the splintering up of teaching responsibilities by the various movements of advocacy teaching: Afro-American, feminist, and so on; one may soon have to add Jewish, Catholic, and so on. Perhaps, after all, these are nothing but a reflection of the Protestant fundamentalisms of the society at large, whose membership is in the millions. Both aggregates, as they see themselves, represent voices of beleaguered dissent from the political culture in America, which has lost its ability to attach them to any promise but that of power.

Myself I find the fundamentalists as noxious in their practical conduct, though not always as hopeless in their declared aims, as the political culture they are revolting against. To one degree or another all these movements tend to be intolerant. Yet, it is sometimes said, the worst they could produce by acting together is an incoherent pluralism. I can imagine a different outcome: a negotiated economy of rival intolerances, in which the active and energetic groups work in concert, and together shape the curriculum of higher education. The sciences, of course, would still go on as they have always done. And the professions would continue to induct students after graduation—an ever more cynical mass of young persons, surer than ever before that society, like the culture they have learned about in school, is a perpetual contest between victims and victors, with no such thing as a common object of admiration. This picture may be far-fetched; I hope that it is. We suppose such an outcome unlikely because we are used to regarding the academy as the freest part of a society remarkable for its freedom. Nothing, however, in the nature of an academy makes it so. If one reads the anonymous attacks on the salons of the French academy of painting in the aristocratic eighteenth century, and again in the republican nineteenth century, or the articles on Pasternak and Solzhenitsyn that have lately emerged from Soviet academicians and that describe a recent milieu of proscription operating in excess of the demands of the state—it is plain from such testimony that academies are well adapted to set limits to freedom of expression, or to fix a conformity of opinion by incentives and rewards.[15]

If academic life in America becomes less free in the near future, one way it may happen is by a series of concessions to the sensitivities of the advocacy groups. Divided by sex, race, class, or geography, these groups have little to say to each other: an educational address by Louis Farrakhan, solicited and admired by one group, will prove to be not what the others had in mind at all. But communication is not what they seek in any case. Beneficiaries of institutional compassion, they want to control the scene of education to assure that nothing wrong, or strange, or possibly injurious to the group-esteem of their members, gets said in the public forum of the classroom or the quad. Success on their terms means that the liberal ideal of tolerance, which drew no comparable limits around permissible speech, will have been exposed as part of the imperial ethic of the West. The defeat of the latter entity will have been worth the sacrifice. But that is to look far ahead. In the meantime, sects like these in their present state can weaken the

resources that make for uncoerced discussion at a university. For
they naturally defend against one kind of knowledge—the kind
that challenges the protective instinct of a group identity.

It was a fear of just this nurturing and sheltering and oppressive
tendency, in every parochial community, that provoked the great
Enlightenment appeals to cosmopolitanism more than two centuries ago. Maybe because their idiom is so dated, those appeals, in
the *Federalist Papers* most memorably, have been less often attacked
in the current climate than the parallel Enlightenment arguments
for free speech. But as moral and intellectual goods, cosmopolitanism and the tolerance of tactless or insulting speech are closely
connected. Both principles refuse to associate the prestige of learning with the brute facts of authority and force. Both set the thoughts
of the individual on an equal footing with the demands of any
group. And both look on the breakup of group practices as an
occasionally necessary side effect of the creation of individuals.
What if it turns out that tolerance, the encouragement of free
discussion, is itself a Western idea? Must we on that account agree
to teach it merely as one more plausible notion among the many
lively alternatives?

To do so would be a disaster. And yet the people who teach the
West as a value seem to me as misguided as those who persecute
the West in the name of other, better, or later values. The whole
idea of values is a mistake I explore at length in the next two
chapters. But it may be asked, if one does not believe the "mission"
of a university to be the inculcation of values, what ought it positively to be? Two short answers seem to me on a better path than
the ones these pages have discussed: higher education is the learning of certain habits, above all a habit of sustained attention to
things outside one's familiar circuit of interests; and it is the beginning of a work of self-knowledge that will decompose many of
one's given habits and given identities. In these respects the aims
of education are deeply at odds with the aims of any coherent and
socializing culture. The former is critical and ironic, the latter pur-
poseful and supervisory.

I find a recent and accurate statement of these aims in Michael Oakeshott's collection of essays *The Voice of Liberal Learning*. Oakeshott writes that education is "an adventure in a precise sense. It has no pre-ordained course to follow: with every thought and action a human being lets go a mooring and puts out to sea on a self-chosen but largely unforeseen course. It has no pre-ordained destination: there is no substantive perfect man or human life upon which he may model his conduct. It is a predicament, not a journey." Of the role the university can have in one's coming to know such a predicament, Oakeshott remarks: "It depends upon a self-confidence which is easily shaken and not least by continual self-examination. It is a somewhat unexpected invitation to disentangle oneself from the here and now of current happenings and engagements, to detach oneself from the urgencies of the local and the contemporary, to explore and enjoy a release from having to consider things in terms of their contingent features, beliefs in terms of their application to contingent situations and persons in terms of their contingent usefulness." And if a historic inheritance comes to be known as a great part of what the universities can exemplify, its effect will be neither dramatic nor even, necessarily, visible: "The notions of 'finished' and 'unfinished' are equally inapplicable to it. It does not deliver to us a clear and unambiguous message; it often speaks in riddles; it offers us advice and suggestion, recommendations, aids to reflection, rather than directives. It has been put together not by designers but by men who knew only dimly what they did. It has no meaning as a whole; it cannot be learned or taught in principle." These terms, for an understanding of liberal learning, may dignify the errors with which I have dealt thus far.[16]

Nevertheless, these have been some of my main clues for the exploration that follows. The next two chapters are devoted to an attack on the ideologists of the right and left who believe that culture subordinates the mind of the initiate; that it speaks in one voice, or in two exactly opposed voices; that in the realm of culture, notions of finished and unfinished are applicable; that men and women have lived, and still do live, who knew well what they did, and who did right or wrong from contingent motives that must be taught precept by precept as an inseparable part of their meanings. These journalists, scholars, disciples, and institutionists believe that the inheritance they are obliged to continue, or to bring to an end, does have a meaning as a whole and that, whether for purposes of revival or of destruction, it must be taught and learned in principle.

PART TWO

2

MORAL EDUCATION
IN THE AGE OF REAGAN

Modern conservatives since Edmund Burke have held a difficult position, at least in part because of the distinctiveness of their view. They defend the things of the past, and are inclined to respect history; and yet, it is a foregone conclusion that history will ratify many of the causes they set out by opposing. John Crowe Ransom described this predicament vividly in a review of Russell Kirk's book *The Conservative Mind*, where he noticed "how conservatives when they return to power do not proceed heroically to undo the innovations of their enemies, as they may have threatened they would; but acquiesce in them, almost without a word of explanation, as if another chapter of history had been written irrevocably."[1] Accordingly, much of William F. Buckley's reputation as the spokesman for a serious movement, or Ronald Reagan's image as a leader in tune with America in the 1980s, depends on our forgetting that these men opposed the civil rights laws of the 1960s and have long been committed to abolishing Social Security if they could. All the way to their assumption of power, they argued for the retrenchment or repeal of a variety of measures which began as innovations, but which the suffrage of American opinion has preferred to keep as traditions. This, however, is a commonplace irony of the sort that all of us confront, simply by virtue of our existence in time. It is no more embarrassing than the liberal's frequent discovery that what the people need does not happen to be what they want. A more persistent difficulty, for American conservatives particularly, arises from their uncritical acceptance of the capitalist market.

For the market is just where the spirit of reckless innovation begins. It is an institution that cannot affect to speak sincerely for public virtue or the common good or any of the more local values that conservatives evoke to shore up against the tidal weight of modernity. The market itself has been the single most volatile and relentless force for modernization in our time. These are platitudes; but the ideologists I will be discussing in these pages, George F. Will and William J. Bennett, have said that they aim to bring to light the platitudes we live by. Given this conception of their role, it is noteworthy that they have professed innocence, and tried to assure the innocence of their public, concerning one main fact about our culture—its relation to the social and economic arrangements of modern capitalism. This has not been the policy of conservatives at other times and in other places. It was William Cobbett's love of an older way of life that in nineteenth-century England informed his attacks on the emergent mores of capitalism. Burke himself disdained any tactic that would have appeared at once to defend an existing order and to favor the instrumentalities of rapid change. Thus, in his speeches for the prosecution of Warren Hastings, on which he labored at the same time that he was writing his pamphlets against the Jacobins, one will find countless passages like the following:

> We dread the operation of money. Do we not know that there are many men who wait, and who indeed hardly wait, the event of this prosecution, to let loose all the corrupt wealth of India, acquired by the oppression of that country, for the corruption of all the liberties of this, and to fill the Parliament with men who are now the object of its indignation? Today the Commons of Great Britain prosecute the delinquents of India: tomorrow the delinquents of India may be the Commons of Great Britain. We know, I say, and feel the force of money; and we now call upon your Lordships for justice in this cause of money. We call upon you for the preservation of our manners, of our virtues. We call upon you for our national character. We call upon you for our liberties.[2]

Hastings was an early imperial entrepreneur, the governor-general of Bengal, and director of the East India Company's operations throughout India, before he was charged, by Burke's party in the

House of Commons, with bribery, embezzlement, extortion, and a systematic abuse of power, and impeached before the House of Lords. But here is his prosecutor, Edmund Burke, a conservative, arguing that a connection exists between the abuse of wealth and power and the corruption of morals. What Burke calls "our national character" and what he calls "our liberties" are not indifferent to the way authority and privilege are given by the Parliament to those who serve the nation.

I have started with Burke because I want to detach modern American conservatives from their claim to a precursor as morally impressive as he is. They do not deserve him. Nor is the disparity solely a matter of intellectual and argumentative strength. Writers like Will and Bennett also define their subject—the defense of tradition—in a far more specialized way than Burke ever did. The sort of questions that the conduct of Hastings prompted Burke to ask, they understand in advance that we will not expect them to ask about an Edwin Meese or a Michael Deaver. To return to such matters often and insistently would be beyond bounds for a party loyalist. But I mean to suggest something more. By a careful consideration of the leading conservative doctrines of moral education in the age of Reagan, I will show that Will, whom I take to be a significant case, and Bennett, whom I take to be a significant echo, have proposed habits of thought to shelter the culture of the past from the influence of the social and economic arrangements of the present. They hope in this way to sponsor the revival of a strong morality and the preservation of a high culture in America. I will give reasons for concluding that their program is impracticable in its details, that it is founded on a shallow idea of tradition, and that it appeals to a superstitious belief in the dependence of a moral consensus on a shared religious faith. But I have to begin by observing that the premise on which the Will-Bennett analysis of culture rests is altogether strange and new. It is, that a culture can save a society from itself.

George Will is best known these days for his work as a television commentator on politics, where he once cast himself as an intellec-

tual apologist for the Reagan administration. But he achieved his
fame earlier and otherwise, in the years of the Watergate investi-
gations and their aftermath. In columns for the *Washington Post*,
the *National Review*, and *Newsweek*, Will mounted a consistent polemic against the liberal ethic of tolerance that he took to prevail in
America. That ethic, he said, had given implicit license to the
disorders of the 1960s and culminated, in Watergate, with contempt
for the law at the highest levels of government. Against liberalism,
Will urged a return to an older tradition of civic virtue, which
required both the inculcation and the enforcement of morals. Such
a tradition was, he conceded, foreign to the history of American
individualism; but it had better be acquired late than not at all, for
what was at stake was America's survival. Many readers who have
followed Will's progress in a desultory way must have felt that his
politics evolved in response to a certain historical moment. At any
rate his writings seemed to offer a reply—whether calculated or
not—to the liberal and radical politics of the 1960s.

   This picture of Will, I now have to report, was not quite accurate.
I have looked up his 1968 Ph.D. dissertation, *Beyond the Reach of
Majorities: Closed Questions in the Open Society*. It is a massive con-
catenation of notes, written in a lively middle-journalistic style,
and, in its leading doctrines, indistinguishable from the mature
writings of George Will. Only a few of his columns (collected in
three books: *The Pursuit of Happiness and Other Sobering Thoughts*,
The Pursuit of Virtue and Other Tory Notions, and *The Morning After*),
and bits of his Godkin Lectures at Harvard University (published
in *Statecraft as Soulcraft: What Government Does*), have been cribbed
from it. But the striking thing is not that points of continuity may
be found; it is that the continuity appears to be of a kind unalterable
by events. Will, at the age of twenty-six, writing in an academic
context and well before what one now thinks of as the more thug-
gish manifestations of the 1960s, was already fully formed as the
opinion-maker that he would become. There are several possible
ways of describing a consistency as thorough-paced as this. Bage-
hot said of Macaulay that he had "an inexperiencing nature," and
I think it would be plain to many of Will's readers in what sense

these words apply to him. It could also be argued—and this is the way Will himself has preferred to see it—that he has both an unusually steady and a peculiarly unfashionable temperament. Perhaps the fairest conclusion is simply that, like many political commentators, he waited for his moment, and with Ronald Reagan's election his moment came.

"A specter is haunting American liberals," Will declared in his dissertation, "the specter of confident politics." And he added that "the kind of open mind the liberal favors is a political menace." The growth of the menace was partly owing to the liberal's reliance on familiar and misleading slogans: the conceit, for example, of a political tabula rasa, in the form of an "open society" or "marketplace of ideas," with which the liberal deluded himself that moral debates in society would tend to their own resolution. Will aimed to replace these untenable notions with some version of a consciously articulated public philosophy. If asked to specify a particular version, Will, at any time from 1968 to 1992, has often retreated to broad allusions to the need "every community [has] for an 'economy of intolerance.'" This means that the citizens of a republic ought to be interested in legislating morality: as a case in point, Will has sometimes cited the civil-rights legislation of the Johnson administration. But much more commonly in the balance of his writings, his own economy of intolerance has sided with such campaigns as those that would outlaw pornography, obstruct abortions, and qualify the legal application of constitutional rights to homosexuals. So, of a proposed city law in Miami in 1977, which would have repealed an earlier ordinance that had banned "discrimination in housing, jobs, or public accommodations based on 'affectional or sexual preferences,'" Will remarked (in a column he chose to reprint in *The Pursuit of Happiness*) that the repeal was "eminently defensible" since the earlier ordinance had failed the test of any law, "to point people toward more human ways of living and to shore up what the community considers essential values." The phrase "more human" is remarkable in itself, and the more so in that it appears to have been thrown in carelessly: a mere Christian moralist would have balked at this, as betraying a pride that may be a greater menace than the liberal's confidence. As an agitator for a public philosophy, however, Will's innovation has been to borrow the authority, without the humility, of the older moralists whom he seeks to emulate.

A common feature of the passages quoted above is that they concentrate their blame on tolerance. This makes for a coincidence, which seems to have eluded Will's reviewers, between his thinking and that of several radical speculators in the 1960s, many of them employed like him in university departments of politics. *A Critique of Pure Tolerance*, the antiliberal pamphlet by Robert Paul Wolff, Barrington Moore, and Herbert Marcuse which kept its cachet on the left through the early 1970s, appeared in time to receive an entry in Will's doctoral bibliography, and its ghost has had a flickering afterlife in his later writings as well. Like Marcuse in particular, Will has no hesitation in assigning to a vanguard in society the practices most worth fostering at a given time. Again, like Marcuse, he does not shrink from the sacrifice of competing and apparently harmless practices.[3] A new name probably has to be invented to suggest the savor of an ideology like Will's. And yet its sources are evident on any page he writes. They are not in the Founding Fathers (from whom he does not pretend to have learned much), nor in Abraham Lincoln (for whom he sometimes has a good word), nor even in Burke or Cicero. Least of all can they be traced to Locke, Hume, or Mill, all of whom Will condemns, in keeping with a general polemic against modernity which he derives, with a minimum of acknowledgment, from the writings of Leo Strauss. The theorist, in fact, to whom his thinking is most directly as well as obliquely indebted, is Rousseau. This seems to me to hold true in everything from Will's talk about civic virtue to his judgments of the naturalness or unnaturalness of mores which, in many post-Enlightenment accounts, would hardly come under public scrutiny at all.

Now an indisputable fact about Rousseau's ideas of virtue and nature is that they are nonempirical. Indeed, the language of the *Social Contract*, the *Discourse on the Origin of Inequality*, and the *Letter to M. d'Alembert on the Theater* makes every adjustment it can to place this fact beyond doubt. Matters like these are less certain with Will. At the point where one feels sure that one has captured him as a theoretical republican, he is apt to put on a different look entirely, that of the empirical and practical-minded observer of a common life. Thus "it is reasonable," he asserts in *Statecraft as Soulcraft*, "to note that we serve good governance by acting on the assumptions that underlie our moral language." Such appeals to ordinary language, in the work of other thinkers, are supported by examples of overheard or imagined speech, the muttered notations of a person weighing a difficulty, or trying to persuade someone else, or actually responding at a moment in a dialogue. The assumption that guides the appeal is that language—as the most subtle and flexible means by which we tacitly, but habitually, realize an understanding of life—incorporates and even anticipates the conscious sense of our relation to our world, our neighbors, and ourselves. Yet nowhere in all Will's writings is an *example* cited from ordinary usage. In him, the empirical-sounding appeal to "our moral language" turns out to be an exordium to a performance that never occurs. One may regret this chiefly on the ground that we all hope to derive instruction from evidence that is indeed drawn from our linguistic usage. There ought to be nothing mysterious about such evidence.

In the question of the legality of abortions, for instance, our language has no common phrase to suggest the constitutional rights of the unborn. It does, however, include expressions like these: "It *isn't right*, somehow"; "It's something I hope I never have to do, even if I don't feel easy about judging others"; "It's almost like killing a person." Our linguistic habits are full of the conviction that abortion is wrong. But then, and equally, one has to take stock of expressions like these: "A woman in that position is going through hell as it is"; "It's no good having the government muck around in people's lives." So one must add that our habits are likewise full of reservations about compelling a mother to bear a child against her will. If one pressed the experiment further, one would very likely arrive at a complicated verdict. In the moral language of Americans today, there is something repulsive, and something to be avoided, in the act of abortion. And in the moral language of the same Americans, there is something repulsive, and something to be avoided, in empowering the government as an interested guardian to assure the full duration of an unwanted pregnancy and the birth of an unwanted child. What the *legal* result ought to be of such a discovery, no sane person will now try to specify in much detail. For the situation is difficult, not because there is moral conviction on one side and tolerant immoralism on the other, but because our moral convictions make opposite claims at a great depth on both sides.

It is characteristic of Will that he should hasten past moments of reflection like this. In a 1978 column (which he chose to reprint in *The Pursuit of Virtue*), he was even capable of summing up the case against government funding for abortions with a remark that though the vast majority of operations "are performed by persons licensed to practice medicine, they serve not the pursuit of health, but rather the woman's desire for convenience, absence of distress—in a word, happiness." He uses polls as he likes, to suit his need of the moment, and without regard to the decadence of plebiscites. Here, then, are statistics that appear unambiguously to bear out the claims of a moral argument: the questions (we are asked to believe) were devised to register the precise distinctions between health and convenience, convenience and absence of distress, absence of distress and "in a word, happiness." I mention this faith in polls as one piece of evidence—we shall come to others by and by—that Will has been touched by the spirit of modernity in spite of himself. The dubiousness of his procedure apart, I find that the lofty tone in which it is carried off has become hard even to describe. Samuel Butler wrote *The Way of All Flesh* a hundred years ago, and showed conclusively the warping effect of moral preceptorship, even where the relation between preceptor and pupil is that of parent and child. To say now what is *for other people*, "in a word, happiness"; to say what is, *for all of us*, "more human":

these accidents of phrasing point to a smugness more settled than mere complacency.

Statecraft as Soulcraft is a short and repetitious book. But it was taken seriously in the Reagan administration; and, since it comes as near as we are likely to get to a full statement of Will's creed, it is worth examining closely. Will announces at the start that he is concerned with the "slow-motion barbarization from within of the few polities which are all that stand between today's worst regimes and the fulfillment of their barbaric ends." As for the American polity, it is less well fortified than Will believes it ought to be as the home base of all resistance. The fragility of our republican life, says Will, originated with an intellectual error by the Founding Fathers. On their analysis of political society, "The scope of the passions is to be circumscribed only by the virtue of tolerance. That becomes the foremost (and perhaps the only) public virtue in a society composed of people endowed with equal rights grounded in their common passions." It may be replied that tolerance is not, and was not meant to be, a virtue alone but rather a practice, which requires daily renewals to sustain its life. It is for this reason that the good of a society's decision to foster tolerance can be seen by its members, few of whom would claim across-the-board tolerance as a personal disposition, but almost all of whom consent to it because they are taught to generalize from what tolerance they do possess and from the benefits they derive from the tolerance of others. Still, this does not dispose of Will's larger point. He thinks we have overestimated the value of tolerance, and so allowed it to drive out other, indispensable, moral goods.

Let tolerance be replaced or, at least, augmented by some sturdier great ideas, from "a core consensus of the Western political tradition as first defined by Aristotle, and added to by Burke and others." Do this, urges Will, and you will be bound eventually to recognize that the maintenance of a society requires giving more attention to the souls of citizens than we in America had supposed. It may be useful to observe close up how Will introduces his key word: "Keats said the world is 'a vale of soul-making.' I say state-craft is soulcraft." The word *soulcraft* is apt to grate on an ear accustomed to English words. It is not quite at home in the language; and yet, it is not immediately clear what foreign word it might be a translation of. But the mention of Keats is awkward for a different reason. When Keats spoke of the world as a vale of soul-making, he meant that it was a place where, with pains, individual men and women could distinguish themselves from others of their kind. Soul, for Keats, implied something very like self, and hardly separable from the body. The background of his phrase, now so famous as to be known even to those unacquainted with his writing, is therefore not pious as Will imagines it must have been. Rather, it is naturalistic and probably agnostic.[4]

We shall have to make other corrections presently, but this will do for a preliminary demonstration that secular morals have had a long history in the West, and have often thrived among the very people whom a casual historian trusts to fall into line as religious types (poets, for example). A corollary lesson ought to be that the "core consensus" of the West is not singular but plural, with not a single tradition but several shifting ones. A tradition, after all, far from being what a few writers "define" and others "add to," is a process that begins elusively, takes on bolder outlines as it is interpreted both by those who admire and those who criticize it, and changes even as its authority grows.

What, then, does Will himself mean by soulcraft? A cultural faculty to supervise education in good morals, pursue a steady surveillance of personal conduct, and, where necessary, censure and punish delinquent morals. This, Will tells us, is just what was never provided by "the liberal-democratic political impulse that was born with Machiavelli and Hobbes." But, at the command of an impulse opposed to that of liberal democracy, "a purpose of politics" has always been "to help persons want what they ought to want." The republican author whom this sentence recalls is, of course, Plato (whom Rousseau exempted from his strictures against philosophy in general). But Will disarms the objection that such custodianship is strong medicine by advising us to think of it on the analogy of a pastor's role in his parish. "Politics should share one purpose with religion: the steady emancipation of the individual through the education of his passions." An emancipated individual will be less narrowly individualistic. He will be socialized by a knowledge of the mutual obligations he shares with others like himself.

So far, this is a familiar sermon; and it may be one that Americans are eager to hear several times in a generation, because they often feel on the verge of forgetting the degree of truth it contains. As a critic of liberal individualism, however, Will belongs to a special class. A moralist of the public good, he has also been, fairly consistently, a defender of the welfare state *in principle*. Nevertheless, it would be wrong to conclude that he is in some sense a social democrat, or even a communitarian. He has a more exalted idea of the state than of the community; and he subjects democracy itself to a satire that he spares the leading bureaucrats of the state. Hence (what may seem surprising in so severe a moralist) his exorbitant admiration for Henry Kissinger, the most successful antidemocratic statesman of our time—the style of whose memoirs Will compared to the style of Monet and praised for covering "a large canvas with small strokes that have a remarkable cumulative effect." A critic, then, of liberalism, democracy, and the forms of solidarity that have made the welfare state attractive to its less eccentric advocates; a believer in the necessity of "soulcraft," and yet a very limited believer, according to the low-church style of the age, in the necessity of a revived Christian orthodoxy to augment the powers of the state: we have only begun to describe Will's politics, but what are we describing? He is, it seems to me, a paternalist, in the sense of the word defined by George Kateb: a holder of the view "that the state is expected to remain indifferent to no sort of behavior, no matter how private, but must endorse what it does not penalize, and become the moral parent and preceptor of otherwise wayward, weak, self-indulgent, or stubbornly transgressive creatures."[5]

The slightest of pretexts will often serve for Will to give a paternalist emphasis to his usual idea of tradition. In *Statecraft as Soulcraft*, for example, he quotes John Maynard Keynes to the effect that in the long run we are all dead. Will comments: "The author of that sentiment, Keynes, was, of course, childless." This is not just a matter of wily sarcasm—though, if one tries the experiment of imagining the same retort in a Buckley column, one may decide that it includes an element of that. But Will has in view an argument about the enforcement of morals that transcends such local skirmishes. "Parents," he says, continuing the exegesis of Keynes's quip, "do not think that way. The great conservatizing experience is having children." For by having them, adults learn "how much this most important of social tasks is a task of transmission. Parents and schools are primary instruments of transmitting." *Transmission*, Will's term for the imitative (not inventive) continuity of a tradition, involves the pouring of a contained substance into a new container. The word seems to call attention to itself; and I beg leave for a digression. At a university where I taught for some years, there was a member of the faculty who greeted a debate on almost any question by intoning a version of the following litany: "A university is an institution that exists for the creation, transmission, and preservation of knowledge, and for these tasks alone." I found these words a calming and almost sedative influence; but in lapses of attention I sometimes considered a plausible extension of the formula. I thought: "The creation, transmission, preservation—and *destruction* of knowledge"; for, of course, knowledge does now and then escape from our tradition, never to return again. This was what happened to the phlogiston theory concerning the elementary matter once supposed to have caused fire. Until it was replaced by something else, phlogiston held the field, it was thoroughly preserved and transmitted. Whereas now, for students who know about it at all, it holds interest only as a dead idea. The same is true of the theory of natural law: roughly speaking, the belief that our moral obligations to our neighbors and to other persons are true, and not only right and binding, because they were written on our hearts by God. Many popular writers like Will, but many academic scholars too, are afraid that morality will be smashed to atoms if natural law ceases to be credited; and they are therefore even willing to cultivate orthodoxies they do not share, as a superstitious outwork of faith. The mistake of such writers is that they underrate the inertia—or, to put it more eulogistically, the interest in order, and the attachment to a common routine—which may be inseparable from human life under every form of government except the most extreme tyrannies. It follows that our moral obligations to one another may not require the aid of natural law theories, any more than the making of fire required the aid of the phlogiston theory. If this is so, what Will takes to be the core of a tradition of *conduct*, and therefore the foundation of the free polities of the West, is in fact as dispensable as the Gothic convention of flying buttresses.

In Will's theory of culture, our ideas, if rightly presented and candidly received, will exhibit a behavior as regular as that of a genetic code transmitted under ideal laboratory conditions. The assurance he wants from his idea of transmission is visible at times in small traits of style, as when he writes that a constitution "presupposes efforts to predispose rising generations to the 'views' and habits and dispositions that underlie institutional arrangements." Burke, who believed that "art is man's nature," would have agreed with this sentence, but would also have wanted to turn it around. Our habits and dispositions do underlie institutional arrangements; but those arrangements also underlie our habits and dispositions. Our virtues, such as they are, flourish in a place, and do not exist until they find their place. This brings us to another curious detail of the same remark, the self-conscious insistence of its *pre*'s: the constitution "presupposes efforts to predispose rising generations. . . ." Only ponderous constructions like these suffice to give Will the sanction he demands. But why? A problem for any constitutional government, and a problem Will would like to evade, is that its conditions at a given time may actually help to decide the "polity's frame of mind." The latter is not entirely separable from its frame of body. At present, for example, there is an unprecedented danger that a generation of Americans will be made permanently cynical, and overlook the things that have been most admirable in our social arrangements, all because an ethic of greed, which they rightly associate with Ronald Reagan, has absorbed or else repelled them but in any case has relieved them of the obligation to think. When they watched that president on television and saw him gift-wrap lies (Our Founding Fathers the Terrorists), dissolve facts (the very existence of Americans who cannot find work), smile and forge ahead, they could hardly still rely on presuppositions and predispositions for guidance. In such circumstances the leading question becomes, whether this man will finally succeed in educating all of us down to his level; and, if so, what adaptations we shall have to make.[6]

As one inquires further into the character of Will's paternalism, its sharper features seem to recede and grow vague in the middle distance. Keen as his instincts are, on the track of any liberal cantterm, he falls here into the cant of the age by exhorting us to heed well the true worth of (unworldly riches? friendship? learning? no, none of these, but)—"Excellence." I do not rise to attack excellence. I cannot help observing that it looks like an effort to split the difference between the old virtues—prudence, fortitude, temperance, justice—and a native utilitarianism that reserves its highest position for the spirit of self-advancing enterprise. Of course, Will writes in a nobler strain: "The abandonment of soulcraft was an abandonment of a pursuit of excellence." And maybe, after all, the native overtones are merely incidental. Maybe we are back with the original paternalist, the author of *The Republic*. The virtue (excellence) of a knife is to cut; the virtue (excellence) of a dog is to hunt or watch; likewise the virtue of a human being is to be more human: a phrase, as we have seen, which Will felt confident of his power to interpret and which, taken literally, meant the state of being *heterosexual* and *not childless*. "A society," he now continues, "that has no closed questions cannot count on remaining an open society. Citizenship is a state of mind. A completely and permanently open mind will be an empty mind—if it is a mind at all. A mind cannot be shapeless; it must be moulded."[7] And the jeremiad, for it no longer has even the form of an argument, ends by asserting: "'He who moulds public sentiments goes deeper than he who enacts statutes and pronounces decisions. He makes statutes and decisions possible or impossible to be executed.'" Though these last sentences appear in quotation marks, they are incorporated in Will's argument almost as if they were his, and it is left to a reader of his endnotes to discover that they come from Lincoln's first debate with Stephen Douglas. I will try to suggest what the words are likely to have meant to Lincoln. But first, it is necessary to surmise what they are likely to have meant to Will.

Recall that in Will's idea of political education, the docility of a good citizen is such that he may be compared to a vessel that needs only to be filled. (If, instead of instructing a citizen in political life, one wanted to teach him how to play a game—say, chess—one would have to break the mold occasionally, since otherwise one would be condemning one's pupil to replay the same moves forever. Political life, however, unlike chess, is a solemn business.) As Will peers into the mind in the vessel, he sees that it not only exhibits behavior but possesses an inner state. Now, this naturally fascinates him, from a censorial point of view: so much so that the subject of his argument seems to change without his noticing it. It began by having to do with the necessity of calling some questions closed. But it has come to center on a different concern altogether, the naturalness of regarding citizenship as a state of mind. The sentence from Lincoln which Will quoted without attribution, as part of the Mind of the West, related in its context not to the psychological process by which minds are closed, but to the social recognition by which debates on certain issues are *implicitly fore-closed*. Burke's whole philosophy was a continuous lesson in how that happens, and in why we ought to care about how it happens. Thus, Lincoln was a careful reader of Burke, just where Will is an impatient disciple; for he saw that such acts of closure were not a matter of setting "ought" before "is." They were a matter rather of seeing how much of what is, how great a preponderance of the sentiments we know as ours, incline us in a certain direction at a certain moment in our history. Will pictures educators building a state of mind which in turn produces good laws. Burke and Lincoln pictured no educators in this sense, but a citizenry coming to self-knowledge, person by person, and seeing where the laws do and do not answer to a state of mind they hold in common. Decisions of this sort (it is part of Burke's and Lincoln's purpose to suggest) often take place in public, and not always at what has been designated a scene of instruction. Wherever they do occur, they teach us to move, in imagination, from ourselves to the little platoon we belong to in society, to a love of our country and of mankind.

The confusion of "closed questions" with a regulated inner "state of mind" has marked Will's thinking all the way from his dissertation to his most recent columns. Indeed, he sometimes makes the jump in the space of a few lines, where it is impossible to miss what is happening. In *Statecraft as Soulcraft*, he commends President Johnson's statement that the Civil Rights Bill was enacted because "a man has a right not to be insulted in front of his children." These are eloquent words, though it would be difficult to say in what their eloquence consists: perhaps they echo a sentiment many people have always felt more deeply than they knew. The aim of the words was to recollect, for an entire nation, certain standards of conduct that its citizens held inviolable. But here is Will's comment: "The theory was that if government compelled people to eat and work and study and play together, government would improve the inner lives of those people." This could not be more wrong. Johnson's statement concerned the limits of what was conscionable in public life; it said not a word about what went on in the minds of citizens. There remains an important sense in which public mores and personal impulses are mutually influential. And yet, to portray this relation as constant and reciprocal would require a complete revision of Will's understanding of a healthy republican education. "Prejudice," wrote Burke, "renders a man's virtue his habit." Without pretending to the full aesthetic mastery of a Kissinger, one may feel that this aphorism suggests a nuance of the moral life which Will has never properly described. For it is always in the power of a government to help certain virtues to prevail, by encouraging some prejudices at the expense of others. In the instance of the civil rights laws, the American government did just that. A prejudice (the kind that makes us favor people like ourselves over people unlike us) was declared to be *legally outranked* by another prejudice (the kind that makes us think a man ought not to insult another man in front of his children). As to which came first, the law or the state of mind, the answer is probably in this case the law. Nor did the law work chiefly because minds had been molded. Minds, in some measure anyway, were molded because troops were called out to enforce the law. And we made the law, not because we had inherited an idea of excellence which it allowed us to realize more truly, but because we thought it was right.

Apart from a family tree of the fathers, paternalism needs to tell a story about the pertinence of their wisdom to the present generation. As we have seen, the fathers in Will's version are the tradition, all core, that runs unbroken from Aristotle to Augustine to Burke. How then does he account for the melancholy fact of its decline, conspicuous in the stunting of so many later, smaller branches? This part of the story begins with the unhappy invention of rights (as opposed to duties), of the autonomous self (as opposed to the responsible social being), and of the personal, symbolic, and disruptive uses of the past which received a first impetus from the success of modernism in the arts. All this is plausible, and a man like Will, whose favorite word is *pedigree,* would scarcely want to claim that it is original with him. The trouble is that he writes the kind of history in which ideas themselves have an agency, as if they operated independently of those who make or change them. Thus Will's bad modernists, like his good traditionalists, are always "contributing" to a project that comes before them, in this resembling the late-coming inheritors of a copyright. "Marcel Proust," he notes in a typical sentence, "contributed the idea (anticipated by William Wordsworth and others) that the self is a retrospective construct of memory." In response to learning cast in this mold, which is usually found in books with titles like *Perennial Problems: Their Cause and Cure,* it is fair to ask whether its narration follows the conventions of grammar. To what did Proust contribute his idea? A close scanning of the previous page will yield a general answer (modern life, the subjective impulse, the decline of the West); though nobody who had read and been moved by reading

Proust would recruit him in this way to the intentions of a nameless global project. It is, however, of the essence of the didactic story Will has to tell that it should reproduce the texture of its episodes in as undifferentiated a fashion as possible.

Near the end of the story, we learn that it holds a moral for American writers in particular. "We have had quite enough Leatherstocking Tales, thank you," Will observes tartly and primly. "We need a literature of cheerful sociability." Prescriptions of a similar pattern are, of course, mandatory in the work of a government critic,[8] whether the republican mores he aims to correct are socialist or capitalist, and whether the state he serves is pluralistic or totalitarian. Why cannot American writers come up with something to meet the order? We *need,* says Will, a literature of cheerful sociability; and from each according to his ability, to each—but let us stop a moment at the phrase "we need." It occurs at the beginning of perhaps two dozen sentences (many of them close together) in the text of *Statecraft as Soulcraft.* It is a phrase most commonly heard at the end of committee reports or academic reviews. And it is a nuisance. To begin with, it does not identify the "we" who need. That it has no intention of doing so makes it a hollow, pretentious, after-dinner nuisance. The truth is, all that we, as participants in a culture, need at any time, and all we can intelligibly ask for, are interested descriptions of our way of life, which set us thinking about how it might be strengthened and how it might be reformed. By contrast, the *topos* of "we need" always has an effect of bullying. It insinuates that the committee member, or reviewer, or professional moralist knows in advance along what lines of force, in what subfield or discipline, the helpful descriptions are likely to fall. Now this is presumption; and it finds its proper reward, many a "Hear! Hear!" later, by the reward of inattention. It is (to conscript Will's favorite example against his favorite way of talking) an easy thing to say "We need a society free of racial bigotry." It is only a little harder to say, "The integration of blacks and whites is a necessary step to that achievement." But from neither of these statements will it follow logically that we need school busing. It is with culture as with society; and Will's pleas for a "thicker" American literature are, in effect, a course in school busing for novelists.

He encumbers himself with embarrassments like these from a motive that remains steady throughout all his writings. I mean his distrust of secularism. This looks at first glance identical with, but proves on reflection to be much hardier than, his almost conventional distrust of individualism. The two issues are brought together revealingly in a passage of *Statecraft as Soulcraft*:

> Writing in favor of religious toleration, Jefferson said something quoted and admired today: ". . . it does me no injury for my neighbor to say there are twenty gods, or no God. It neither picks my pocket nor breaks my leg." Yet in the same essay (*Notes on Virginia*) he wrote: "And can liberties of a nation be thought secure when we have removed their only firm basis, a conviction in the minds of the people that these liberties are the gift of God? That they are not to be violated but with His wrath?" How can religious convictions, or their absence, be a matter of indifference if the liberty of the nation— and hence the safety of his pocketbook and even his limbs— depends on a particular conviction? Whether Jefferson is correct about the connection between the security of liberty and the prevalence of a particular conviction is an empirical question, and perhaps still an open one. But the logic of his position is awkward, as is the logic of modern politics generally.[9]

One may as well start by correcting a secondary but by no means trivial error. The "connection" Jefferson believed he saw was *not* an "empirical question"—not, that is, testable or open to testing— for the reason that no society, including ours, was ever formed by postulating such connections in a mood of experiment. Jefferson held an uncompromising belief, which he wanted to strengthen, and not to test, by carrying it into action. The belief was that in a free society, liberties could only be secure in the presence of a deeply shared common morality.

Because the only practical instance of such a morality in his time came from religious belief, Jefferson wrote the sentence about God's wrath which Will finds awkward for his position. But it was the regulation of conduct, more than the content of the regulative beliefs, that mainly concerned Jefferson, as his sentence about one God or twenty gods makes clear. And we, the beneficiaries of his thinking, are free to sustain his belief as we choose, in keeping with the best plan we can devise for the coexistence of the two goods mentioned in these sentences: the survival of our liberties, and the survival of our morals. There is only a natural difficulty, rather than a logical awkwardness, in trying to combine these goods. There would be the same difficulty whether we chose a religious or a secular principle of combination. Indeed, it is perhaps merely an instinct, or an instinct informed by a reading of history, that finally decides one's choice of one principle or the other. Like most paternalists, Will has an instinct (which looks to me like superstition) that tells him morals cannot survive without the prop of religious faith. Like most individualists, I have an instinct (which looks to Will like the blindness of enlightenment) that tells me morals can in fact survive without such support.

To frame the argument so may seem to reduce it to a contest between two irreconcilable prejudices. Yet it is striking that Will, as much as Jefferson, appears indifferent to the content of the faith he believes to be necessary. This suggests a germ of antipaternalism in his thinking, and its failure to develop betrays, at least, as awkward a logic as anything in Jefferson's *Notes on Virginia*. The most curious aspect of this encounter is not, however, that Will's position is closer to Jefferson's than he wants to admit. It is that Jefferson's statements may themselves be read as harmonizing with a secularism which he only anticipated in part. The first sentence Will quotes is about the nation; the second, about the individuals who compose it. Of the latter Jefferson supposes only that they must share a strong belief in a common morality, a belief that religion alone in the eighteenth century seemed to support in the lives of most people. Does the same hold true in our own time? If so, to be a faithful Jeffersonian will mean advocating religion as a truth of private life; but this, in fact, is already a smaller demand than Will and his party now make. On the other hand, if a coherent public morality can be sustained free of religious sanction, then one may as a good Jeffersonian advocate secular private beliefs, in addition to a secular public philosophy, and still suppose that one is helping to resist every imaginable form of social chaos.

Since Will is among the very few persons who now occupy anything like the role once filled by Walter Lippmann, Stuart Chase, James Burnham, and a host of other useful intellectual popularizers, one may regret that he has settled for a story as four-square as that of tradition versus modernity, virtue versus tolerance, classical republicanism versus American individualism. Still, most of his predecessors did the same thing. It is only when one looks more closely at Will's educational methods that a vague initial sense of doubt changes to something sharper. For a columnist even more than for other writers, mannerisms are an index of character, and Will's writing from the first has been notable for two: the ventriloquized gruffness of a downright Oxford slang ("Moynihan's basic point is to bang on"), which inadvertently carries the Gatsby trademark ("old sport"); and the studding of his text with the names of learned authorities, whom Will brings forward much as an *arriviste* displays silverware, to dazzle, stagger, oppress, and sicken the visitor to his study, his emporium.

The hard-earned, half-found Anglophilia is innocuous, in Will as it is in others, though some Americans may find it rather a tease, like his thin smile and his walking stick. The pre-Montaigne style of enlisting, for one's own provisional cause, the sayings of any number of sages, is a more dubious practice, because it strikes a slightly dishonest bargain with the unlettered reader's piety about tradition. Plainly Will does think in lists of names, but lists of names do not think. "Jean Cocteau said . . .", "As Emerson says . . .": never mind what Cocteau has to do with Emerson, it is a commonplace occurrence for the reader to be led by Will, with distinguished and ill-sorted companions like these, through a pathless wilderness of sententiae, to emerge suddenly into a clearing some-

where near eight hundred words, at the prospect of a decided
opinion on the advisability of sex education in Ferndale, California.

We may now come to a more vivid sense of the design of Will's
methods by observing how they are brought to bear on a particular
occasion. On June 18, 1978, he devoted a column to Alexander
Solzhenitsyn's Harvard commencement address. In that speech
Solzhenitsyn had attacked the intellectual promiscuousness of the
West, and raised doubts about the unconditional acceptance of
freedom of speech in a secular society, as distinct from the condi-
tional acceptance of it in a religious order. In a comment in *Dissent*,
I remarked that there were great writers whom we could not use
all of, and on the evidence of this diatribe Solzhenitsyn was one of
them: he himself had not been rescued by his great force of spirit
alone; he had been rescued by a principle, the principle of freedom
of speech; and in proportion as we admired him, we were obliged
to continue upholding that principle.[10] Will took a very different
line. He was disposed to appreciate both Solzhenitsyn's strictures
on "America's flaccid consensus" and his proposal of a more rigid
exclusionism in morals. This could not have been meant to suggest
Will's assent to the politics of agrarian messianism that underlay
Solzhenitsyn's criticisms, as a program well suited to modern
America. But he did go the length of announcing that Solzhenitsyn's views were "congruent with" those of "Augustine, Aquinas,
Richard Hooker, Pascal, Thomas More, Burke, Hegel, and others."
Briefly pausing to cheer the warm, if distant, handshake between
Hooker and Hegel, the reader to whom these names are not just
names may return uncertainly to "congruent with." That phrase
works hard to conceal the wide difference between an analogical
affinity which may be shared by discrete things, and a total identity
in the aspects of things as interpreted by a strong-minded observer.
In what ways, however, could Solzhenitsyn be supposed to have
conformed to the views of any one of these thinkers? Consider his
doctrine that great souls are formed by suffering against the grain
of their times: that much alone excludes Hegel. Or his belief that
the policies of a nation ought to be shaped by a cooperative un-

derstanding of theocratic edicts and the wisdom of the folk: Burke, and probably also Pascal, drop out of the picture here. Indeed, only in a very contingent sense can the remaining names be said to share a pattern of thought; we have to keep shifting about different features of all of them to rearrange the composite likeness. This is not a manner in which history can afford to be written. Is it, nevertheless, a manner in which a popular education in the history of morals can afford to conduct itself, in the format of twice-weekly seminars on the opinion page?

What makes Will so weak a skeptic in an encounter like this is his notion that traditional culture, if absorbed intensely enough, can repair the corrupt mores of a republic, the way a vitamin injection revives the spirits of a depressed patient. This is what I meant at the start by the illusion that a culture can save a society from itself. Will's argument proceeds as if we could recover by cultural means the very things we lost in the processes of social development or decay. At the same time, his sense of the texture of social life is rather abstract: certainly no more resourceful than the average person's, outside the class and milieu to which he or she belongs; and positively dull when compared with the nervous inquisitiveness of a rival columnist like Russell Baker.

It is perhaps the same constitutional delicacy, combined, as it is, with theoretical assurance, that makes Will suspect our daily lives have no solidity, that they are capable at any moment of dissolving into something insubstantial and possibly anarchic. And this is where religion enters the scene: to complete the work of culture, by assembling the fragments and restoring the substance of our experience. "Mankind," Will writes, in the last chapter of *Statecraft as Soulcraft*, "has needs—call them spiritual, moral, emotional." It does matter what we call them; but soulcraft anyway embraces all three: "The soulcraft component of statecraft has one proper aim. It is to maintain the basis of government that is itself governed by the best in a 2,500 year legacy of thought and action—social arrangements known to be right because of what is known about human nature." The date Will picks as a point of origin takes us back to Plato. And there already is a first complication. What Plato knew about human nature—not suspected, but knew—included an idea of the necessity of slavery. Will himself would renounce that part of "the soulcraft component." But are we as free as this to alter bits of the cultural legacy? To the extent that we are and to the extent that we press our advantage, our self-interested use of tradition exemplifies the same pragmatic and modern approach that Will deplores in the Founding Fathers.

Here is the climactic paragraph of Will's peroration, concerning the definition of man that we Americans, on pain of extinction, are now obliged to relearn in full:

> When man is defined in terms of his nature, he is prey to tyrannies that frustrate his nature by making him subservient to the tyrant's will. But worse comes when man is defined not in terms of his nature but in terms of his history. What comes is totalitarianism, which aims to reconstitute man to reduce him to raw material for history's processes and purposes. Thus, for example, Soviet totalitarianism cannot be considered an accident of Marxism, the result of a wrong turn by Lenin or Stalin. It is the result of doing what Marx did when he defined man in terms of man's experience rather than his essence.[11]

These sentences make a confused web of assertions to which I can only begin to do justice. But their most inventive touch is to have lined up historical consciousness and an interest in human experience *on the same side with* totalitarian politics; and to have lined up a theory of man's essential nature and of a stability that reposes outside history *on the same side with* conservative politics. This is an extraordinary error, and shocking to find in the last pages of a book of political philosophy (however condensed). If we know one thing about the totalitarian governments of modernity, it is that they have sought to obliterate all consciousness of history, and that they have done so in the name of a theory of man's essential nature. By contrast, Burke, when he wrote against the French *idéologues*, wrote above all as the defender of experience *against* theory—which was, as he described it, the work of "refining speculatists," "political aeronauts," "smugglers of adulterated metaphysics." To the dismay of the pamphleteers and columnists of his day, who altered their calendars the year of the revolution to begin again at zero, Burke spoke for history and nothing if not history. How then—by what feat of political aeronautics and smuggled metaphysics—can a modern conservative propose to write off history and experience together? They belong, says Will, to the totalitarian party now. But here again he takes a shocking, an extraordinary, and, if one may say so, a *historically* false view. Leave aside the question whether Lenin and Stalin are the legitimate successors of Marx—as depressing a question ultimately as whether George Will is the legitimate successor of Burke. It remains worth saying that Marx, as the subject of active and not just scholastic discussion, was heavily criticized in the 1950s by several *anti*-totalitarian writers, on the ground that he sought to determine the limits of experience too narrowly. To Will, however, this characteristic alone would serve to recommend any thinker. To be sure of numbering Marx among his enemies, Will has to blame him for procedures he happens to share with Burke.

The exposure of errors like these is a slow business. But what has distinguished Will's career thus far is the pertinacity with which he has survived exposures of a much swifter sort. He has sometimes appeared to flout even the decorum that urges a temporary silence in the face of public embarrassment. He published, for example, in March 1979, in the week before Three Mile Island, a resonant endorsement of the whole nuclear industry, a bill of health so comprehensive as to leave its critics on a par with believers in miasma, witchcraft, and other precivilized phantasms of pollution anxiety. Understandably, he does not reprint that column in *The Pursuit of Virtue*; but he does, oddly, reprint the self-vindication that he published a few weeks later, when the worst possible short-term disaster had been averted. "Events," Will reported, "have not contradicted most of what was said here about nuclear safety. . . . The record of commercial reactors remains what it was: no one has been killed and public-health damage, if any, is unmeasured." Was

this after all the voice of prudence? Or was it rather a reflex sentiment of commercial optimism, in the service of a corporate good
which the genius of public relations has lately captured with the
phrase *damage control?* Seldom before at any rate, in the work of a
republican moralist, have the ancient words *caveat emptor* been
given so euphemistic a gloss. But Will's poor judgment in his Three
Mile Island columns was an occasional and adventitious matter;
and readers faithful to a given opinion-maker will pardon such
faults until they come to seem qualitative and essential. This was
not yet the case with Will when he wrote of a well-known leader,
"He has relied so much on merchandising novelties that he has
devalued the theatrical dimension of politics." And yet, the president to whom Will applied those words was not Ronald Reagan
but Jimmy Carter. Even the staunchest of Will's loyalists, as they
look at the theatrical appreciations of *The Morning After*, may be
puzzled to reconcile the milder words with the grosser offenses of
the Reagan years.

When I had finished writing the last paragraph, a fresh example
came into view. There on television was George Will defending
President Reagan's nomination to the federal bench of the barely
literate Birch Society enthusiast and law school graduate Daniel
Manion. Why does a man like Will venture so far that one may
now reasonably charge him with practicing a double standard? I
believe the answer is that he himself, these many mornings after,
across the boundary from the Carter to the Reagan administration,
has become part of the "merchandise" in the "theatrical dimension"
he began by criticizing. To restate the fact in more familiar terms:
he himself has been partly responsible for a recent innovation in
American politics which seems to have changed republican mores
for the worse. As a purveyor of instant commentaries on David
Brinkley's "This Week," Will has been helping to shift the intuitions
of millions of Americans; and not about issues only, but about the
comparative status of elected or appointed officials and the journalists through whom their positions are mediated. Like his fellow
commentator, Sam Donaldson, Will by his conduct habituates view-

ers to a treatment of public servants that ranges from benign dandyism to insolence. The lowest habit that the new opinion-makers
are adding to the customary practices of an interview is that of
interrupting the guest without apology; and my impression is that
in this, as in the assumption of a competence at once above the
people and their leaders, Will has been among the worst offenders;
though all, from Rather to Brokaw to Koppel, are disgraceful by
the standards of American television journalism only a decade ago.
Neoconservative writers have pointed out some of these abuses for
interested reasons of their own. But they still keep a soft place for
Will, and exempt him from every stricture they correctly apply to
the rest. They take him at his word as a public educator on the
neglected subject of our need for a public philosophy. Up to now
I have treated him in much the same way. Yet it appears that in
the years of Ronald Reagan's ascendancy, Will may have become,
behind our backs and as it were behind his own, a different moral
quantity from what he set out to be.

The *Wall Street Journal* in 1986 carried a long article on Will, which
mentioned his frequent and sympathetic meetings with Nancy Reagan, and reported that the Wills had the Reagans to dinner about
once a year "just to relax." Other Washington journalists have
prepared the way for this sort of thing and anticipated Will's standard reply to challenges: conflict of interest is in the eye of the
beholder. Even at the start of the eighties, when he arranged a
party to introduce the new president to Washington, it could be
said that Will was simply making the most of his contacts, and
thus following a pattern which had never damaged the reputations
of columnists like James Reston and William Safire. In one choice
of his career, however, Will moved outside the norms of journalistic
conduct. He coached Ronald Reagan for his debate against Jimmy
Carter, then went on the record with praise for Reagan as the
superior debater, without ever declaring that to do so made him a
double weight in the scale, the first time as a participant and the
second time as a reporter. This did not cost Will any of his syndi-
cated outlets; and from the point of view of circulation why should

it? What it ought to cost him is some part of the reputation he holds for personal probity and public virtue. For, if this act of collusion was unscrupulous, even by the standards of the Reston-Safire insider tradition, it was beyond conceiving by the standards of a tradition Will affects to cherish more dearly.

In the summer of 1797, Burke was on his deathbed, and Charles James Fox, with whom he had broken ranks over the French Revolution, made inquiries in order to pay his last respects. Burke would gladly have seen Fox if his sense of honor had allowed the pleasure, but he sent a message through his wife,

> to inform Mr. Fox that it has cost Mr. Burke the most heart-felt pain to obey the stern voice of his duty in rending asunder a long friendship, but that he deemed this sacrifice necessary; that his principles remained the same; and that in whatever of life yet remained to him, he conceives that he must live for others and not himself. Mr. Burke is convinced that the principles which he has endeavoured to maintain are necessary to the welfare and dignity of his country, and that these principles can be enforced only by the general persuasion of his sincerity.[12]

Will's defense, when questioned about his coaching of Reagan, was that he was wholly sincere in estimating Reagan the better man in the debate: whatever his commitments, this was also his honest opinion. Yet he neglected every measure to assure "the general persuasion of his sincerity." It is the steady pursuit of good conduct, under the eye of such persuasion, where no division is recognized between public knowledge and private reassurances, that chiefly distinguishes the ethic of virtue which Will admires from the ethic of self-interest which in theory he despises. As Burke wrote in another place, of an advantageous private connection which he believed himself obliged to refuse: "The operation of honour (as separated from *conscience,* which is not as between man and man but as between man and God) is to suppose the world acquainted with the transaction, and then to consider in what light the wise and virtuous would regard it. I am sure such men would not justify my conduct." Will has come to ask himself less and less whether such men would justify his conduct.[13]

In turning from George Will to William Bennett one is conscious of a change of atmosphere in several respects. Bennett's position as secretary of education might have situated him to become an even more efficient publicist than Will; and he appears to agree at every point with Will's stress on the need to propagate a traditional culture closed to criticism. Yet Bennett is the less skillful writer of the two, as well as the less agile thinker, so that he often brings to light, by stating quite unguardedly, assumptions that Will has taken care to hold in reserve. Indeed, in Bennett's best-known campaign, his public sponsorship of a "core curriculum" for higher education in the humanities, the resemblances to Will's "core consensus" of tradition are so close as to warrant quotation in detail. "The late twentieth century," writes Will, "needs what the mid-nineteenth century had, a Matthew Arnold to insist that everything connected with culture, from literature through science, depends upon a network of received authority." This is the challenge that Bennett means to take up: he will address, he says in his 1984 pamphlet *To Reclaim a Legacy,* "the great task of transmitting a culture to its rightful heirs." To assist him in defining that task, Bennett assembled a "study group" of teachers and administrators with long experience in higher education, among them David Riesman, Hanna H. Gray, Wayne C. Booth, and William Arrowsmith. Yet, perhaps deliberately, Bennett leaves unclear the role that this group played in preparing the text of his pamphlet; in any case, he tells us that he solicited contributions from another forum and by other means: "The general public was also invited in a newspaper column by George F. Will to send me their lists" of "ten books that any high school student should have read."

Bennett's stylistic affinities are with Will, too, more than with any of the eminent persons whom he summoned to his study group. In seeking to give a vivid shape to their idea of education, both writers tend to picture the process as one of *combustion:* "the fuel that carries a social tradition forward is tradition," says Will.

But sometimes their figures of speech offer an alternative view of
the process as one of *siphoning:* the aim of reading great books is
"to tap the conscious memory of civilization," replies Bennett. In
spite of their announced design, these metaphors imply just the
practical, optative, and head-on approach to tradition as a business
of technical know-how, which has characterized the more lugu-
brious American plans for the reclamation of culture over the past
two centuries.

The latest decline of standards, Bennett thinks, has been visible
above all in the humanities, which are now often taught "in ways
that discourage further study." Others have argued that American
society itself does not encourage further study of the humanities,
and that the problem is daily exhibited at the highest levels of
presidential government. *You can get this far without knowing anything,* was the message sent to millions of viewers by the ignorant
old charmer himself. It was stamped on their minds by every
improvised word he spoke and by every stupefied answer he made
in reply to an honest question. To pursue this line of attack, however, is irresponsible from Bennett's perspective, which stops inside
the school gates. In order to limit the grounds of argument, I prefer
to concede the point, and will confront Bennett's analysis on its
own terms. As a main cause of the crisis in the humanities, Bennett
adduces the negligence of teachers. They have, he believes, lost
sight of "life's enduring, fundamental questions: What is justice?
What should be loved? What deserves to be defended? What is
courage? What is noble? What is base? Why do civilizations flourish? Why do they decline?" Some of these questions, of course,
have room for several more within them. For they have been asked,
at different times, with implications so widely disparate that one
may feel the questions were really changing, even if the words
stayed the same. But it is the last two of Bennett's "enduring,
fundamental questions" that give the game away. They are in fact
anything but perennial questions.

Civilization as a conscious enterprise, or an unconscious process
susceptible of conscious helps; a past accomplishment which has
now become fragile, and the destruction of which may be hastened

by the neglect of its inheritors: civilization in this sense is a concept special to the historical thought of the past two hundred and fifty years. It started with the invention, by Burke, of an idea called "Europe" and the invention, by nineteenth-century Russians, of a dream called "the West." Hegel and Carlyle fortified it with dramatic accounts of a hero who alone embodied the distinctive good and evil of a race. Now, Bennett's narrowly inspirational sense of the word derives from theirs, but at two more removes. Talk about civilization as a matter of pedagogy began in earnest with Ruskin. It was popularized by Kipling and reached its height in the years between the two great wars of this century. "Why do civilizations flourish? Why do they decline?" Spengler, Eliot, Yeats, Pound, Aldous Huxley, Christopher Dawson—all took a crack at it, and one had thought that period was over for good. It is understandable that a revival of the cold war should prompt a revival of just such questions as these. What is scandalous is that they should ever be placed on a par with "What is justice?".

A civilization, says Bennett, is transmitted by its teachers— "transmit" being a favorite word with him, as it is with Will. Accordingly he does not speak of teachers as "expounding" or "interpreting" their subjects. These last words would imply for the student a kind of *thinking* that Bennett wants to supplant by *reception*. Proper transmission, then, with proper reception, is to rescue from utter decadence a pedagogy which, at present, offers students a choice between two unpleasant extremes. It can be "lifeless or tendentious, mechanical or ideological." These make a curious pair of antitheses, as Bennett himself appears to recognize later on, when he writes that teachers "cannot be dispassionate about the works they teach." If we take this last remark as somehow consistent with the descriptions cited above, we arrive at a distinct but perplexing sense of Bennett's proposals. Teaching is to be passionate in some way, but tending to no conclusion, and least of all an ideological one. As to why we need a revival of the humanities at all—let alone a revival so carefully enclosed and supervised—Bennett gives a familiar justification for his appeal. He is disturbed by the narrowness with which students today regard their future vocations (an attitude that can hardly be called either passionate or ideological). They are "preoccupied (even obsessed) with vocational goals at the expense of broadening the intellect."

But whose fault is this? Bennett wants very much not to blame it on the social and economic arrangements that have made a career in a large corporation appear almost inevitable to any student who cherishes worldly ambitions. Such a student naturally wonders what a few books of history or literature or philosophy can do for one's earnings. Whose then is the failure of nerve? Bennett wants to say: the modern liberal's or radical's. Involved, as he is here, in a difficult tactical maneuver, he travels lightly and talks in code, and we shall have to interpret him as we can.

It would seem to follow from Bennett's analysis that we ought to demand, for the sake of our culture, a broader and deeper education in the humanities, however that may be brought about. Yet at this point Bennett seems to stop short: "I must emphasize," he warns, "that our aim is not to argue for more majors in the humanities, but to state as emphatically as we can that the humanities should have a place in the education of all." If one were to try to parse this complex of intentions, the result would perhaps be something like, "Stimulate them with the humanities, but not too much!" (Or, "A place for the humanities, and the humanities in their place.") Having stepped forward so boldly, why does Bennett now step back so timidly? One may read him as enforcing a constraint dictated in part by a rational sense of limits. Yet, as the clause about the numbers of majors suggests, in doing so he aims for a conclusion altogether congenial with the spirit of humanistic consumerism. And that is a spirit full of concessions. Of course, it says, we still need more personal injury lawyers; more real estate developers; more copy writers for public relations firms; more cosmopolitan influence peddlers. But please, while you are transmitting on their frequency, at least fill their heads with the right names to drop at cocktail parties. It would be shallow to suppose that Bennett sympathizes with this point of view. But, in his political position, serving the people whom he serves, he is cautious not to offend those who do.

Once the social determinants of the crisis have been safely nul-
lified, Bennett's story about liberals and radicals can go into full
swing. In his account there have been two separate phases of our
decline. These are "ideology" and "subjectivity," and he calls them
opposite poles. But the description is, as we shall see, slightly
disingenuous. For Bennett does not believe that ideology and subjectivity are the twin perils of a single epoch. Rather, subjectivity
came first and prepared the way: it is, in effect, the liberal parent
of a radical child. Bennett will say as much when he feels sure of
a familiar and appreciative audience. In *To Reclaim a Legacy*, published for general distribution by the National Endowment for the
Humanities, he adopts a more diplomatic tone. He tells us that his
"study group"—by speaking in whose name, Bennett leads us to
believe that he sought their permission for every statement—were
"alarmed by the tendency of some humanities professors to present
their subjects in a tendentious, ideological manner. Sometimes,"
he continues, "the humanities are used as if they were the hand-
maiden of ideology, subordinated to particular prejudices and valued or rejected on the basis of their relation to a certain social
stance." But, "at the other extreme, the humanities are declared to
have no inherent meaning because all meaning is subjective and
relative to one's own perspective. There is no longer agreement on
the value of historical facts, empirical evidence, or even rationality
itself." As one who believes in the value of historical facts, and
who knows that the facts say nothing without a perspective, I will
try to explain more clearly than Bennett what is at issue here.

Let us start by accepting Bennett's premise that "the highest
purpose of reading is to be in the company of great souls." Further,
let us, in imagination, place ourselves in that company. Finally let
us take note of the respect we feel for, but also the distance we
feel from, a revered presence we will never wholly come to know.
Well, but what then? We can watch the company hold a colloquium
among themselves, in a language foreign to ours, and with sounds
as strange as those of any conversation from which we have been
excluded. Or we can try to join the company (deferentially still, it
goes without saying); and ask them questions, with the aim of

learning something; and even give replies, in the hope of suggesting an unexpected counter-statement. This has always been one
convincing picture—it is at any rate an old picture—of what happens in education. But once we join a conversation like this, we
necessarily work in a medium that includes prejudices (ours, and
those of the company) and that yields perspectives (determined by
our time as well as theirs). When we try to make sense of the ideas
that form such a perspective, we may generalize about them by
speaking of "ideology." There is, as all teachers know, an educational use of ideology and a repressive use of it. The mark of the
former is that it assumes something may be learned from the past;
the mark of the latter is that it is concerned only with framing a
rebuke to the past. In Bennett's view, however, both practices are
equally vicious, since they license the same elementary act of irrev-
erence. They allow us to join the company in a conversation. Somehow, Bennett has concluded that the move from listening to joining
is also a move from impartiality to bias.

To help decode the more abstract features of Bennett's program
in *To Reclaim a Legacy*, I have found it useful to compare the sometimes evasive language of that document with the always forthright
language of his speech, "In Defense of the Common Culture." This
was an address given by Bennett on May 15, 1986, to the American
Jewish Committee in Washington, D.C. If I have interpreted the
argument rightly, it not only supplies some of the missing details
of his educational policy, it also suggests that a strong motive of
the policy from the start has been a reaction against the radical
politics of the 1960s. Already in *To Reclaim a Legacy*, Bennett had
noted that "intellectual authority" in the 1960s "came to be replaced
by intellectual relativism as a guiding principle of the curriculum.
. . . We began to see colleges listing their objectives as teaching
such skills as reading, critical thinking and awareness of other
points of view." Bennett, in short, already treated the adoption of
these ends—reading, critical thinking, and an awareness of other
points of view—as more or less catastrophic, and likely in themselves to induce an adversarial relationship to authority. But the

same theme is resumed less temperately in his American Jewish Committee speech. "Campus radicals," he says there, "nowadays tend to see the university as a kind of fortress at war with society, an arsenal whose principal task is to raise 'revolutionary consciousness,' frustrate the government, discredit authority and promote a radical transformation of society." The key word is *nowadays*. It was written in 1986, by a sentient being, a reader of the newspapers, the secretary of education of the United States. The 1960s are a nightmare from which Bennett cannot awaken. However becalmed the life may be on campuses today, however many radicals of an earlier decade give up the *hortus siccus* of dissent for the *hortus conclusus* of Wall Street, Bennett will not rest content until he is cured of his memories; and nothing will ever cure him. I believe there is a connection between the obsessional quality of thinking like this and the proposition, advanced by Will and now seconded by Bennett, that civility alone no longer affords a strong enough sanction for the morals of a republic.

Bennett in this speech argues that to preserve our way of life we shall have to inculcate religious belief by the agency of government itself. It is an extraordinary proposal and, therefore, its reasons have to go a long way back. Of the core tradition to which we can still choose to belong, Bennett remarks "We are part and a product of Western civilization"; and he cites, as earlier resting places of our tradition, "Enlightenment England and France, Renaissance Florence, and Periclean Athens." These were our precursors in coming to live by the ideas of justice, liberty, equality, and government with the consent of the governed, ideas which are "the glue that binds together our pluralistic nation." Here one may be conscious of a gratifying symmetry. Just as the morals that bind us to each other gradually congeal into religious doctrine, so the little allegories that describe the process of cohesion itself appear to harden. They began (in what we may now call Will, Stage 1) with a Burkean trope: "conservatism teaches the dignity of government that grows organically from the native soil." Then (in Will, Stage 2, which corresponds to Bennett, Stage 1) came the revised view of tradition as a capacious fuel tank, or a reservoir to be tapped.

But now, in a still more striking, if also more puzzling idiom, we have (Bennett, Stage 2) tradition as a sort of *glue;* with the hint that here, as in the paper chains that students make with library paste, to take up a single link is to encumber ourselves with the whole.

Still, it is noteworthy that Bennett's list of precursors—Athens, Florence, Enlightenment England and France—adds up to a largely secular tradition. Why then does he not follow the advice of the Founding Fathers, and opt for an American version of out-and-out secularism? After all, as we saw when discussing a similar turn near the end of Will's argument, an American secular morality can be rendered sufficiently binding by the enforcement of a strong nonreligious consensus. To discover the reasons for Bennett's choice, we have to move outside the field of education and culture entirely. For his ideas have been shaped to fit the larger policies of the Reagan administration. Nor have they been designed, by conviction, in keeping with its politics of principle alone. They have likewise been trimmed for expedience, to shore up its alliances of the moment. These are serious charges, but they are charges for which, it happens, Bennett himself has volunteered all the evidence.

In his address to the American Jewish Committee, this secretary of education spoke of something even more important than our system of schools, something he called the "common culture" of Americans. Our culture on his analysis has three distinguishable elements: first, "the democratic ethic"; second, "the work ethic"; and third, "the Judeo-Christian ethic." The division of the subject itself betrays a remarkable imprecision, like that of the baseball coach who split the game into three parts: first, playing; second, batting and fielding; and third, fear. It is, however, the last, vaguest, and most doubtful of Bennett's elements that occupies most of his attention. The Judeo-Christian ethic "provides the fundamental ideals that underlie our entire political and social system— ideals like respect for the individual, standards for individual behavior, and a commitment to decency and to service to others." After Will's thoroughgoing paternalism, this defense of individualism is almost invigorating. I can agree with, and indeed would

like to live my life by, all of Bennett's "fundamental ideals." But I
am uncertain in what sense any of them is Judeo-Christian. Perhaps they are if one adds, "in heavily reformed versions of both
religions." Nevertheless, respect for the individual, standards of
individual behavior, and commitment to decency are as much
Roman-Republican as they are Judeo-Christian virtues. What for
that matter *is* the Judeo-Christian ethic? Bennett is no help. It
"isn't," he says, "something manufactured by the upper stratum
of society in the elegant salons of Washington, New York, or Cambridge." By contrast, it flourishes in the common culture of "most
Americans."

When pressed for details, Bennett replies that the ethic has to
do with "moral imagination"; and "the moral imagination of most
Americans is," in his opinion, "sound." This last word, *sound*, does
much the same work in Bennett's analysis that the cover-virtue
excellence did in Will's. As applied to moral imagination, the adjective *sound* is merely a solecism. Moral imaginations are not sound
or unsound, they are alive or dead. To imagine a thing morally is
an individual act and a positive exertion; it is not to be accomplished
by sharing a condition, like a state of health. But Bennett needed
to misconstrue the English language, and pay irrelevant compli-
ments to the audience who stood him as proxies for *most Americans*,
because his business on this occasion was not to educate but to
raise morale. The year being 1986, our common culture was under
assault by an adversarial culture; and "one important feature of
this adversarial culture . . . is the theme that the U.S. is the
incarnation of evil, the common enemy of mankind." Bennett went
on to characterize the adversarial culture in a manner that more
prudent conservatives have avoided since the anti-Semitic campaigns of Europe in the 1930s. He compared its agents to a kind of
virus: "Most Americans, of course, reject the perverted culture of
our adversaries. . . . Our common culture serves as a kind of
immunological system, destroying the values and attitudes pro-
mulgated by our adversaries before they can infect our body poli-
tic." Burke was at once less dramatic and more cogent when he
conceived of this power of resistance as inertia. The very presence

of habits, and a way of thinking and feeling to which people have accustomed themselves, explains, far better than immunology does, the ability to survive which their culture may exhibit even in the absence of their knowledge of reasons why it should survive.

After sharing some plausible evidence that our failures of cultural reception begin long before college, Bennett renders this demonstration pointless by urging a defense of our culture and morals by other than educational means. "Last summer," he recalls, "in a speech to the Knights of Columbus, I argued that 'Our values as a free people and the central values of the Judeo-Christian tradition are flesh of the flesh, blood of the blood.' For this," he laments, "I was called an Ayatollah." Whoever thought of calling him that was a wit; and the label ought to stick. Flesh of the flesh, blood of the blood: this is bizarre language to be applied to religious belief, by the holder of a nondenominational office, in a secular nation whose pledge of allegiance omitted the words "under God" until the mid-1950s.[14] What did they make of this at the American Jewish Committee? We must go slowly here, for there are further signs that Bennett's sense of his occasion was somewhat murky. Students today, he informed his listeners, "may grow up ignorant of the role of religion, of religious freedom and religious faith in American life." Now, religious freedom is not quite the same thing as religious faith, however much the unifying phrase "role of religion" may try to make them so. At bottom, William Bennett appears to be saying that the sentiment of religion in general is more vital to Americans than the particular tenets of a believer's faith. We have seen a similar thought framed by Jefferson for pragmatic reasons, and by George Will for reasons which he insisted were more than pragmatic, but of which he could not give a coherent account. What all earlier thinkers on the subject have acknowledged, however, is just what Bennett cannot afford to admit: that religious liberty may, as a matter of fact and precedent, have shown itself to be at odds with "the role of religion."

The strangest twist of Bennett's reasoning comes at the end of his speech. Here I must quote at some length:

All surveys show that most Americans today believe in "the father of all mercies." But, whether individuals give personal assent to a father of all mercies or not, the extra gift of our common culture is this: the mercies—rights, freedoms, liberties—belong to us all. It is the heritage of our common culture, grounded in the Judeo-Christian tradition, that helps to support not just religious liberty, but our free society as a whole. Again, one does not have to assent to the religious beliefs that are at the heart of our common culture to enjoy its benefits. For example: "We hold these truths to be self-evident: That all men are created equal; that they are endowed by their Creator with certain inalienable rights. . . . And for the support of this declaration, with a firm reliance on the protection of divine providence, we mutually pledge to each other our lives, our fortunes, and our sacred honor." Whatever one's personal views, the religious tradition at the heart of our culture does require, in our time, common acknowledgment, respect, attention, nurture, and defense.[15]

When Bennett agreed to speak to the American Jewish Committee, what exactly had he been told about his audience? Was he under the impression that they numbered themselves among the believers in a "father of mercies"? (The phrase occurs once in the King James Bible, at Second Corinthians 1:3.) Or did he mean to suggest that these mercies included a protective tolerance of Jews in spite of their unbelief?

It is true that the rights, freedoms, and liberties to which Bennett alludes may count as mercies on a broad construction of that word. But then, one may well feel that one belongs to the "us" to whom they are given, without therefore supposing that they were given by the Christian God. Evidently, Bennett wanted to assure this moral but not Christian gathering that the founders of America associated the good of their way of life with a religious sentiment rather than a religious doctrine. Yet he supplied the assurance by quoting, as an example of "enjoyment" without "assent," the famous words of the Declaration of Independence, which do mention

a Creator and "the protection of divine providence." Into a very
short stretch of argument Bennett has here managed to compress
two non sequiturs. For, to the Declaration as a whole, the founders
did believe that we must assent in order to enjoy the benefits of
American society. But they did *not* believe, and it is a matter of
record that they did not believe, religious faith played any important part in the assent that they required. On the contrary, they
gave much thought to religious freedom, but left no provision for
"the role of religion" in the forms of loyalty that they inculcated.

Thus, as someone who believes our common culture ought to be
predominantly secular, I have a better claim than Bennett to be
counted as a moral and intellectual descendant of the signers of
the Declaration. The evidence is not only in that great document
but in the Constitution of the United States, the Bill of Rights, the
Federalist Papers, and in other works by the authors of all of these,
especially Jefferson, Madison, and Hamilton. The America to which
I feel a strong loyalty began to exist two hundred and fifteen years
ago. The America to which Bennett wants to divert my loyalty has
been cooked up in the past few years, on curious occasions like
that of the secretary of education's speech, with its appeal to a
Father of All Mercies under the auspices of the American Jewish
Committee. The heart of this new, fake "common culture" is a
stillborn marvel of the ideological laboratory, with no utility outside
the parlors of Heritage Societies. And yet "whatever one's personal
views," Bennett insists, it requires nothing less than "common
acknowledgment, respect, attention, nurture, and defense." All
these, he must be saying, are possible *without assent*. And here I
believe is an interesting problem for the modern conservative adepts of character-building. What kind of person is it who can attend
to, acknowledge, respect, defend, and even nurture an entity from
which he or she withholds assent? Someone anyway far gone in
casual deception and an apathy that borders on self-contempt.

Difficult as it is, we have to go on trying (hardest of all where
the new cultural scientists do most to make cartoons of our creeds)
not to confuse tradition with imbecility, or moral soundness with
moral idiocy. Ideas matter: Bennett and Will, like many weightier

thinkers, have said this again and again, and they are right. It is because ideas do matter that it is wrong to defend and even to nurture ideas one believes to be deeply in error. For those who accept Bennett's truth about culture, he holds out the promise that "this truth will keep them free." Those who both know what they think and assent to what they believe may prefer the older saying as the better one. The truth will make them free. It is not a secret that was found long ago but a gradual discovery that is still going on.

I have to conclude with what may seem an awkward confession. In the most general form of a great many issues that Will and Bennett raise, I feel a certain sympathy with their warnings. A common sense of the past is rapidly vanishing, from the educational curriculum as it is from the culture at large. More than any other agency of the change, the mass media have been responsible for the pace of this obliteration; and even within the academy, their influence is growing every day. One result is the displacement of old books by new ones, and if I had to choose I would side with the old. But my reason is not that I regard them as "cultural capital" (to borrow a symptomatic phrase of Will's) or that I believe by learning their lessons I will be better able to protect my culture against reading, critical thinking, and other points of view (to return to Bennett's leading signs of decay). It is rather that books which have been tested by a lot of people for a long time seem to me precisely those that teach the most about reading and are likeliest of all others to foster critical thinking. They can make other points of view so vivid that even our shared life seems foreign to us for a while. Great books, much more than timely ones, suggest a detached and therefore an unpredictable view of our culture. Their good derives from their peculiar power to make us think, and the right use of that power is to reform, and not to console, the culture and society in which we are at home.

Yet Bennett and Will, instead of ever suggesting a vindication of culture along these lines, have preferred to teach the great ideas as a master clue to the defense of the West.[16] The latter cause in turn has become for them, in a very confused way, identical with the maintenance of religious beliefs against the onslaught of secular ideals. Throughout their polemics, therefore, they are obliged to be reticent about, or else cryptically to disguise, the political concerns that preoccupy them both. In the body count of their mimic wars between the ancients and moderns, they have started and finished wrong for a visible reason. They have had to take Ronald Reagan, and the culture that he represents, as a more than implicit exemplar of tradition. But he is the reverse of that. The greatest of all modernizers, the unexampled master and servant of images, the destroyer of the past and the effortless deformer of memory: these are the terms in which he will be remembered, if a culture markedly different from his survives to remember at all. From such a future perspective the motives, as well as the judgment, of men like George Will and William Bennett, will be difficult to recover or imagine.

In one respect, however, both their motives and their judgment are intelligible even now. I mean the service into which they press religious doctrines as the necessary bulwark of an otherwise secular culture. This demand propels them to the outmost bounds of sophistry, far from their own sources in the Enlightenment tradition they cannot help invoking. But they take these risks for the sake of an ad hoc coalition of the Republican right that merges Christian fundamentalists, whose main political idea is that the Constitution needs to be scrapped, and neoconservative intellectuals whose hatred of the left supersedes every consideration of empirical prudence. Temporary as the alliance may be, the reaction it exhibits is part of an enduring pattern in America. It remains a commonplace view now, as it was two centuries ago, that secularization cannot be had without demoralization. The anti-Enlightenment argument against America has always begun here. It says that we had better act as if we believed religion's claims, even if that forces us to do some fancy bookkeeping. But the reply of our native tradition remains what it always was. It grants that the state Jefferson and Washington founded is hard to live with now, as it was from the first. But the role of an intellectual may sometimes be to challenge the common view of things. As Jefferson and Washington believed, America's unique mission in the world was also to challenge the common view, by showing that a moral life could be established without metaphysical tests or sanctions. A conservative plea may now perhaps be allowed after so many words in reply to those who take the name of conservatives. Our constitutional and secular state, and the individualist culture that has reflected many of its complex qualities, are doubtless not the best we can envision, but they are what we have to begin with and they are worth defending today.

3

THE LIMITS OF
INSTITUTIONAL RADICALISM

Can a great tradition of art or thought still command interest apart from the political interests of our moment?

Two distinct topics have been involved in the recent debate about the future of the humanities, and the worst failure of the debate is that it hardly seems to notice the distinction. The topics in question are the traditional study of the humanities and the study of tradition in the humanities. Attacks on the first tend to shade into attacks on the second, without understanding the very different challenge this entails. At the same time, defenses of the second often try to cover the first as well. Because I want to sketch a position that I have not seen argued elsewhere, it will be best to start with a disclaimer. I have nothing to say for or against what is now called the traditional study of the humanities; though, in the United States, few scholarly practices are of more than three generations' standing: a fact that ought to make us suspicious of theories which hold such practices to be either altogether oppressive or altogether sacred. At any rate I offer no argument here about the older patterns of teaching and research. Rather, I aim to defend the study of tradition as such. If I am right, the humanities are the proper place for that study to go on. And the future of that study may have something to do with the future of political liberalism and of the Enlightenment ideals of rational discussion and individual choice. I write in the belief that political liberalism and these particular Enlightenment ideals are both, on balance, good. I cannot imagine a good society that would not assure their survival. But in the current discussions of higher education, in the crude satire of the right and the protective clichés of the left, it has often seemed unclear how strong a consensus remains in favor of the survival of these things.

Another name for the subject of the debate about the humanities today is "liberal education." The phrase is still in common use because it has a sound that is flattering to Americans. But, in practice, the thing has never been as common as the phrase. The process it names cannot, in fact, be formulated as an official policy or embodied in a state curriculum, for it describes a tacit way of thinking and acting in a moral community. A liberal education tries to assure the persistence of a culture of responsive individuals—people who, in the course of a long experiment in learning, will have discovered the habits of attention that make it possible to be at once thoughtful and critical citizens. Where the future of the university is discussed, or just the future of the humanities, what appears to be most under challenge now is precisely what this understanding of a liberal education had presupposed: the value of coming to know a tradition that is not the property of any party. A tradition on this view, far from being fixed forever, may be shaped by the voluntary choices of readers and thinkers. Indeed, it exists not only as something to know but as something to inter-pret and reform. But a difficult paradox holds together the idea of a nonrestrictive tradition. Before it can be reformed intelligently, it must be known adequately; and yet, unless one recognizes first that it *can* be reformed, one will come to know it only as a matter of rote—with the result that the knowledge of a tradition will seem as unimaginative a business as the knowledge of an alphabet or a catechism. Complex as it is, the liberal understanding of tradition was for a long time promoted by American politicians, shared by public servants, exemplified by artists, critics, and freelance citi-zens. The process of sifting the tradition still continues, or we would be dead as a society. Our agreement that it ought to con-tinue, however, is weaker now than it has been for several gener-ations.

Given the practical need for coherence in education, what could ever replace the idea of tradition that I have been summarizing? There is a possible answer: an idea of authority. One must be partial here for the subject, properly pursued, would take us the length of a separate book; and a few examples will have to support the claim that an appeal to authority is often the opposite of an appeal to tradition. We are familiar with the sort of authoritarian (Jerry Falwell) who knows that it is wrong to teach children the theory of natural selection; and with the sort (William Bennett) who knows that it is wrong to teach grown-ups the history of thought without a religious overlay: the former has more-than-scientific, the latter more-than-historical, reasons for the authority he invokes. But there is another sort of authoritarian, only now becoming familiar, who believes "professors should have less freedom of expression than writers and artists, because professors are supposed to be creating a better community." This was said by Professor Barbara Johnson, of the Department of English, Harvard University, in the course of an undergraduate orientation-panel sponsored by the university.[1] Doubtless Johnson too has her reasons. But they are no more the reasons of a liberal or an educator than are Bennett's or Falwell's. Extremes meet: the fundamentalist of the parochial religious community has the same foresight regarding what is "better," and the same methods for achieving it, as the fundamentalist of the parochial academic community. Both ignore, or deride, the teaching of a strong tradition of tolerance in politics and learning. This seems the place to declare a polemical intent in the pages that follow. I hope to sharpen a certain general anxiety about what the authoritarians *say* into an active distrust of what they are likely to *do*. It would, I think, be a good thing if universities did not follow the example of some other institutions and become a staging ground for contests between rival communitarian orthodoxies.

One further preliminary word about tradition and authority. I have spent much of the last five years reading the pamphlet wars on higher education in America: on budgets, demographics, first principles, open-mindedness, and "the souls of America's young people"; the proceedings of left-wing think tanks and accounts of the same proceedings in right-wing journals of culture; with assorted *cris de coeur* from editorial writers and unattached observers, as well as exchanges of bewildered anecdotes in the letters columns of newspapers. In all this vast body of recent literature, the words *tradition* and *authority* are used pretty steadily, and they are used interchangeably. The confusion seems to be widespread. Yet a tradition may itself supply grounds for appeal against the exercise of arbitrary authority—the deeper the tradition, the better the chances for success in the appeal. It is instructive in this respect to compare the broad social influence of the Protestant ministry, in the abolitionist period, with the narrow exposure of the Marxist professoriate in the 1980s. In pursuing the subject anyway, it will be useful to hold in mind an aphorism by the great art historian Erwin Panofsky, who described a humanist as someone who "rejects authority" but "respects tradition." A troubling fact about the humanities today is that so many on both sides of the argument respect authority but reject tradition.

The crisis affects the humanities most of all because traditions are made from books. That does not mean a set list of great books. Few institutions have ever adhered to a single such list for more than a generation. And yet, educated Americans tend to feel that there are good books that students ought to know—a reason for universities to exist is that you read the books there, and learn to think about them. Maybe the books have gone on being taught in some measure from sheer habit. But it is a good habit. Such was the common perception of the humanities around the end of the Second World War; and on the whole the picture was right in its mingled sense of purpose and routine. About the structure of the humanities in 1992, the same educated Americans are apt to have a much less confident picture. But they seem to feel sure of this much: that in the humanities generally, and in literature departments above all, strong arguments have been mounted against teaching many of the old books. The habit of teaching them still survives because the numbers (of teachers, of students) are still on its side. Yet the opposition to such teaching is active and energetic, and it seems to grow stronger as defenses of the remembered routine grow duller.

To say why this should be a cause of anxiety will require a digression on how universities got into the curious business of teaching culture. John Stuart Mill invented the idea of culture in our modern sense when he spoke in his essay on Jeremy Bentham about the good of "self-culture."[2] The essay appeared in 1838. For a long time after, it was assumed that the culture of individuals might be formed without much conscious aid from institutions. Mill, however, had in view a middle-class public so much more conversable than ours that it takes some imagination even to recall the milieu he was working from. When one looks back at Victorian England and the America of Whitman and Lincoln, one is impressed by the consensus a majority of the educated observed in the arts and moral sciences. Not, indeed, a consensus of judgment, but a consensus about the grounds of judgment. That culture had its touchstones—serious monuments, local monuments—many of which have dated badly. But their familiarity was the outcome of shared ideas, of a knowledge of people and things and reputations to be reckoned with (whatever one finally made of them), all to a degree that we are now likely to find incredible. Incredible—and, many would want to add, elitist, exclusive, pernicious. But the first reaction I think is the true one. This was the milieu in which the author of a radical defense of liberty could look forward to seeing his arguments reviewed in *Fraser's Magazine* or the *Athenaeum*, the *Edinburgh* or the *Quarterly Review*, any of a dozen journals neither academic nor popular, which kept a cultural conversation alive.

We live in a different atmosphere, from which the available signs of a public culture have for the most part been withdrawn. The deterioration has sped up noticeably in the past two decades, and the ground note of American culture, as it is experienced by a literate person today, is television—at best the national network news, or some grave and newslike talk show. The news magazines are done in the same style and written by the same people who go on the shows. This change has been quite marked even in an autonomous publication like the *New York Times*, which once seemed a great resource for discussion and information, and which cannot trace its decline to any apparent sense of rivalry with television. What there is of a live debate on issues of current importance goes on in journals of opinion like the *New Republic* and the

Nation. These are run by factions, and their coverage outside politics is limited, but they are the only feature of our landscape that gives a remote idea of the intellectual life that Mill could rely on, when he trusted culture itself to be acquired as "self-culture." Consider, as a symptom of our different milieu, the fact that we have not a single journal that still makes a practice, as the *TLS* does in England, of reviewing a great many new books soon after they appear. What intelligent reviewing we do have occurs sporadically, often in the pages of small academic journals. That means that if works of art or complex argument hold much interest for you—painting or fiction or moral philosophy or political theory—you are thrown back on your own resources to make what selection you can. People in this position tend to look for help.

And, mainly, they look to universities. For it is an unhappy fact that most of the conversation about culture in America now is carried on in universities. Almost alone, they perform the function Mill and his contemporaries supposed no single institution would ever have to perform. No one can quite remember when they assumed this responsibility, but without them certainly nothing else would fill their place. They induct students into a life of reading, looking at, and discussing works of the mind. What troubles the pamphlet-writers and letter-writers about the humanities is that this function might, in the not very distant future, be suspended. Not that a disaster is on the point of occurring—but that it might, gradually, occur—because we have forgotten the arguments for preserving a state of things we took for granted. The anxiety I mentioned earlier is thus linked to a particular fear: that we now run the risk of thoughtlessly surrendering, in a piecemeal fashion, an educational practice which in turn strengthens a kind of social coherence we believe to be valuable. The government accuser who frames the matter in this way will receive from the academic comforter a ready reply: "Schools are much the same as they always were—just come and see."[3] But one ought not to forget a third character in this dialogue, who is present at least as an observer— the aggrieved parent who asks (or wonders if it is still permitted to ask), "Why are my son and daughter watching MTV for a class requirement instead of reading Tocqueville on the tyranny of the majority? I think television is a way of death. And what do they mean when they talk about an 'interpellated discursive body hierarchy'? What is going on?"

When a tacit consensus starts to break down, a panic reaction asks, How can we hold on to it? By what rituals of consent or symbolic allegiance can we make it mandatory? But in a free society, tests of adherence or assent are only warranted in a crisis that demands of citizens an intense, complete, reciprocal trust. We are not at a moment like that, and besides education does not feel like that, not even at moments of low self-confidence.[4] In an area where our habits and opinions were never meant to fit us snugly, we ought instead to be asking questions that lead away from tests. How did the older pedagogy lose some of its animating purpose? And what can we do to restore as much of that purpose as is now worth having? A safe consensus cannot be induced by artificial means, in intellectual any more than in moral life. What is sometimes possible, in the intervals of a controversy, is to offer reflection on a change that is already in progress. One thereby improves the odds in favor of reflective change.

A curriculum based on certain books is not as silly a therapy as it is often made out to be. Yet such a curriculum is, at most, a therapy. After all, the titles with which we fill our "required" reading lists make only the details of a collective portrait—the sharp outlines of which are decided by a story we want to tell about ourselves as a culture. Logically, this last element in a curriculum comes first, but it may be the hardest of all for us to think about now. A loss of articulate energy and even of demonstrable prudence in our political leaders; a tendency among citizens generally to follow protest, grievance, and other acts of occasional citizenship into the paths of legal redress and not public persuasion—these phenomena are both a cause and a consequence of the growing distrust in America of any common discourse concerning the daily choices of politics and morality. For students now in their teens and early twenties, the genuine struggles of this society, over civil rights in the fifties and sixties, over Vietnam in the late sixties and early seventies, can seem a thing of the past. So, too, can the very idea of a speaker or writer who addresses a chosen audience. The public discourse now is fashioned by front men and anchor-persons who read expressively from an electric roll of words and address an audience of everyone. The representative figures of the culture are lawyers—especially those paid to plead a cause behind the scenes. Taken together, these developments betray a weakening of the belief that citizenship requires an active competence.

Humanities scholars tend to resist thinking of themselves as exemplars of a meaningful discourse that is missing elsewhere in their culture. They resist from a decent modesty, and perhaps also from a sense of inadequacy. At most, they portray the life they have chosen as an interesting line of work, something intelligent students can "go into" if they care enough. The obvious worldly competition, people also known for their adeptness in the uses of words, consists above all of lawyers and journalists, but scholars seldom rank themselves anywhere on this scale. At the same time, they have felt pressed by the usual expectations of the academy itself to identify their work as far as possible with special credentials. This concern has led away from public engagements and into a professional—even, at times, an esoteric—ambition for the refinement of a knowledge all one's own. Professionalization along these lines has been going on for most of the century, and yet here again the past twenty years have seen a remarkable acceleration of the process. It says something about the consequent state of mind that no word in the academic humanities is used more frequently and uncritically with the intent to praise than the word *marginal*. We want a new knowledge, and we want a knowledge no one will accuse of pretending to be central. Still, some common belief is needed to enforce agreement and to excite enthusiasm. At present the belief is that the codes of professionalism and its customs at any time are good in themselves, since what one learns by standing outside them is not knowledge. The more closely one looks, the more conspicuous is the tenacity with which the last view seems to be held. It is a kind of staring faith—half cynical, half relieved.

Scholarly discovery in the humanities does now and then produce new knowledge. That is only one of the interesting things it
does. It may also (by a fresh arrangement of facts) help to create
the intuitions of a whole generation. And it may (by a stroke of
interpretative acuteness) serve as a stimulus to further discovery,
or as an incitement to thinking. It is true that thinking is an elusive
and indeed a nonutilitarian good. Until recently, one could have
said that it therefore had a home in the humanities. But an advanced student of literature now who justified a project in this way
would risk being sent to the provinces for reeducation. The sudden
fortune of *knowledge* as an ideal of the humanities is all the more
puzzling when one recalls that, ever since the early sixties, a majority of scholars in departments of literature have been trained not
as historical researchers at all but as critics. Yet for people doing
intellectual work, the way to social acceptance in America has
always been through imitation of the sciences. By which was
meant, originally, the natural sciences.

Here the social sciences were merely the first to go; it has taken
some time for the humanities to follow. For the first of these shifts,
from the natural to the social sciences, chiefly a methodical language was taken over. In passing from the social sciences to the
humanities, only the memories of such a language are needed. A
few habits still remain in the way of a clean sweep for "knowledge."
You cannot predict the behavior of someone suffering from an
anxiety disorder in the same manner that you predict the behavior
of a planetary body. It is not clear that you would *want* to read a
novel by Flaubert in the same manner that you read a chart of
socioeconomic status. Nothing, in either instance, stops us from
forcing the transition anyway; or rather, nothing stronger than
social and moral conventions: a convention about the difference in
character and dignity between astronomical entities and individual
persons; a convention about the way to look at works of art, as
distinct from other sorts of social documentation. These are, to
repeat, only conventions. But they are what we have—nothing
better—to tell us how to spend our time well or ill.

An important use of literary theory in the 1970s and 1980s was to ease the rigors of this scene of legitimation-by-knowledge. Once the analogy with science has been accepted, the humanities can move very fast in any direction. For the objects of research here offer a very perfunctory resistance—they have an almost infinite amount of "give." The profile of a voter group, however preposterous its inferences, can in the end be falsified by additional or contradictory evidence, but how can a novel answer back? A concise professionalist thesis in literature departments now runs as follows: "We need to teach not the texts themselves but how we situate ourselves in reference to those texts."[5] It is pointless to object that nobody ever taught "the texts themselves," whatever that may mean; rather, teachers conducted a class on a book for the sake of showing a way of thinking and talking about books. The point of the statement above is less to argue or persuade than to announce that the subject has been changed. Correctly translated, it means: "We need to teach not interpretation but the sociology of knowledge."

I do not much like the atmosphere or the effects of the professionalist move in literature. But the emphasis on literature in attacks on the humanities seems to me misplaced, and if one allows the blame to fall there, one must do so entirely as a matter of convenience. In fact, what is happening now in literature happened earlier, over a longer period, elsewhere in the humanities. That is why *only* literature departments are relied on to teach a canon of works that have been read for generation after generation. Teaching on this pattern became a marginal option long ago in more thoroughly professionalized fields like philosophy and history. The classic texts out of which those disciplines grew, the disciplines themselves honored by atomization or polite oblivion. It is made out to be a scandal that advanced students in English today may have read only a few plays by Shakespeare. It has been a long time since even the most eminent professional philosophers or historians were expected to have read all of Hume or Kant or Thucydides or Gibbon—unless, of course, their particular interests happened to incline them that way. Our crisis, then, feels like a crisis because, by an accident of institutional arrangements, the teaching of humane letters has for some time been entrusted to departments of literature; and now, prominently at a few institutions, literary scholars show signs of wanting to give up their traditional work for novelty and a clear reward. "Don't jump off that cliff!" say a host of concerned citizens, but we know better. There is a warm sea of publications below.

A definition may now be needed to suggest what the humanities ideally ought to represent. The one I like best was offered by William James in "The Social Value of the College-Bred," a 1907 address to the American Association of Alumnae:

> You can give humanistic value to almost anything by teaching it historically. Geology, economics, mechanics, are humanities when taught with reference to the successive achievements of the geniuses to which these sciences owe their being. Not taught thus, literature remains grammar, art a catalogue, history a list of dates, and natural science a sheet of formulas and weights and measures.[6]

For James it is the historical approach to events, texts, and persons—telling a story about phenomena otherwise linked only by family resemblance—that turns a field of study into one of the humanities. On his view, the difference between the humanities and other areas of learning is not to be explained by the presence or absence of a method. It has more to do with a choice between interpreting the achievements of the past in a steady relation to the present and digesting the molds of contemporary knowledge with occasional dips into the past for comparison, contrast, and condescension. James's definition also shows why history and philosophy now belong to the humanities only provisionally. They moved away at the bidding of strong internal motives—in history, distrust of the ideal of a single story about a common past; in philosophy, the pressure always to redraw the outlines of a given problem in response to discoveries in the natural and social sciences. In departments of literature, the pull away from the humanities has had weaker but still sufficient internal motives. Against the critical appreciation of great works, a skeptical pressure has been placed on the words *appreciation* and *great*—the former being put down as the eulogistic name for a blind habit, the latter as a judgment of value that can be altered when and as we please.

Many readers will agree that *none* of these developments has been altogether happy for education. But they will then ask, "What is the alternative to continuous professionalization, and to the usual professional devices for regulating knowledge?" The only possible response has often seemed to be "a genial amateurism"; or "the culture of common sense"; or "just reading for the pleasure of it." These phrases are all in the same style and no one has ever believed that they answered the question. But different answers have also been given from time to time. Michael Oakeshott, for example, quotes in this connection the master of Eton William Cory, who distinguished the mere acquisition of knowledge from the making of "mental efforts under criticism."

> A certain amount of knowledge you can indeed with average faculties acquire so as to retain; nor need you regret the hours you spend on much that is forgotten, for the shadow of lost knowledge at least protects you from many illusions. But you go to a great school not so much for knowledge as for arts and habits; for the habit of attention, for the art of expression, for the art of assuming at a moment's notice a new intellectual position, for the art of entering quickly into another person's thoughts, for the habit of submitting to censure and refutation, for the art of indicating assent or dissent in graduated terms.[7]

Concerning the inheritance that is thus passed on to a student, Oakeshott himself offers the skeptical judgment I have already quoted in chapter 1: "It has been put together not by designers but by men who knew only dimly what they did. It has no meaning as a whole; it cannot be learned or taught in principle, only in detail." These remarks by James, Cory, and Oakeshott all suggest a nonscientific defense of education. James thought that learning of every kind, which was otherwise just a compound of an age's favorite facts and theories, joined the humanities when it became the subject of a story about the past. Cory and Oakeshott draw some consequences for a liberal education generally. For such an unrehearsed intellectual adventure (to borrow Oakeshott's phrase) is constituted by something less than knowledge and something more: the learning of arts and habits. Knowledge, without these, though it may lead to intricate speculation, will never pass into self-knowledge.

But this view only offers a sense of the purpose of education for students. It is a different matter to say how far it might apply to teachers as well. Presumably they have gone to school already, and so are already acquainted with the arts and habits in question. If the things that later interest them are specialized topics of research, why not confine the bulk of their teaching to just such topics? That has long been the model of academic work in the sciences. Until lately, however, it was a model scorned by the humanities—where, from personal interest as much as dedication, many professors often chose to teach outside the area of their current research. But in the last decade literature has taken the path of the rest of the humanities. Even a first-year instructor will now be advised, by the cleverer sort of colleagues, to negotiate as early as possible for a sequence of seminars that follow an intended sequence of publications. Maybe the only good that is lost in the process is a certain ideal of "range." But when that happens, it quietly changes everyone's feeling about the kind of place a university can be.

It would be wrong to draw a nostalgic picture of the general life to which the humanities have lent themselves in earlier periods. The refutation lies in a history of the academy itself: the teaching methods of the old grammar and rhetoric created, for most of two centuries in America, as desolate a waste as a pervasive anti-literary theory of literature may now create again. One version of the story is nicely told in a recent book by Gerald Graff, *Professing Literature*. And on the whole, once the focus has been restricted to the academy alone, it comes to seem a story of merely cyclical crises in the humanities. But such an account of the curriculum cannot reflect the disparate functions that a given study may have served for the culture of different periods. In the nineteenth century, the academic humanities were chiefly to be relied on for grammar and rhetoric, both "dripped in" to the student's head with a stupendous dullness. Dullness apart, that may have been pretty much what was looked for then. Something wider and deeper is looked for now.

Universities, of course, cannot be held answerable for the defects of a general life they did not make by themselves. The new academic professionalism shows that the schools at this level are just one more casualty of an ethic of market rationalization that controls our society today as never before. And yet, precisely if one does look at the whole society with the same degree of realism, one will want to take with some caution the usual advice to follow professional development wherever it leads. Professional development really has no more moral claim on us than real-estate development. The forest is plowed under to make a dozen shopping malls, for which a corporate agent puts up the first ten million, a neighborhood pays with its life—and now, as the last extortion of victory, a graduate tutor is asked to interpret the original blueprint in class as a paradigm of a "social text." The truth is that with much refinement and convenience, professionalization has brought much damage everywhere. *Everywhere:* in the medical and legal professions, too; in every discipline the creation of which requires the creation of a new laity. What it has most destroyed in America is our common sense of a public life.

Professionalism in itself is without charm. Its success as a working doctrine in the humanities owes everything to its alliance with another, and at one time a quite distinct, force. I have in mind a mood of belief that fiction could do more with than polemic can: I will be calling it—with a sense that the phrase somehow fails to be satisfactory—"institutional radicalism." This mood has its own tightly regulated conformities. But I think it is fair to begin by looking at institutional radicalism as a nonconforming reaction—a spirit of partisanship brought in to cure something as virulent on the opposite side. The conservative great-books plans that I described in chapter 2 have come to be associated with a design of assuring assent to a political and economic establishment. For the conservatives offer a distinct image of culture. It is a culture in which people can always be trusted to derive much the same truths from the same books—a culture of assent. William Bennett's paragons of acceptance, who "respect" and "nurture" a culture without assenting to it, have now been requested to go the whole length after all. Let us, for contrast, think of the institutional radicals as people who aim to exemplify an opposite ideal—a culture of suspicion.

Members of the culture of suspicion see through all the possible mystifications of "the given," whether that means a given pattern of interpretation, a familiar social order, or a received habit of distinguishing political education from political recruitment. They know that an unreflective tradition, of the sort the conservatives plead for, is not a medium of thought but rather a lulling therapy for acceptance of things-as-they-are. When they challenge such a therapy, they are apt therefore to appear as the defenders of a liberal freedom of conscience. This posture, however, is misleading.

Institutional radicals begin with an uneasy truth: that meanings in any culture are arbitrary—produced, that is to say, by choice and circumstance and the accidents of power. Once those meanings take on the apparent solidity of conventional truths, they serve to keep in place all the hierarchies of social, economic, and sexual subordination. These sound like the kind of data that any reformer would want to use. But here they are used with a disdain for every practicable design of reform. Faced with a choice between the conservative belief that culture is sacred and the liberal belief that it is a common possession of some utility, the truly suspicious assert that it is always partial, always compromised. Or—to adapt the police-blotter slang that has helped to make these discussions sensational—a work of art is *complicit* in crimes it does not confess; accordingly, it must be not interpreted but *interrogated*. I take these words from a recent public lecture in which "literature itself" was said to bear "some of the responsibility" for the inadequacy of the sanitation laws of Victorian England.

There is an intelligible pattern of motives for this moralizing disapproval of literature. The freedom that works of art now enjoy in a few societies was won, with difficulty, as an effect of the triumphs of Renaissance humanism and the Enlightenment. But the prejudices of institutional radicals tend to be antihumanist and anti-Enlightenment. Combined with a distrust of "the West" (here identified with the project of empire) is a distrust of the individual (= capitalism) and of tolerance (= repressive tolerance). Some of these predigested beliefs go back to Fanon and Marcuse. Closer in the foreground is Michel Foucault, whose works are mined for words that seem to telegraph a truth about whole epochs ("circulation," "currency," "surveillance") and for the clinical irony of his prose in translation. But the scripture of institutional radicalism—a work so available that many readers can accurately reproduce its argument without having read the text—is Max Horkheimer and T. W. Adorno's *Dialectic of Enlightenment*. As Horkheimer and Adorno argue there, all Enlightenment knowledge presumes, and believes its own presumption of, impartiality. Yet it does so for the sake of conquering the objects of knowledge (among which are included other people). Everything that comes to light in this way is known in order to be assimilated and therefore exploited by the knower. In the process an alternative or contrary truth is cut off, and the task of theory is to recover what has been lost, by exposing the dead-end of what has been gained. Jürgen Habermas, a responsible and skeptical expositor of the Horkheimer-Adorno thesis, observes in *The Philosophical Discourse of Modernity* that the aim of the *Dialectic* is to exhibit the perpetual relapse of enlightenment into myth; so that for the authors, "the permanent sign of enlightenment is domination over an objectified external nature and a repressed internal nature." Indeed, the adjective most commonly paired with *enlightenment*, by academic writers of this tendency, is *totalitarian*.

It needs to be emphasized that such a use of the *Dialectic of Enlightenment* leads to an oddly distorted picture not only of the Enlightenment but of the views on aesthetics that Adorno evolved over a long career of thinking. In *Aesthetic Theory* he writes: "To instrumentalize art is to undercut the opposition art mounts against instrumentalism." He had nothing but contempt for those who sought in art the fluent and translatable meanings of propaganda. But most readers at any time use a body of writing for what they think they will find there, and what literary theorists have been drawn to in Adorno is the part that looks *simply* iconoclastic. Some of the consequences for practical criticism have been sketched with great acuteness by David Norbrook. In recent "historicist" discussions, writes Norbrook, where a general reaction against the liberal culture of modernity is presumed in advance, even the English Revolution

> can be seen as a key moment in the installation of the logo-centric, repressive, bourgeois subject [who is] the source of most evils of the contemporary world. Thus Jonathan Dollimore's *Radical Tragedy* . . . sees the Enlightenment one-dimensionally as a fall into essentialism that paved the way for racism, and manages to move in one page from Kant to a Nazi ideologist. For Herman Rapaport, in *Milton and the Postmodern*, Milton's defense of the regicide marks him as a predecessor of Himmler.[8]

Habits of thought like these are now dominant, if not yet exclusive, in two areas of literary study, the Renaissance and American literature. And they bring with them a copious and explicit vocabulary of praise and blame. For blame: *essentialist, canonical, thematize, containment, ideology.* For praise: *decentered, marginal, reproblematize, subversion, ideology.*

The points of accord I have listed above are negative and minimal—necessary and not sufficient elements of an orthodoxy that may never crystallize. But together they give a distinct tone to current reflections on the function of literary scholarship. It is a tone that connects a left-wing antihumanist like Fredric Jameson with a right-wing pragmatist like Stanley Fish, and in turn connects both with a utilitarian relativist like Barbara Herrnstein Smith. In all these writers, though in each for different reasons, the liberal idea that knowledge is a cosmopolitan good has been displaced by the professional idea that knowledge is an institutional good. Not the free discourse of equals, they say, but the licensed discourse of peers, creates the conditions for an advance in knowledge. And what is true of knowledge is true of thought itself. This last deduction has acquired such currency that it can be stated flatly as an axiom: "Professionalization makes thought possible," write the authors of a recent pamphlet, *Speaking for the Humanities*.[9] Are there also some kinds of thought that it makes impossible?

With statements like this, one feels that the circle, not only of worldly advancement, but of mental life itself, has been prematurely closed from within. A step further along the same path lies the proposition I heard advanced, without irony, at a recent symposium on the humanities: "There are no ideas except in institutions." If, then, a scholar (say, an intellectual historian in a department of social historians) should leave her institution but go on writing books, she would be doing something in those books, but we could no longer say that she was having ideas. It is an odd and unhappy terminus for thought to arrive at. Combine, now, these typical "inside" statements with the rarer "outside" statement I quoted at the start—"Professors should have less freedom of expression than writers and artists, because professors are supposed to be creating a better community"—and it will be plain how the anti-elitist humanities elite could come to be oppressive in some of its daily effects. But how did things ever reach this point?

There used to be a morality of scholarship that warned the interpreter or commentator or historian (all of whom were pictured as impartial) never to seek through scholarship to influence the world outside of educational institutions. I do not accept this morality—it is hard to see how it could be lived. But it was an understandable product of liberal self-confidence a generation ago, of pluralism in politics and positivism in science. As illusions go, it was not a bad one. Maybe it helped to induce a degree of conscious fair-mindedness even in scholars who knew exactly where they stood at the beginning of a plan of research. A longer scanning of the evidence for conflicting testimony, a greater reluctance to impute low motives to scholarly or political antagonists: these, at least, are imaginable effects of such a belief. With the unmasking of the disinterested ideal, which many humanities scholars now *assume*, every choice, whether conscious or not, is easily exposed as "implicitly a political choice." Critical practice along these lines follows from a deliberate policy of crude thinking. It also begs a number of questions, as the following parallel assertions may suggest:

1. Milton was making a political choice when he wrote *Paradise Lost* in a complex idiom that few readers could follow even in 1670.
2. The professor is making a political choice when he says the good of studying *Paradise Lost* is to expose the elitist pretensions of its author.

Do these two assertions, in fact, describe the same kind of choice?

An institutional radical will want to say that they do. A pretty predictable moralism is at work in assessments like these—a moralism that one naturally associates with active public commitments. But for the past decade or so, the activist tone in scholarship has been found compatible with a restriction of politics to the universities themselves. Indeed, the standard defense of institutional radicalism in the humanities, and increasingly in the study of the law as well, is that scholars can have their deepest influence on public discourse simply by doing what they do anyway. One works in the classroom in the hope of achieving some effect in society; but, by a happy symmetry, the social effects are already there in the classroom; to pass outside it is to risk the strangeness of a new routine, without the promise of any reward. *One must cultivate one's garden.* At no earlier period, perhaps, would this have been taken to mean: "Talk long enough about that flower and you will succeed in changing the plant-structure of the universe."

Feminism, the one academic-political movement of thought that might be supposed an exception to these strictures, also goes some way to prove the rule. The movement is impossible to dismiss as merely academic—unlike Marxism, unlike most "culture criticism" and all the varied phenomena that come under the heading of "social text approaches." It has made converts, changed lives, found inroads into the structure of the laws, in American society at large. But for whose benefit?—outside, of course, the ranks of the middle class to which academics themselves belong. It is symptomatic that the enemy of choice for the movement, on its intellectual side, should be the nineteenth-century bourgeois man of genius. He *was* a great offender, his works being in better taste than his life, and deserves all the posthumous shame we can heap on him now. But to what end do we continue to pile it high? After a point surely he will cease to feel the wound. This insistent return to a dead antagonist is part of the unreal intellectualism that feminist theory shares with academic theory generally.

When one considers the larger political causes with which academic feminism has been associated, the picture is more encouraging and yet limited in comparable ways. The ends aimed at have been high, and the advances remarkable by any measure. But how have the ends been chosen? Think of the way two evils in particular have concentrated the attention of every reformer of this milieu: on-the-job harassment and the right to have an abortion. These are reforms of tremendous moral importance. A society that achieves them fully will be a freer society. But what do they mean to the mother of five in the inner city who has seen two of her children shot by stray bullets from handguns?—an issue in which the movement in question has been distinctly, but secondarily, interested. Once again it is not clear what, apart from the limits of social imagination, governs the choice of an issue here. For women are frequent victims of guns in America, though they are rarely the killers. This would seem to be a "gender issue" if ever there was one. It is men who go mad for guns; that is one of the most dangerous things about men; and the countenancing of it by our society is one of the most impressively sexist facts about that society. And yet, all this hardly comes home to an academic as it does to someone who may live just a few hundred yards away.

This brings us to a general point about the curious thinning of the garden in its third decade of cultivation. Of the triadic mantra *race-class-gender*—about which such a lot is heard these days, from the university application form to the professional conference schedule—it is *class* that is likely to be most often neglected.

Meanwhile, race and gender are our great diversions, race most of all. The institutional radical of the eighties continued to pay ritual deference to the significance of class; but, except in a few courses on social history, the subject had dropped from sight: nobody remembered how to think about it. Yet if one had to choose tomorrow the life of a Harvard Law student who happens to be a black woman from a professional family or the life of a high-school graduate who happens to be a white man in a company town that General Motors owned and closed, which of us would hesitate for even a moment? The usual failure of analysis here is part of a general malady. The radical knows how to behave in the presence of the law student: deferential interest and concern will be shown, even, or especially, when that student says that the language of law must be revised to accommodate the new beliefs she holds about the authenticities of race and gender. Put the same radical side by side with the out-of-work white man and the response will be indifference amounting to boredom. After all, for what experience of "otherness" could that man be an advocate?

Thus a prescriptive compassion for those who carry the *mark* of victimhood—something class never did for anybody—pulls in an opposite direction from the actual sense of social justice. To the extent that institutional radicalism has fallen in with this trend, it is at fault in all its varieties. They seem united for now in a single impulse: to associate themselves with the group that is conspicuous biologically or otherwise, as against the claims of the less visible group, or for that matter the persecuted individual. The failure of imagination is on a scale so staggering that it is hard to conceive what method such people even in power could devise to respond to the grinding matter of commonplace deprivation. Their wisdom has traveled the whole round from affirmative action to sensitivity training and back. Personal sympathy, social sympathy for those who stand at a distance that may be hidden by apparent similarity to oneself—these possibilities are nowhere on their charts.

Of institutional radicalism as a social phenomenon, the only analysis so far has come from neoconservative journalists, in articles for *Commentary* and the *New Criterion*. All the articles agree that the new tendency grew out of sixties radicalism; that what is happening now is the inward migration, on campus, of the leaders and followers of the student revolt; and that the people in question still think the way they always thought—which means that they are a nuisance and ought to be abated. There is a particle of truth in the analysis; the truth of a profile just glimpsed in an unlit room. To see where it goes wrong, one must have spent time lately on the faculty of a college or university, as most of the article writers have not done. It is true some of the sixties people are still around; and true, sometimes now they have tenure. These facts say nothing about how they conduct themselves. There is great variety here, but one may say as a rule that their bureaucratic manners are impeccable, while their generosity and opportunism occur in about the conventional mix. So the puzzle remains: even as the language of academic study has been politicized, politics itself has been coded back into the language of academic study. If I say in a lecture, "The figuration of Prospero's last speech in *The Tempest* betrays a slippage from subversion to containment which the occlusive presence of Caliban tends to undermine," I may, in some fantastic dialogue of the mind, be singing the equivalent of a Sandinista Wedding March, but what it means to you practically is, "Look at a slightly different list of secondary works, this time, and don't turn in the paper late."

Russell Jacoby, in *The Last Intellectuals*, wrote well about the obscurantist habits of institutional radicals, but he saw their predicament as part of a larger story about the vanishing from American culture of the public intellectual. His thesis I think explains why a single article of faith from the sixties has passed unchallenged into the eighties—namely, the idea that the university is a microcosm of society. That is why what one does at a university will suffice as a complete account of what one does in society. At times of relative tranquility this means that "the politics of interpretation" can be pursued with only the usual iconoclasm. At times of social unrest it may well mean, as it did in the sixties, that turning the university upside-down looks like an appropriate gesture of solidarity with causes that have nothing to do with education.

One further motive seems to unite the several available versions of institutional radicalism: a belief in the priority, no matter what the context, of the twin ideals of equal representation and universal rights. These are radical aims that many Americans endorse—in politics. Carried into every human practice, they work against a strong principle which says that merit ought to be judged separately in separate spheres.[10] To the institutional radical, however, that kind of separation can only be defended as a tactical move. For culture and politics involve not the moral good of discrete virtues but the fighting of successive battles in a single war: the two activities are infinitely translatable into each other. Suppose, for instance, I want to increase the political representation of some person, or class of persons. I can enter the political fray with congressional representatives, editorial writers, and so on, and try to get some legislation passed. Or I can increase the representation of the same person or class of persons by altering the reading list for a course I teach. That, I will say, changes the "image" of things as much as any political action could—and perhaps more so, because more elusively so.

Thus by a kind of extended pun, the structure of representation in a political order is said to be linked directly with the choice of objects for representation in art. This axiom, commonplace in the humanities today, belongs to a pedantic populism that is more typically found in state-run academies. Every such academy beginning with France in the eighteenth century has enforced a criterion of value based on subject matter and appropriate "treatment." The situation is not the same yet in American universities. But in defense of critical autonomy, as in defense of free speech, principles are seldom invoked that could stand in the way of just this drift toward conformity. A polite silence is the rule here, and that is a pity, for the pedantic-populist view of culture forgets an important fact. Literature owes what prestige it still commands to the idea that it is a sphere where influence cannot be bought, or leveraged, wheedled or bullied for, in quite the same way it can in politics through the machinations of skillful lobbyists. Doubtless this idea is to some extent an idealization—even in the heyday of romantic and modern art, it was partly that—but we hold on to different words for culture and politics because the idea has continued to serve a human need. Now, if the lobbying for representation in culture ever reached a pitch where it was clear what was happening, at that point all the advantages of iconoclasm would have been played out, for culture would have been emptied of its prestige. We could then cut back to a regimen of politics that needed no translation, and have one fewer set of virtues to worry about.

And yet the left-wing plea for a supervised culture rests on evidence open to doubt. The truth is that nobody knows, or ever has known, how works of art dispose us to act. All we can reasonably be sure of is that they do have some effect: it would be odd if one part of human life were alone exempt from such hazards. What to make of this possibly fortunate and possibly appalling fact remains a matter to be settled by convention. The belief of the suspicious, that culture has a pervasive influence in politics and so ought to be thoroughly translated into politics, is as defensible as my belief that its influence is nothing like pervasive and that to pretend otherwise only leads to coarse sloganeering. In making some estimate of the risk on both sides, democratic principles have not until lately been at a loss. They permit no test of right representation in a work of art, any more than of right perspective in a licensed interpreter. They allow the possibility that we may even build up minds so free as to cherish, for generation after generation, some books more than others, without from that long experiment catching the taint of a superstitious reverence. Is there a social cost or a social benefit in keeping the experiment going? Probably something of both, and we will never have the instruments to measure them.

But the argument is likely never to come to a head. No matter what their program, the adepts of institutional politics seldom encounter members of the general public whom they have written off. In consequence they are poorly placed to know how their opinions sound to many of the people who might read, or hear, or even be affected by them. It will be instructive therefore to look at a rare occasion when institutional radicalism—or, as it is sometimes

called, the "oppositional practices" of a profession—did briefly and
memorably come face to face with public opinion. The academic in
this case was Robert Bork, a professional man of the *right*—a different type from the scholars I describe here, on the face of things.
Yet the logic of his position was the same as theirs. I believe the
defeat of Bork's nomination to the Supreme Court—not only that
it was accomplished, but the way it was accomplished—was a rare
hopeful event of our recent politics. And how was it done? By
affirming a certain traditional interpretation (as it happened, the
liberal interpretation, which in civil rights has become traditional)
of the impact of modern history on public life. Against this, Bork's
main defense rested on the assumption that his repellent views
belonged merely to oppositional practices within an academic
profession. His explanation, had it been accepted, would have
cleared him from the kind of scrutiny by the representatives of a
common tradition to which he was in fact exposed. I select the
example to make a point about the drawbacks of institutional radicalism generally, without respect to party. Some time in the future,
the judicial nominees who try to explain away their opinions with
just this logic may turn out to be members of the legal-academic
left. If the defense they give is as evasive, and the public sentiment
against it as strong, as happened in the case of Bork, then those
nominees too will deserve to be defeated.[11]

The last two sections have been a necessary excursus; it is time
now to return to the practical issues they point to. For the foregoing
remarks could hardly claim much interest if the new movements
had not produced a striking change in the shape of literature departments. Some main innovations are:

- The teaching of a canon of great books as one continuous record
  of deception and betrayal; literature, so to speak, with a minus
  sign in front of it;
- The teaching of alternative canons in black studies, feminism,
  and other subjects;

- The teaching of literary theory for an up-to-date access both to the great-books canon and alternative canons;
- The teaching of mass culture (including television sitcoms and shoot-'em-ups, *USA Today*, "Postmodern Standup Comics," and so on).

These enterprises look like an odd assortment, and it might be supposed that they would not have much to say to one another. Nothing, for example, about the perspective of alternative-canon teaching should make it in the smallest way sympathetic to the concerns of anti-canon teaching, and it is possible to admire much of the work done in the former area and none in the latter. Yet hardly a single telling criticism has been ventured by any of these tendencies against the interests of any other. However vastly the character and justification of the enterprises may differ, their practitioners appear to feel that they must stand or fall together.

I think this feeling is mistaken. But it has led to occasional displays of unity, and on an interesting front: the worth of teaching mass culture. If enough people want to slow down the trend, maybe it can still be done. Not merely an initiative but an argument will have to be challenged here. Anti-aesthetic theory can prove very handily that there is no intrinsic difference between high art and mass art: the only difference that counts has to do with habits of interest and perception. Grown-ups, including many grown-up students, are likely not to want to allow television-for-credit in universities. But until that preference is widely known, professionalists in the humanities will, as far as possible, take the high democratic ground and identify mass culture with popular consciousness. The confusion of "mass" with "popular," and of "popular" with "democratic," shows a decay of the social sense of scholars on a par with their new self-sufficiency. It is as if Colonel Sanders, because his products are consumed by millions, were to be treated as an authentic representative of Southern military folk cuisine, and as if to question his practice by cooking something better or going to a real restaurant were the expression of an anti-democratic elitism. Yet counter-arguments will scarcely make much headway where a professional convenience is at stake. High theory, in the humanities, *needs* mass culture to test its concepts on, just as a scientist needs a control condition in an experiment.

The current defenses of mass culture are in no way novel, and when a surer consensus prevailed they were simply beside the point. For a long time, television was refused a place in literature departments—not because of a metaphysical belief in its rottenness but from a general agreement that its goods were inferior. By contrast, the practice of teaching it now, and so giving students in the classroom more of what they can find outside, has acquired a shock value that is hard to top. The gesture makes a direct score against the older democratic belief in the liberating uses of culture. And it does so quickly, familiarly, without apology or explanation, as only a gesture can. If, in fact, as the culture of suspicion asserts, the Enlightenment did not enlighten, if the liberal idea of tradition was always and only a mask for oppression, and if, in the invention of an aesthetic sphere a little apart from science and politics, the Enlightenment and modern liberalism together must be judged a cheat and a swindle, then the kind of interest we have come to associate with works of art is only the result of a single long unhonorable error. Then, too, the best way to overcome the aesthetic prejudice against mere packaging will be by teaching in a solemn spirit works of commerce that profess to be nothing but packaging.

It is, on the face of it, a creed of social despair. Still, a leading precept of liberal education holds that no subject in itself is low, and none is ruled out in advance as a basis from which genuine learning might start. That must be true of television, at least as a potential subject. The question is how, and where, to approach the thing intelligently. To study it in a language that matters, you need some knowledge of how the shows are "created," streamlined, and sold; of the corporation executives, advertising agencies, and on-the-scene liaison personnel who sell the audience to the sponsors; of the influence of marketing, and of production constraints, on many details of the final package, such as the timing of plot climaxes for commercial breaks; and so on, far into the domain of economics and sociology and behavior modification—assuming all the while a fair acquaintance with statistical analysis and the newer techniques of audience demographics. Having equipped yourself in this way, you may eventually be in a position to work for a profit in television; you will at any rate be well situated to unmask its products, if you have a taste for doing so. None of this knowledge is at home in the humanities, and no one yet has offered to transport it there.

There is an irony in the recent professionalist effort to legitimate television that can hardly be savored too much. For the products of television are themselves produced by a market culture far more debased and far more powerful than the bookish tradition that some academics hope by this alliance to destroy. Nowhere do we see the face of that culture more in the real glare of its mastery than in an election year like 1988. It was the last step of a long downward path when George Bush (or was it Michael Dukakis?) quoted the Chevrolet motto "the heartbeat of America" without quotation marks, to evoke all the pathos he could find in an idea of public service. It was part of the same step when Dukakis (or was it Bush?) quoted the network Olympics logo "Go for the gold," in answer to a question about economic policy. All this the culture of suspicion has taken in, and wants to teach, and wants students to consume, more and more. To what end? Perhaps that of some day evolving a wholly negative "knowledge." But a cynical assumption as well appears to play its part here. Television has the perfect charm to suit a style of affectless dandyism that now flourishes among the prospering intelligentsia of the West. It is the thing you can always be "with," without being of it. Mixed in with the other motives of the style may be a touch of envy for those whose suspicion has climbed to the higher stage of unqualified cynicism—those who work in the industry of television itself, yet reserve the right to say how little they are of it.

When I first heard a theorist praise the militant intertextuality of a soap commercial, I thought that to have made the ad was the next best thing to interpreting it. Or was it just the next, better thing? That was the year before the humanities conference about television at Johns Hopkins University, to which some of the show-makers themselves came to answer their (quite sympathetic) explicators. A professor who went said afterwards, "The industry people were really very nice." Well, the industry people *would* be nice. Occasions like this give them some free advertising and add to their products a gloss of respectability that even the most whimsical sponsor cannot bank on. There is not, yet, at a major institution, a Don Johnson Professor of Lifestyle. But if the endowment were offered to a state-of-the-art program in theory and communications, it is hard to see what standard anyone would cite for turning it down.

But that is to project rather freely from current tendencies. And one should not underrate the element of costume here, or the extravagant tokens of normal insincerity. At the 1988 convention of the Modern Language Association in New Orleans, the undeclared general theme was mass culture, as applied anachronistically to any place or period covered by the curriculum of scholarship. The intertextual soap crowd and the anonymous ballad crowd got together and theoretically serious exchanges abounded on such topics at the Marriott and the Hilton. But on the Friday afternoon when the convention began to thin and was replaced at the same hotels by the bigger, rowdier, and (I think it fair to say) more popular clientele of a football weekend, it was not clear, from the results of one informal canvass anyway, how many of the Association's avant-garde could name even one of the teams in the Sugar Bowl. The populist affectations of a teacher at any level make for benign entertainment. But the effects are never edifying, and the public in a democracy has a natural interest in those effects.

I believe in any case that discussions about the humanities ought to be widened to include people outside both the culture of assent and the culture of suspicion. It is too important a matter to be handed over exclusively to far-right journalists and hard-left professors of literature. At present, the curious airlessness of the debate is typified by a trimming proposal that has just emerged from a group of moderate, humane, and thoroughly optimistic professionalists. Gerald Graff, in the book I mentioned earlier, together with Jonathan Culler, Catharine Stimpson, and a number of others argue that universities can best adjust the innovations of research to the older habits of pedagogy by teaching the curriculum-controversy itself. This certainly looks like the path of least resistance and will therefore recommend itself to many university administrations. Also, it implies a high-minded estimate of undergraduate students, as of their peaceably arguing professors—a flattering picture all around until you think about it. But what can it mean, for the most gifted student imaginable, to "learn the conflicts"?

The timely books and articles that take a position on the conflicts are not built to last; there will be another debate, with different books and articles, for the early 1990s and for the late. Where a pedagogy like this has been tried, in the more arid tracts of the social sciences, it cuts down the generations of students to blocks of five or six years, and one generation is reduced to talk with the last about the fraying ends of a half-dead quarrel. It is true that such a proposal envisions a student generous enough and inquisitive enough to thrive in any atmosphere. But suppose we imagine a student more remarkable still: one who sees just how far his or her teachers stand for unharmonizing points of view; who even takes pleasure in arranging mental wars between them (in which, perhaps, some perish forever); but who, far from wanting such an exchange to be formalized in every class, thinks of education as something more than a professional debate. This student will already have read some works of history and philosophy and fiction that prompted a fresh kind of thinking about life: one reason that he, or she, went on in school and took the humanities instead of the sciences was to think about books like that in a more organized way. By the proposal we are now considering, such a student is sold short.

In sum, one cannot help feeling that the teach-the-conflict idea is a device of convenience worked out for scholars themselves, to give a live constituency to talk that would otherwise be muffled in the iron lung of subsidized quarterlies. Things are bad, yes; the talk has become tedious and fractious; but not so bad, yet, as to warrant an expedient like this. Besides, there is in fact a line of recent inquiry in the humanities, or rather a convergence of interests, from which a curriculum might be built to serve the education of students. I have in mind the growing agreement that historically important books ought to be read across genres, even when that means passing across the boundaries of departments. For example, it should be possible to read *Leviathan* and *Paradise Lost* in the same class, just as they were once read by the same culture, without having to be taught by a scholar who makes up in a hand-to-mouth fashion a whole history of poetry or of political theory. The odd thing is that such an experience is not now broadly possible.

Here again one may blame the lapse in some measure on the effects of rapid professionalization: on one hand, a loss of confidence in areas where some real competence might still be fostered; on the other, a tremendous widening of scope in areas where no departmental talent can serve as a guide. These difficulties are now being felt above all in departments of literature.[12] And yet the difficulties themselves suggest a shared belief that books talk to each other in subtler ways than the existing map of the departments can reflect. Everyone hears scraps of this conversation, but it is hard to find the teacher, in a single body anyway, who can keep up with what books of such different sorts are saying. I do not think the solution lies in bending to the fast answers supplied by the avant-garde in a given department—answers that, as I have argued, tend even in the short run to be parochial and in the long run both anti-traditional and authoritarian. It may lie rather in creating a permanent place for collaborative teaching in the humanities. To be well sustained, teaching on this pattern requires that the collaborators come to know texts that feel initially strange to their understandings. In doing so they may be reminded, not of the sense in which their students are proto-professionals, but of the sense in which they themselves continue to be students.

There exists now at many institutions, though in an unorganized way, a community that might some day give a vivid character to teaching and research along these lines. It does not usually occur as a group with a fixed place of residence, for its interests do not

correspond to the chosen emphasis of a single department anywhere. But it has a clear identity; and it has a history. A generation
ago some classics of historical narrative, which a new-modeled
discipline had pushed aside (Hume, Carlyle, Macaulay), were
found to be leading a second life in English departments. It was a
halfway solution, but it did allow some fresh scholarship, and it
kept something good alive. The same sort of adaptation is now
occurring across a wider range of subjects and with more regular
support. The history of philosophy at a number of schools has
partly migrated into departments of religion, and moral philosophy
is often at the center of the curriculum in departments of politics
and law schools. It seems very probable that if, in keeping with
the same pattern, departments of literature ever decide in earnest
to unload their great books, somebody else with different motives
will want to take them up. It would be a fine stroke of poetic justice
if the next generation of philosophers elected not to read a word
more on "weakness of the will" from professionals until they had
consulted several thousand pages of Tolstoy, George Eliot, and
Henry James.

I have mentioned the worth of a community that may exist in
no special *place*. For the argument I began with, it seems worthwhile to add that this is a community that exists at no special *time*.
It can be a liberating discovery to feel that there are thoughts one
has in common with people who lived and worked, acted and
suffered a long time in the past. Indeed, many of the strongest
feelings of solidarity for a thinking person are likely to be of this
kind. Such "elective affinities" are interesting in themselves but
they serve a deeper purpose of scholarship. To believe on reasonable grounds that in a given cause, though one may have few living
allies and perhaps no visible ones, somebody in a similar predicament once felt the same intuition, can be a sustaining knowledge
and the beginning of a persuasive self-trust. There are, that is to
say, kinds of discovery foreign to one's contemporaries, knowledge
that neither a sect nor a school professes, which one can feel called
upon to bring to light alone. And the only way will sometimes be

through a personal reading of the past. Dependence and group-narcissism are the paralysis of genuine scholarship; but scholars, like citizens, to whom that seems a healthy state of things will always invoke *the argument of growing solitude.* "A cold look," as Nietzsche describes it, "a sneer on the face of those among whom and for whom one has been educated is feared even by the strongest. What is it that they are really afraid of? Growing solitude! This is the argument that rebuts even the best arguments for a person or cause."[13] Maybe the only aim that Nietzsche ever had in common with John Stuart Mill was to disarm of its sting the "argument of growing solitude." Nietzsche's reason was a distrust of the herd, Mill's reason a trust that it would not stay a herd forever, provided all thinking did not come to be identified with the conventions of a certain time and place.

Professional institutions are defined from within by their socializing codes. Traditions are made of something more. They offer, in fact, a kind of solitude, and a kind of company. The unity one looks for in a tradition is the loose fitting together of lots of facts, stories, and the shadows of strong impressions. Of course the more adhesive unities are good for something; they must be, or so many people would not cling to them; but they cannot grow and they cannot change. What remains perplexing about their appeal is that the wish for permanent stability and the fear of an endless panic should so often be joined in a single mentality. The culture of assent and the culture of suspicion have done well at least in reminding us that America is all one society and that a deep sickness somewhere will eventually be felt, though under a different name, everywhere. We have our *academic* junk-bond dealers, perpetual negotiators, inside traders sailing close to the wind in several markets at once; we may, just now, be entering the era of the hired raider, and the leveraged buyout of whole departments.[14] The crisis of the humanities is an episode in the internal development of an area of study. But it is also part of the history of America in the eighties.

This chapter itself has been a casualty of the very institutional parochialism that it describes. I have written steadily of "the humanities," and yet I write as a teacher of literature. The mood of a related discipline like art history is so different that the same generalizations hardly seem to apply. Or anyway, not yet: the literary humanities embody large numbers, they command many journals, fellowships, and institutes for advanced study, and a volatile tendency is always more likely to spread than an inert condition is to stay inert. Anyway the calm and imperturbable voices here, who say that changes have always happened, that things will shake themselves again into an accustomed shape, miss the whole point that their overexcited neighbors have somehow grasped. Culture does relate to society, after all: to say more would be portentous, to say less merely false. Some time ago the universities took on the work of showing by example what the connection might be, and how the connection might vary from person to person. They are now some way down the road to putting aside that work; which is why people worry about the humanities. The mistake of the professionalists, I said at the start of this chapter, has been to exalt knowledge-as-such at the expense of arts and habits. Yet knowledge, the knowledge of the sciences, if it adds nothing worthwhile to human conduct, still gives us the mixed benefit of progress. What do arts and habits give us?

A provisional answer is that the benefit relates to the ideal of an open, informed, and reflective discourse. It was in deference to some such ideal that a few modern philosophers—among them R. G. Collingwood in *The Idea of History*, Michael Oakeshott in *Rationalism in Politics*, and Richard Rorty in *Philosophy and the Mirror of Nature*—came to think of inquiry in the humanities on the analogy of "conversation."[15] Why conversation?—as opposed to, say, contest, or market, or stockpile? Conversation is the right metaphor because it marks an event, in time, that had a beginning and perhaps will have an end, though no one afterwards will remember just how either occurred, or why. Conversation, because each speaker frames a statement in the belief that someone listening is capable of a reply. Because all of the speakers have an interest in common that none can easily describe. And because the good of conversation is not truth, or right, or anything else that may come out at the end of it, but the activity itself in its constant relation to life. Though the subject changes and the participants do too, the sense persists that a certain place is there for belief and doubt, and this somehow keeps smaller projects going forward, with a sureness more utilitarian enterprises give as a forfeit to more immediate ends.

Above all, conversation offers a place for coming to know something quite different from what one had known before. This may mean a different way of living, of thinking, of being. But for a citizen of modern America, the largest, almost the only unimaginable difference, is between the new which we inhabit and the old which we have never seen enough of to forget. It is because the distance between our lives and those of the past seems to be so commanding a fact—greater than the difference that separates us from any alien culture today—that I have kept coming back to the arts and habits associated with the study of the past. I quoted earlier a passage from William James's "Social Value of the College-Bred," in which all the humanities were praised as modes of history. The rest of the same thought in James's lecture says briefly what I have tried to say at length.

> The sifting of human creations!—nothing less than this is what we ought to mean by the humanities. . . . Studying in this way, we learn what types of activity have stood the test of time; we acquire standards of the excellent and durable. All our arts and sciences and institutions are but so many quests for perfection on the part of men; and when we see how diverse the types of excellence may be, how various the tests, how flexible the adaptations, we gain a richer sense of what the terms "better" and "worse" may signify in general. Our critical sensibilities grow both more acute and less fanatical. We sympathize with men's mistakes even in the act of penetrating them; we feel the pathos of lost causes and misguided epochs even while we applaud what overcame them.[16]

If one asks what it would feel like, in practice, to respect tradition even while rejecting authority, these words offer a vivid clue.

4

REFLECTION,

MORALITY, AND TRADITION

For the scholar as for the citizen, there is a common sense of liberalism concerning the uses of tradition, and I mean to defend it here. I have in mind a way of thinking that associates personal reflection with social morality, and that sees both as modified by a tradition which can reform itself. Accordingly the subject of this chapter is a tradition of liberal thought, which incorporates a modern idea of what tradition is. This common sense about learning and practice remains available today as a habit of feeling and as a possible motive to action. Yet it is a sense that has seldom been given conscious formulation. The liberal idea of tradition has never become a *familiar* abstraction: in times when it was accepted and used, it was too firmly established to require such help; and now that our contest is fought on the ground of institutions rather than individuals, it is forgotten because it is useless to both sides. I do not claim to have made any discoveries; the present attempt is rather one of recovery. The idea in question belongs to a broad inheritance from the Enlightenment which we draw upon even when we pretend to defy it.

From the latter part of the eighteenth century to the start of the twentieth, a few moral philosophers, together with poets and novelists and psychologists, developed the historical and evolutionary idea of tradition which associates morality with reflection on customs and practices. This general view is defined by the sort of reasons it allows for the justification of belief and of conduct. Such reasons, which we cite individually to suit an occasion, have their meaning against a background of reasons already given and choices already made. The subject matter for moral reflection becomes, first, the continuity between past and present which makes a given society what it is, and, second, the continuity between present and future which helps it to survive as a particular adaptation of human nature. Tradition in this view is the gradual accretion of reflective practices. It follows that a morality shaped by the knowledge of a tradition must give peculiar force to my thought of myself as a survival of some past. It will give the same force to my thought of the future as a survival of the moment that I now represent by my thinking and acting.

Many elements of the argument go back to Hume's *Enquiry concerning the Principles of Morals*. A more dramatic and explicit source is Burke, in his *Reflections on the Revolution in France*, but in other works, too: the *Letter to a Noble Lord*, the *Speech on Conciliation with the Colonies*, and certain passages from the parliamentary debates on India. Burke himself, it seems to me, owed a large debt not only to Hume but to Joseph Butler, the founder of natural theology and author of the *Analogy of Religion* and *Sermons Delivered in Rolls Chapel*. It will be plain why, in its broad outlines, this is an Enlightenment argument. On the other hand to treat Hume and Burke as heroes of liberalism may seem perverse. It has been usual to dispatch both, with the rough-and-ready confidence of the platitude, as "conservative." Yet the Hume who interests me is a secular moralist; the Burke who interests me is a reformer whose most persistent instinct is anti-absolutism: the truth of these characterizations will emerge in the quotations that follow. Closer to our time, William James and Michael Oakeshott have made a liberal idea of tradition still seem vivid and still, to borrow James's words, a "live option" for theorists of society. What these thinkers share is an interest in human nature and a belief that every discussion of individual or collective identity implies a reading of human nature. They share, too, a demand that talk about human nature should be answerable to experience. Whose experience? That question need not bring us to a dead stop. We do not have to choose between a vision of human nature as "One clear, unchanged, and universal light" and a vision of countless separable egos, each with its own interests. Nor are we thrown back upon the determining idea of social groups, themselves as consistent as individual egos, which one finds in anthropological relativism. None of these choices looks plausible to Hume or Burke or the others I have named. They prefer to write instead about a social group of some size, within which persons have some points of common experience, and more points of tacit common reference. Within the group it is supposed that the work of individual judgment and individual conscience may be formative for the group.

Some terms that seem essential to this way of thinking are *nature, habit, probability,* and *constitution.* We hear rather little from Hume or Burke about *tradition.* Indeed, an excessive concern with that word, and a tendency to mystify the idea which comes with the word, are often the marks of a scholar who only partly sees what the argument has at stake. But my own interpretation will be partial, too. The summaries that follow, of Burke and to a lesser extent of Butler and Hume, are arrived at by abstracting a few broad features from the circumstances of their writings. One cannot, in reading their works, find a single statement of exactly the view I trace. Granted that initial liberty I think the procedure justifies itself. If one imagines Burke free of a context in which the defense of property and the defense of mixed constitutional government were his central motives; if one imagines Butler free of a context in which Church of England doctrine must be vindicated against the assault of Deism; in such imaginary states they would likely still recognize themselves in my portraits of them. As, of course, would Hume—who to a considerable extent has been my guide in interpreting the others. What makes their analysis of tradition seem prophetic today is that it has a psychological motive.

This motive they must themselves have understood well enough. But in the nature of the age when they wrote, and the crises that they faced, it was a motive they felt little need to bring to the foreground of the argument. What motives then stood in the foreground, for them? Butler's thought of morality and survival comes from the need to defend a Christian belief in immortality; Burke's, from the need to defend an aristocratic moral code that still has links with Christian sentiment. By contrast, the psychological motive that is implicit in their thinking must seem to us today a great subject in itself. The question one asked then was, What am I in

relation to what God has determined I ought to be? The question
one asks now is, What am I in relation to what I myself can possibly
be? The answer delivered by the liberal tradition has not varied
much over two centuries. It is that I am, at any given moment,
more than the sum of the instincts of a narrow self-regard. I have
more resources, or am apt to be more resourceful in relation to the
thoughts and actions of life, than I can know as a matter of introspection or of identification with a "significant group." More than
this composes me. And here Butler and Hume and Burke still speak
to us. For they tell a new story about the human need for a moral
order of some sort, whether Christian or not; and they offer a new
picture of the deformations that human nature must sustain in the
absence of such an order. The way our need for a moral design is
met, they say, always affects our idea of who we are. That idea, in
turn, has a decisive influence on our powers of moral judgment
and conduct.

Burke's *Reflections on the Revolution in France* is usually read as an
anti-revolutionary tract. Taken as a political document, that is what
it is, and it marks a departure from his earlier writings. But taken
as a natural history of society—an irregular sequence of moral
reflections on how societies are made, modified, or broken—the
book is continuous with the rest of Burke's thinking. He argues for
slow reform. Gradual, constant, incremental change is the path of
endurance best adapted to human nature, in associations of large
numbers of people who have lasted together for a long time. Such
associations are neither voluntary nor compelled. They are simply
the result of things that have happened—chance developments,
the grounds of which we have no interest in questioning and the
consequences of which have become a second nature to us. We
thus take for granted most of the circumstances of social life. For
Burke, the only exceptions to the rule are people who live in
conditions of misery or necessity. With them, social life has not
become a second nature, and in a nation where they form the
majority or the overwhelming plurality, a revolution may be warranted. "An irregular, convulsive movement may be necessary to

throw off an irregular, convulsive disease." Burke, however, supposes that in modern Europe the people themselves know that
such a movement is not commonly in their interests. Periods of
acute misery can usually be dealt with by a specific remedy. Continuous suffering is to be dealt with by principled reform. By these
means we avoid revolution, and most people at any time, in any
station of society, want to avoid a revolution. "The people have no
interest in disorder." Our lives together are kept going by custom,
by habit, by inertia and accommodation. To the extent that the
usual order of existence is varied, we want to have some control
over the variations. But a revolution must take such control away
from almost everyone. It is an imposition on our experience—
indeed, it makes this a point of pride, saying: "Nothing will ever
be the same again." It wants not just to influence but to define our
imagination of experience; and so, for as long as it is a revolution,
it is bound to be illiberal.

The continuity of social life from one generation to the next is
sometimes pictured by Burke in metaphors of organic succession.
Ever since the settlement of 1689, the subjects of Britain have
wished "to derive all we possess as *an inheritance from our forefathers.*
Upon that body and stock of inheritance we have taken care not
to inoculate any scion alien to the nature of the original plant." He
anticipates a challenge to such heavy dependence on precedent:
"But you may object—'A process of this kind is slow. It is not fit
for an assembly which glories in performing in a few months the
work of ages. Such a mode of reforming might take up many
years.'" In defense of the procedure he recommends, Burke says
that "it might; and it ought" to take a long time. "If circumspection
and caution are part of wisdom when we work only upon inanimate
matter, surely they become a part of duty, too, when the subject
of our demolition and construction is not brick and timber but
sentient human beings, by the sudden alteration of whose state,
condition, and habits multitudes may be rendered miserable." His
idea of reform, as a process of reflection "in which time is amongst
the assistants," implies a rejection of the idea that political theory
is an experimental science—an influential belief among pioneers of

social thought like Condorcet and Godwin. The knowledge that belongs to politics, says Burke, is separate from the knowledge that belongs to religion or metaphysics on one side and to physics and chemistry on the other. For him the practice of statesmanship cuts across the distinction between science and art. Yet Burke also wants to detach politics once and for all from the language of philosophical "speculation"—according to which a man working alone, on materials supplied by human nature, can arrive at a permanent truth about human nature. The maxims of classical prudence, he thinks, come as close as we will ever get to such truths; and the maxims derive their current authority from a suspicion that the "private stock of reason . . . in each man is small, and that the individuals would do better to avail themselves of the general bank and capital of nations and of ages." By contrast, the political "speculatist" is guided by a scientific faith that one's private stock of reason may give sufficient grounds for judging any old or new social arrangement.

In his *Speech on Conciliation with the Colonies*, Burke had said that "the character of judge in my own cause is a thing that frightens me." This does seem a decisive objection against the theorist of society who works from his private stock of reason: that he is, in a sense, setting up as the judge in his own cause. Burke anyway feels a steady distrust for the man of speculation who is cut off, by the very authority of his theory, from the experience of a life shared with others in society. He feels an equal distrust for the man who, by a therapy of sudden enlightenment, chooses to cut himself off from the experience of the past. Utter privacy and utter contemporary-mindedness have the same disadvantage. But the latter condition may have the wider appeal. Many people have thought some time or other that it might be attractive to try to live entirely for the present moment. And in a crisis of authority, a new government may test its credit by putting this idea into practice.

Burke's *Reflections* offers itself as the personal record of such a crisis. In this book of 1790, one can see a great moralist of the arts and society troubled by a nightmare that has its prompting in history. The nightmare is that a whole generation might come to

feel so marooned, yet so euphorically attached to their common
fate, that they act as if they had no ties with any previous time or
with times to come.

> One of the first and most leading principles on which the
> commonwealth and the laws are consecrated, is lest the tem-
> porary possessors and life-renters in it, unmindful of what
> they have received from their ancestors or of what is due to
> their posterity, should act as if they were the entire masters;
> that they should not think it amongst their rights to cut off the
> entail or commit waste on the inheritance, by destroying at
> their pleasure the whole original fabric of their society; hazard-
> ing to leave to those who come after them a ruin instead of an
> habitation—and teaching these successors as little to respect
> their contrivances, as they had themselves respected the insti-
> tutions of their forefathers. By this unprincipled facility of
> changing the state as often, and as much, and in as many ways
> as there are floating fancies or fashions, the whole chain and
> continuity of the commonwealth would be broken. No one
> generation could link with the other. Men would become little
> better than the flies of a summer.[1]

Burke's perspective here may have started by being nostalgic and
paternalist; in the end, he offers a defense of history that is inseparable from a defense of human nature. Yet Burke guards his
analysis with a bitter irony that concedes something to his oppo-
nents: "They who destroy every thing certainly will remove some
grievance." As, when you kill a man, you certainly do cure him of
the influenza from which he had been suffering. Burke is not
interested in preserving the monuments that serve as a symbolic
inheritance of human nature—or rather, he would not preserve
them for their own sake. Reverence of this sort seems to him
admirable only when it comes from a natural piety which will
preserve an environment for the creation of future monuments: "I
do not like to see any thing destroyed, any void produced in
society, any ruin on the face of the land." To imagine that one has
a right to commit to waste any object that others have found

beautiful and useful is to imagine that others later will have the same right with respect to one's own possessions or associations. It is a gesture of contempt in which self-contempt must always be deeply involved. "Something they must destroy," Burke will say in a moment of deep psychological insight into Jacobinism, "or they seem to themselves to exist for no purpose." And yet it is in the nature of all reform that some things will be changed finally. In the long run few memories will survive of how an old hospital used to look, or how an antiquated parliamentary ceremony used to be performed. When Burke writes of deliberate habits of thought, and of slowly maturing directives for action, we are aware of the catastrophic dangers he helps us to escape. But there is a risk that, with criteria as severe as his, we may fail to recognize a change for the better when it is offered.

Burke thinks that we can, in practice, recognize a change for the better, that we can make such weighty judgments both rationally and prudently. We do it by invoking a standard of probability—at first, a standard of dramatic probability. Would *that* follow *this*, would that seem a likely next step from this, if the two were offered in a narrative sequence and our belief were solicited as members of an audience? He gives a remarkable, almost reductive, example of such a judgment in his *Letters on a Regicide Peace*—urging, as a point against the treaty with France, that no reader of a book of history, after a narrative of the relations between the two countries through the 1780s and 1790s, would on reaching the present chapter find it credible that peace should break out in the very next. It would be improbable. The reader would stop reading the book. So far, Burke's definition of probability is no different from Hume's in the *Enquiry concerning Human Understanding*, where probability is said to be the state of "being determined by custom to transfer the past to the future, in all our inferences." This suggests that where we fail to transfer the past to the future, it must be because there was something inconsequent and disjunct, or something crooked and wrong, about the next historical action in the proposed sequence.

How we move from dramatic judgment to moral judgment becomes clear in the celebrated passage of Burke's *Reflections* about the October days—a description of the mob that threatened the life of the queen in her private chamber at Versailles. English radicals like the Dissenting preacher Richard Price, who were in sympathy with the revolution, had rejoiced at the event or seemed to do so, and Burke remarked the strangeness of their response. It sprang from a failure of "prejudice"—in the positive sense of prejudice, which he defines as *untaught feelings;* and a failure of "nature"— again, in the positive sense of a fitness of things beyond challenge, which Burke calls *wisdom without reflection.* He says of the imaginary spectators at this moment on both sides of the Channel: "I thought ten thousand swords must have leapt from their scabbards to avenge even a look which threatened her with insult." The proper next action in sequence is to be taken unconsciously, but instantly, as a matter of course by those whose judgments have become to them a second nature.

What are we to make of those ten thousand swords? From Burke's day to ours, the image has seemed to many readers not just quaintly provocative but overheated, self-indulgent, absurd. The risk he took is the more puzzling in the light of his actual feelings. He had spent much of a long career thwarting the aggrandizement of George III, and felt little general fondness for the cult of kings and queens. "A high and dry anti-monarchist"—such was the summing-up of his public character by a master of the field of eighteenth-century politics, Richard Pares. If Burke had no trite leaning to ceremonial displays, he also knew that to imply, as he did, that the gentlemen of the age were *chevaliers,* was a compliment more inscrutable than flattering. He let the picture stand nevertheless because he wanted to search out a faculty of response in his readers and the extreme case made for a genuine test. There is no short name for this faculty—the ability to be shocked by a wrong use of power, whoever its agents happen to be; and, in the practice that follows feeling, a readiness to execute the reaction with punctual energy.

Still thinking of the threat from which the queen should have been protected, Burke asks himself, "Why do I feel so differently from the Reverend Dr. Price?" And he answers, "For this plain reason: because it is natural I should." Here the standards of dramatic naturalness and moral naturalness are explicitly joined, and an idea is brought forward which has controlled the comparison all along: history is a theater of judgment, and human nature itself is embodied in the responses of the spectators.

> The theatre is a better school of moral sentiments than churches, where the feelings of humanity are thus outraged. Poets, who have to deal with an audience not yet graduated in the school of the rights of men, and who must apply themselves to the moral constitution of the heart, would not dare to produce such a triumph as a matter of exultation. . . . No theatric audience in Athens would bear what has been borne, in the midst of the real tragedy of this triumphal day. . . . They would soon see, that criminal means once tolerated are soon preferred.[2]

The theater is a school of moral sentiments because the interest which we learn to take in the imitation of a complete action can teach us to applaud the reward of virtue, the punishment of vice, and the instant operation of revenge or of self-defense which Burke associates with chivalric morality. Art, in showing nature under ideal conditions, partakes of an instinctive order like that of chivalry. But why should we grant that the theater is a *better* school of moral sentiments than churches? Because it deals in a variety of probable human actions under different circumstances; whereas churches offer only a repeated reflection on one or two paradigmatic actions. It may be an unstated part of the argument that in the theater we are conscious of the other spectators, of the importance of the praise or blame they give to what passes on the stage, as we are not conscious of the other members of a church congregation. Yet, at the moment of judgment, I do not look at those others. My eyes are on the action that is taking place on the stage.

By my own response, I am made to reflect on the human nature that composes me and that I help to compose.

It is sometimes said against Burke that the authority he respects must defer to an ultimate source, and that the source in this case is of his own devising: the "Ancient Constitution" of the British people. *What* constitution? asked early skeptics like Paine. One cannot point to a single contractual agreement in the history of Britain wherein are set forth definitively, and for mutual acknowledgment, the duties of rulers and the rights of subjects. From a political point of view, I think this criticism is fair, and that Burke does mystify the ambiguous entity he calls the constitution. He does it because he wants to show that the British have earned by centuries of reform all that the French can claim to have plucked down in a year of revolution. Yet, if one reads his argument as a general statement about how a tradition of moral thought can survive, it will appear that he does not mystify at all, for he relies on something less palpable than a constitution taken as a positive document. When Burke speaks of the "constitution," he really has in mind the constitutedness of a society, the sense of coherence that supports its members when they approve certain actions and disapprove others. In the passage I have just quoted, he turns out to be referring not to an agreement signed and accepted some time in the past, but to "the moral constitution of the heart." In the *Letter to a Noble Lord* he will defend "the constitution of the mind of man."

This sense of a natural authority that comes from the way we are constituted is not quite original with Burke. But he sees its political uses, and distinguishes it alike from arguments that appeal to mere utility and to rights. He is most original, as well as risky, in associating our moral constitution with an idea of sensibility—a feminine kind of responsiveness which is felt to supply a motive for the exertions of masculine honor. This last element of a natural constitution was decidedly absent from Butler's *Dissertation on the Nature of Virtue*—the work from which I think Burke drew the metaphor of the constitution. For Butler, the sentiments by which

we praise or blame the conduct of others or of ourselves, and by
which we know we are right to do so, have no relation to a
softening of manners or delicacy of feeling. Instead, our constitution is a single grand mechanism that weeds out vicious conduct
and allows sociable conduct to flourish. By sociable conduct it is
clear that Butler means the sort that helps humanity to survive as
a whole, and by vicious conduct the sort that would, if pursued
far or by many, tend to the extinction of humanity as a whole.
Moral thought, for him, means a natural selection, over time,
among competing human instincts. At the same time, each individual judgment is an act of conscience without regard to an outcome either of individual or of general happiness.

Writes Butler: "The fact then appears to be, that we are constituted so as to condemn falsehood, unprovoked violence, injustice,
and to approve of benevolence to some preferably to others, ab-
stracted from all consideration, which conduct is likely to produce
an overbalance of happiness or misery." What, then, of the possibility that "the Author of nature" may *not* have joined the consequences of individual judgments with a scheme of general happiness? Butler considers the possibility and adds, in a remarkable
sentence, that whatever the outcome may be, "still, *since this is our
constitution;* falsehood, violence, and injustice, must be vice in us,
and *benevolence to some preferably to others,* virtue" (emphasis added).
Recall, now, the inescapable claim of just such natural feelings on
Burke, in his judgment of the violence of the mob against Marie
Antoinette: "Why do I feel so differently from the Reverend Dr.
Price? For this plain reason: because it is natural I should." It is the
same with Butler and his constitution: the judgment it delivers is
right for us, because the constitution is ours. The individual or
collective act with which judgment makes us respond—the giving
of a charitable dole, the refusal of support for a revolution—may
turn out well or ill for society as a whole now or in the future. We
seem to have, at the moment of choice, very little to say about how
those habits will go to work. And moral choices in general, as
Butler and Burke present them, always have something of this
reflexive quality. They say to us, "But still, because this is our

constitution . . . ." The good that is promised by acting in its light is that we shall know who we were when we acted. At the end of the story, for a society or for a person, the narrative one can make of many such associated actions will carry the conviction of probability.

Butler says of *"the principle of virtue"* that it is capable of being *"improved into a habit."* The same train of thought seems to lie somewhere in the background of Burke's defense of prejudice: it "renders a man's virtue his habit." When we see a woman assaulted, a woman who holds the highest place in the system of our country's laws and manners, we react at once without reflection. We do not pause to inquire into the faults of her life and how they may balance the wrong that she suffers now. We do not for a moment speculate on the possible good effects of failing to protect her, or the possible ill effects of protecting her without due consideration of all sides. To insist on the intervention of some such impartial mood is to usurp our own constitution. If we do allow such a pause, it is bound to occur to us (as it has occurred to the new citizens of France) that the queen is only a woman and any human being is only an animal and not, at that, an animal of the strongest or most serviceable kind. Burke frames his passage on the queen as a test to find out readers of whatever party who "have chosen our nature rather than our speculations."

If we have so chosen, we will look in a crisis to the instant mandate of prejudice: "Prejudice is of ready application in the emergency; it previously engages the mind in a steady course of wisdom and virtue, and does not leave the man hesitating in the moment of decision, sceptical, puzzled, and unresolved. Prejudice renders a man's virtue his habit; and not a series of unconnected acts. Through just prejudice, his duty becomes a part of his nature."[3] Burke believes this with sufficient earnestness to intensify the thought in a dangerous paradox. He regrets that the loss of chivalry has meant the departure of "that chastity of honour which felt a stain like a wound, which inspired courage whilst it mitigated ferocity, which ennobled whatever it touched, and under which vice itself lost half its evil by losing all its grossness." The idea of beauty as a garment that softens vice is a startling variation on the idea that prejudice renders a man's virtue his habit. Burke makes us conceive of virtue as perhaps only a covering, a habit, literally something that one wears. Suppose what lies beneath to be the inward and inveterate character of a person or an institution. Even so, he thinks, virtue is actually made stronger by being confirmed into a habit. Vice in turn is made weaker by having to counterfeit its nature and wear the cloak of virtue. Most readers are so transfixed by the paradox Burke has fashioned to palliate "vice itself" that they forget his interest in the process by which vice also has "lost half its evil." I take his to be an ingenuous and not an ironic praise of hypocrisy. Hypocrisy is, he reasons, a *deep* homage that vice pays to virtue. As long as hypocrisy exists, as we may be sure that a sense of shame is still alive, and this is so because manners are civilizing through and through.

Some commonplace observations may remove any sense of unnaturalness that lingers with the paradox. Even a mostly vicious life that has been taught by right prejudice will be forced to the expedient of hypocrisy: the habit, or mask, of such a life will be that of virtue to some extent, though its conduct obeys all the familiar patterns of vice. And yet the unconscious habit does affect the conscious person. The necessity of submitting oneself to a prohibition against shamelessness, also acts as a downright inhibition, and so from sheer expediency one may be forced to give up half the shameless deeds one would otherwise have performed. Manners are in this sense more than the costume or outward expression of morals. They are themselves a source of morality. But perhaps we can make the thought more vivid by a contemporary illustration. Lieutenant Colonel Oliver North was asked by a committee of the Congress whether he had wrongly destroyed thousands of memoranda pertinent to an inquiry into his conduct by a legal arm of the government he had sworn to uphold and protect. He replied: "I think I shredded most of that. . . . Did I get 'em all?" Watchers of the televised hearings will recall the curious experimental smirk that followed this utterance. The smirk was asking, How much shame is left? Vice, here, had lost none of its grossness. So complete a failure of hypocrisy can occur, Burke argues, only where a vast demoralization has weakened the contract of a society.

Yet to speak of a social contract at all can be a misleading clue to the liberal idea of tradition—as Burke himself understood it, and as his successors have understood it. Burke, in fact, does not believe in the practicability of a positive contract (a contract written out and agreed to by contending parties), and this sets him on a different path from a liberal theorist like John Locke. There is, however, one sort of contract he does believe in—except that he calls it, more simply, a partnership. It is "a partnership not only between those who are living, but between those who are living, those who are dead, and those who are to be born." No one in such a partnership will strive to be singular or inventive much of the time, in acts that affect citizenship or participation in society. I think this is the real sense of Burke's saying that "we know that *we* have made no discoveries, and we think no discoveries are to be made, in morality." If one has become a member of a moral community that persists over time, even the linguistic usage by which one registers approval or disapproval will wear the look of something precedented, undiscovering, almost circular in its obviousness. In the *Reflections*, Burke helps us to imagine what this way of judging may feel like by his reliance on a single rhetorical scheme. Meanings are elaborated in this scheme by disposing a single root-word into different parts of speech. Burke says, for example, of the Jacobins that "their liberty is not liberal." He says of manners in general that "to make us love our country, our country ought to be lovely." The effect is of a mere memory or confirming echo which seems nevertheless to involve a recognition.

The idea of society as a continuous partnership has a clear intuitive appeal. Yet Burke may seem particularly vulnerable just here, where a contractual or utilitarian thinker would not be vulnerable. His argument, it can be said, gives a realistic account of human nature in society, it reveals with great acuteness the points at which we may discover a social order to be weak or strong, but his whole way of thinking is unprincipled and irrational. I want to defend Burke from this charge by enlisting in his defense the moral philosophy of Hume. The procedure is warrantable because Burke did borrow from Hume a great many features of his argument. He places a tacit reliance on a Humean morality to fill the background of a picture he himself has left unfinished. With this background accounted for, he hopes to satisfy his reader that the result is, within limits, principled, and as rational as the subject of human nature permits.

Hume begins his analysis of morality by distinguishing between the understanding and moral sentiments. The understanding perceives relations between things—actual or probable relations. By contrast, the sentiments associate a feeling with the relations described, and enable us to act on a given perception: "The end of all moral speculations is to teach us our duty; and, by proper representations of the deformity of vice and the beauty of virtue, beget correspondent habits, and engage us to avoid the one, and embrace the other." It is the power of representation alone that teaches the look of deformity and beauty; and in this way, the sentiments must always be auxiliaries of the understanding. Nor is the work they perform somehow subordinate. Of the following two sentences, the first describes the characteristic action of sentiments, and the second the way the moral world would appear in the absence of sentiments: "What is honourable, what is fair, what is becoming, what is noble, what is generous, takes possession of the heart, and animates us to embrace and maintain it. What is intelligible, what is evident, what is probable, what is true, procures only the cool assent of the understanding; and gratifying a speculative curiosity, puts an end to our researches."[4] A judgment free of sentiments therefore would be animated by no motive to action.

Similarly, a judgment from which too many of the pertinent sentiments have been shorn may prove a stimulus to wrong action, or to a wrong self-exculpation by the agent. Hume uses a familiar illustration from antiquity:

When Nero killed Agrippina, all the relations between himself and the person, and all the circumstances of the fact, were previously known to him; but the motive of revenge, or fear, or interest, prevailed in his savage heart over the sentiments of duty and humanity. And when we express that detestation against him to which he himself, in a little time, became insensible, it is not that we see any relations, of which he was ignorant; but that, for the rectitude of our disposition, we feel sentiments against which he was hardened from flattery and a long perseverance in the most enormous crimes.[5]

The picturing which the sentiments are asked to supply, in order to evoke an adequate response to virtue or vice, makes their activity depend on the exercise of taste. Hume speaks, indeed, in the language of taste, of our need for "nice distinctions," "the most minute discriminations between vice and virtue." He employs the word *delicacy* in a multitude of contexts, always with deliberate double stress, to imply a quality of feeling on which morality and taste undistinguishably draw.

The tone of his analysis throughout is matter-of-fact, almost unmoved: "morality is determined by sentiment"—that is the way things are. But Hume's largest hopes for such a morality are inseparable from his hopes for enlightenment. The principles, though "somewhat small and delicate," from which moral sentiments must spring, are to be understood finally as "social and universal; they form, in a manner, the *party* of humankind against vice and disorder, its common enemy." This prophecy makes sense in the light of Hume's treatment of self-love and benevolence, which he sees as mutually cooperative, and not as mutually repellent. In the Humean scheme, self-love is a small circle placed concentrically within the larger circle of benevolence. It may be artificially darkened by habits of self-regard, or of an overwrought delicacy. Still, it would be wrong to conclude that one's feeling for oneself is different in kind from one's feeling for others. On the contrary, Hume thinks we come to know our own worth only by passing in review ourselves and others, and seeing both in the light by which worth is ascribed to people in general. The major sentiments of approval, as he interprets them, follow the same pattern as the sentiments of disapproval or qualified approval.

What advances the general utility is good for everyone in society. But Hume's idea of "general utility" is to be sharply distinguished from the calculation of the pleasure or pain that a given act will bring to greater or lesser numbers of persons—the calculation that lies at the heart of reductive utilitarianism. General utility was Burke's sense when he said to the revolutionists of 1789 what no utilitarian reasoner could ever say: "You began ill because you began by despising every thing that belonged to you." A social thinker ought to begin by trying to appreciate the things that belong to himself or herself, as one, characteristic, both typical and anomalous member of a society. What benefit does such an exercise confer on the thinker? On this point Hume is clear: "This constant habit of surveying ourselves, as it were, in reflection, keeps alive all the sentiments of right and wrong, and begets, in noble natures, a certain reverence for themselves as well as others, which is the guardian of every virtue." It looks from his phrasing as if there were some danger of the moral sentiments going dead inside us. The therapy of keeping them alive is the work of reflection and sentiment together.

It is no contradiction for Hume to speak of reflective sentiments, because the action of moral judgment goes both ways: reason correcting the work of sentiment; sentiment sometimes ratifying, sometimes significantly failing to "animate" the verdict of reason. As he remarks in another passage that deliberately mixes metaphors of taste and judgment: "In many orders of beauty, particularly those of the finer arts, it is requisite to employ much reasoning in order to feel the proper sentiment; and a false relish may frequently be corrected by argument and reflection. There are just grounds to conclude, that moral beauty partakes much of this latter species."[6] Where does this reasoning come from? In large part, says Hume, from customary practices and denominations which, in daily life, still have an axiomatic force. Within a given society "common interest and utility beget infallibly a standard of right and wrong among the parties concerned," and the person who enters a society will want to find the standard solid at many points. The most elementary social facts break down under analysis if we abstract them from general utility. This is true, says Hume, even of property; for apart from such utility, "it must be confessed, that all regards to right and property, seem entirely without foundation, as much as the grossest and most vulgar superstition. Were the interests of society nowise concerned, it is as unintelligible why another's articulating certain sounds implying consent, should change the nature of my actions with regard to a particular object, as why the reciting of a liturgy by a priest, in a certain habit and posture, should dedicate a heap of brick and timber, and render it, thenceforth and for ever, sacred."[7] Thus, general utility runs only as deep as a tissue of conventions that have practical force; but the conventions themselves are not the founding elements of the practice; on the contrary, they were evolved to represent a general trust that mostly needs no expression.

Hume takes as an example our common reliance on promises. Are such miniature contracts really necessary? They are, he says— but only as a token of our faith in something else. A promise therefore is not my saying to someone, "I will do as I say, or else." It is rather both of us saying to each other (though only one of us speaks): "We see that this business will be done as things of the same sort have been done before." It is an insight shared by Hume and Burke that this account of promise-giving can be extended so as to cover a society bound only by prejudice, by duties that have come to be second nature, and by a history of common feelings like the love of honor. The views that Hume and Burke hold of society differ in what can sometimes seem a point of emphasis (though it sometimes seems much more). When he talks about reflection on common sentiments, Hume draws attention to an interest in general utility from which every thoughtless impulse seems to have been purged. By contrast, Burke offers his defense of prejudice in order to strengthen a suspicion that no sentiment can ever become thoroughly reflective.

What Hume and Burke say about morality holds true as well for the continuity of moral thought and conduct with which education is always involved. From a modern point of view, the most remarkable thing about their argument is its sense of attachment to inherited practices—a sense that survives every skeptical doubt regarding the comprehensiveness of a given object of attachment. Burke and Hume alike reject universalism; yet the idea of human nature is real to them. "Mankind" or "humankind," they seem to say, is an ideal object that makes it probable for reflective sentiments to extend over time, across the generations of human life, just as they extend over space, among the persons in a given society. I said earlier that in a Humean judgment we pass in review both ourselves and others, and see both in the light by which worth is ascribed to persons in general. But for both thinkers, this must include not only the living but those who are dead and those who are to come. Once we include the generations to come, the idea that what is good for me must, to pass my approval, be good for others also, will itself yield an idea of progress. The idea depends on the force of personal imagination as one casts one's eye over society. And it finds its true ground not in a universal imperative but in the continuous acts of individuals who have a regard for general utility. This consideration alone justifies Hume in speaking of moral sentiments as "the *party* of humankind"—a party whose interests advance only with the advance of human nature. It also justifies his readers in conceiving of a tradition of moral knowledge—a tradition to which the knowledge of taste is related.

But the Humean argument does something more unpredictable. In its view of our motives of judgment, there is a socially justified place for the person who acts alone; the person whose judgments lead away from either a rising or an established consensus, and whose acts may seem cast adrift from the going versions of general utility. This point has been made with eloquent clarity by Annette Baier—a moral philosopher whose writings on Hume have greatly

influenced my treatment here. In an essay called "Secular Faith,"
Baier speaks of the dilemma any dissident person must face in a
society where sentiments of approval and disapproval have been
fully socialized. To whom, or to what other society, can such a person
appeal? For "only a fool supports widely unsupported institutions
whose only good depends on their getting wide support." But
then—remembering the sense in which the society of human nature
extends over time—Baier asks, "support from whom? From my
contemporaries and only them? It is fairly evident . . . that the
support of the majority of his contemporaries is not *sufficient* to
guard the conformist from being taken in by fool's gold, especially
when the institution is one which *conserves* goods for future generations. Whole generations can be retroactively made into cullies
of their joint integrity by later generations' waste and destruction."[8]
But the support of one's contemporaries turns out to be not only
not sufficient but not necessary, once the field of moral reflection
is taken to include the past and the future—that is, once a living
tradition has been heard to speak in a voice different from that of
the existing political or cultural authority.

Baier offers a defense of someone acting within a human tradition—against the suffrage of contemporaries and for the sake of a
vivid posterity—by invoking the promise of Kant's idea of a "king-
dom of ends." Yet a similar defense is also derivable from Hume's
idea of action. When I make a moral judgment, my field of reflection includes other persons, and the action itself will touch other
persons. It is this truth, writ large, that produces the effect Baier
describes elsewhere as "the asymmetry of care"—"an extended
version of morality in which there are more who are cared about
than there are doing the caring." After all, the asymmetry of care
is another name for what happens when we go beyond the constitution of a society to embrace the constitution of human nature;
on this account,

> apparently futile unilateral and possibly self-sacrificing action
> is neither futile nor unilateral. Not futile, because it keeps alive
> the assurance of the possibility of qualified members for a just

society. Not unilateral, because the one just man has "a cloud of witnesses," all those others whose similar acts in other times kept alive the same hope. The actions of individuals who, unsupported by their contemporaries, act for the sake of justice do not necessarily hasten the coming of a just society, but they do rule out one ground on which it might be feared impossible. In this very modest way the just man's actions confirm his faith, demonstrate that *one* condition of the existence of a just society can be met, that human psychology can be a psychology for sovereigns.[9]

The reasoning applies equally to a protest on behalf of a just but unsupported institution and to a protest against an unjust but widely supported one.

Let me try to sum up the broad argument about morality with which I have been concerned. The argument, in Butler, in Hume, and in Burke says that the knowledge of tradition is a partial but necessary expression of the self-knowledge of human nature. A tradition only works through its constituent individuals—people who offer their judgments by means of the existing institutions; but also, people who are capable of separating themselves from institutions. The model here for one's attachment to a tradition becomes not Louis XIV asserting "L'état, c'est moi," but John Keats saying "English ought to be kept up." When a tradition speaks through us, it passes into conscious thought only to pass beyond conscious thought. We ratify by reflection what we will confirm as prejudice. In the moment of action or creation, we are not left skeptical, puzzled, and unresolved.

Yet an enlightened tradition must include as one of its possibilities a return to reflection; an estimate, or revaluation, of principles, which may lead to a modification of practice. Burke himself exemplifies this possibility in some of his speeches on American affairs: when, for example, he says, "I do not know the method of drawing up an indictment against an whole people"; and again when he says, "An Englishman is the unfittest person on earth to argue another Englishman into slavery." It is important for the moral judge in Burke's position to be able to say to his audience, "I give you nothing but your own; and you cannot refuse in the gross what you have so often acknowledged in detail." Still, this hardly exhausts the possible grounds of a reformer's appeal. If a social order were not susceptible of change, if it did not permit us to see that some of its organs have grown old and to realize that they should be allowed to die out, tradition itself could scarcely survive as a medium of self-reflection. A changeless society might nevertheless persist in some form. Yet Burke also said that superstition is the religion of feeble minds—implying, I think, that only a tradition which can modify itself deserves to be called a faith of active minds. There are, in any modern society, active minds of another sort, whose energy makes them press for change after change, with the desire that others conform to each new shift in the principle of conformity. This kind of character Burke associated with the profession of lawyers; we ought, he said, to try to live without too many of them.

To see one's thinking against the background of a tradition is the habit of a mind that does not aim to constitute a class in itself. Rather a mind like this supposes, when it reflects on general issues at all, that it aspires to membership in some such elusive entity as Wordsworth invoked: "There is / One great society alone on earth: / The noble living and the noble dead." How does a tradition engage enough minds in a generation to *appear* so substantial a power? We are reduced here to the mysterious fact that people do labor to inherit ways of thinking and feeling. That they do may relate to the almost impersonal appeal of certain motives to action. Fame, Hume tells us, is a motive like that; honor, Burke adds, is another.

In many respects our democratic society does not resemble the society in which the liberal tradition in morality evolved. Burke, though he wanted to preserve the good will of the American colonies for the sake of the empire, looked with ambivalence on the social experiment that began in 1776. In private, he said there was bound to be a civil war in the new republic. It was the good fortune of his moment that he could see the politics he aimed to defend (mixed monarchy with a strong republican element) and the community he aimed to defend (the empire of Britain) as agreeable with each other. In support of both, he referred to a single tradition. For us in America today, the ideals of political liberalism and communitarianism have grown distinct, and a single tradition cannot be supposed to unify them. But why should this have happened?

One reason, it seems to me, is that we have had to regard certain theoretical ideals as if they themselves could be an inheritance, in a way Burke thought impossible for a morality of "untaught feelings" such as he endorsed. He believed that whenever a theory (say, the theory of democratic equality) came to override a prejudice (say, the prejudice in favor of an old aristocracy) its effects would th eaten the traditional life of society. We in the United States have lived for a long time by just such a theory, and amid the wreck of many prejudices. And so the question recurs: if political liberalism is the only lasting tradition we have had; the only one that has persisted, across generations, from the beginning of the republic, and that seems to represent us well; does it follow that liberalism in the broadest sense implies a way of thinking and feeling we must inherit if we are to survive? I think it does. We are in the position of using Burkean means to achieve a non-Burkean end.

Maybe the difficulty of our position is only the difficulty of all original hopes. It feels odd for an American to talk to Americans in the conservative language of customs, habits, and time-honored practices. Shaw said that if you found the word *morality* in the Bible, you would be as surprised as if you found *automobile* or *typewriter:* we feel much the same when we see *tradition* in a portrait of ourselves. The truth is that our system of laws was made against all Burkean precept, and our success seems to tell against his view on two separate counts. He believed that no nation could derive its government and sustain its legitimacy from a system of ideal and abstract rights. But the constitutional founding of the United States did just that. He likewise believed that a nation's morality would always be in force before the lawmakers arrived on the scene. The existing code of manners would offer a "dense medium," which a code of laws could only aim to ratify. Yet, in America, with the aid of a written constitution and a bill of rights, we have successfully legislated a morality the basis of which is respect for individual rights, and religious and didactic toleration. We have refined the prescriptive code to an impressive minimum, and we have done it in a society where manners appeared to offer a thin medium. There, it must strike us, is the commonwealth theory, and here the post-commonwealth fact. We have kept up for two centuries the experiment of a political order that binds itself as lightly as possible to a remembered past or an imagined future.

Yet in alluding like this to a reversal of moral probabilities, one comes close to a usual mistake about American democracy. If the people begin with nothing but hopes in common, because they lack the rooted faith of a shared cultural memory, it does not follow that they find their support only in an undistinguishing miscellany of habits. American society does not feel like that; probably it never did. Abstract principles (it is true) make a weak sustenance for the daily affairs of people who must be ready of judgment as well as quick with reasons. But in the history of the United States, talk about abstract principles led to complicated results—produced, in the long run, a moral life of sufficient depth and sufficient texture. A revealing habit of this life is the casual conviction that "everyone has the right to speak his mind." In the films of the thirties where the line occurs, the preceding line often is, "Give him a chance!" And perhaps the two sentiments have more to do with each other than an inspection of their dictionary meanings could show. Together, they are not far from the reason President Johnson gave for the moral necessity of the Civil Rights Bill: "A man has a right not to be insulted in front of his children." These almost proverbial beliefs do carry, of course, deep traces of Enlightenment ideals, yet the beliefs themselves are held as tenaciously as prejudices. The strange result has been the making of citizens who are proud up to the point of equality, and who thereby embody a new virtue in the history of human nature. That is why constitutional loyalty is taken to supersede other motives in the conduct of public affairs. The idea of a community abstractly rooted, far from defeating the

parochial attachments Burke and Hume took for granted, makes
the most high-minded start imaginable for the system of morals
they described.

How well is the experiment working? I see two recent developments about which the tradition of secular morality may have
something instructive to tell us. The inherited republican theory,
concerning the treatment of one's fellow citizens as rights-bearing
persons, exists now under a pressure to which it has not been
subjected before. The theory itself flourished with the high individualism of commerce and the arts in the nineteenth century. It
was a dream more than a social fact, but the dream was given a
lucky second wind by America's world dominance in the 1940s and
1950s, and only in the last generation has its credit begun to wane.
But with the weakening of individualist habits of thought (except
as a rationalization of sheer market power and mobility), a new
kind of social expectation has begun to be discernible. Many people
today who enter the system of American society do not expect to
survive unaided and are not conscious of wanting to achieve what
they can by merit alone. Loosely speaking, these people are communitarians. Yet the communities that they represent are many,
dispersed, and shifting all the time.

Sex, class, race, ethnic origin, sexual persuasion, or religious sect,
almost any criterion that can define a group is taken to lay down
the possible hints for a separate entitlement. Many of the groups
in question are struggling for the rights of democratic citizenship.
The scandal that these rights still have to be fought for may obstruct
a view of how far the struggle aims beyond citizenship. It frequently aims instead at public support of a group identity. And
this suggests a movement away from the liberal ideal of a community in which men and women were to be treated as ends. Treat
me (says the communitarian today) as a means of course, but one
whose dignity will be cared for by the group in which I hold
membership. Thus group sentiment has detached itself once and
for all from the idea of solidarity in human nature which liberalism
took from the Enlightenment. But, with us at least, it does not
therefore move toward the kind of national identity that Burke saw

as the alternative. What we are witnessing is an American inversion of American individualism. Groups have become the contenders. And yet the groups retain the traits of the old egocentric bargainers on whom they are modeled.

Whether or not the flux of communitarianisms persists for long at its current strength, it will have been clear from the illustrations in chapter 1 that the group ideologies thrive at considerable cost to the general utility: life to them is death to a republican morality like ours. To continue the democratic experiment with any chance of success, Americans need to be Burkean spectators regarding their own implication in morality, Butlerian constitutionalists regarding the good of membership in humankind as a whole, and Humean reflective agents regarding the consistency of personal with social welfare. This may mean that we shall have to abridge our habit of poring over every inherited custom and convention in the spirit of the Russian schoolboy in Dostoevsky: given a map of the stars, he hands it back with corrections. Politics has helped to supply Americans with the dense medium of a tradition, and the weaker the coherence of a society in other respects, the stronger its political ties must be. Joseph Butler once asked in conversation: "Why may not whole communities and public bodies be seized with fits of insanity, as well as individuals?" We suffer not from insanity but from the effects of a decade-long interval of self-imposed immaturity. We seem to have inherited a politics fit to survive, but are looking on while, in the interests of everyone as a group litigant, in the interests of no one as a citizen, the knowledge of politics which with us was once a distinct competence and even a calling begins to pass from memory.

The offense to memory would be merely a sentimental loss if it were not at the same time an offense to imagination. But an ignorance that eradicates our sense of the past must also diminish our relation to any conceivable future. In Burke's stricture against those who "commit waste on the inheritance," there is implied a leading maxim of the liberal tradition—one with much meaning now, both in relation to right-wing political innovators and left-wing cultural innovators; for Burke was concerned with the destruction of works of nature as well as with the destruction of works of art, and he supposed the habits of piety that preserved the one would also preserve the other. A maxim Burke seems always on the point of formulating is that *no generation has the right to act as if it were the last generation on earth*. (It may be a corollary that no generation has a right to think as if it were the first generation on earth.) If so, we can notice another use of shame: it makes us wary of crossing certain boundaries in the presence of unseen judges. The predicament of these years in America is that we appear incapable of electing leaders appropriate to a people who aim to have successors as well as ancestors.

The solidarity of generations is a formative issue for the liberal idea of tradition, even though it comes to consciousness late in the history of the tradition. The survival of a creed like liberalism, whose leading social virtues are toleration and personal autonomy, depends on joining what is good for me with what is good for others in the long run. This means a time long after the expiration of my short, self-favoring, views. Yet to think as if for others—the well-being and not the demands of others—is alien to the habits of market liberalism. It may seem almost as improbable an exercise for political liberalism. The very idea of such an experiment is enough to incite feelings of strong resentment in the experimenter—as if I were being denied some promised portion of my own well-being. Kant, who saw clearly the part such resentment could play in deforming thought, gave the best answer to any generation's impulse to follow self-interest alone. In the *Idea for a Universal History with a Cosmopolitan Intent*, he writes:

> It remains perplexing that earlier generations seem to do their laborious work for the sake of later generations, in order to provide a foundation from which the latter can advance the building which nature has intended. Only later generations will have the good fortune to live in the building. But however mysterious this [conclusion] may be, it is nevertheless necessary, if one assumes that an animal species is to have reason,

and is to arrive at a complete development of its faculties as a class of reasonable beings who die while their species is immortal.[10]

To act as if for a progressive impulse of the species is not to act without self-love. And what holds true for one person's grasp of motives not strictly selfish may also hold for a generation's power to act with regard to posterity.

John Rawls, in a chapter of *A Theory of Justice* which deals explicitly with justice between generations, evokes a similar idea of progress to console the defensive fear that one may be cheated of "the pursuit of happiness." That fear can easily unleash the reckless actions of people who suspect that all they accomplish (in ventures of cooperative savings, or of salvage for the general welfare) will redound to the benefit of people like them in later times. The consequent revulsion from an unequal burden can be cured, Rawls believes, by the thought that generations "are not subordinate to one another any more than individuals are. The life of a people is conceived as a scheme of cooperation spread out in historical time. It is to be governed by the same conception of justice that regulates the cooperation of contemporaries. No generation has stronger claims than any other."[11] This argument certainly carries some force as long as we have in view the progress of a society. It falters when we bring into view the progress of an individual—as an equal good, or as a good that is greater because less likely to deceive the hopes and fears that people do cherish on their own behalf.

Here the greatest defender of liberal individuality turns out to be the greatest defender of tradition. The relevant passage occurs in John Stuart Mill's *On Liberty*, at the point where Mill considers the evil of silencing opinions of which one disapproves. For whom, after all, will this be a privation? Mill rules out the silenced person who in this case would be the judge in his or her own cause. He then offers a utilitarian answer: that such a restriction on speech artificially shrinks the free market of ideas. And this by many interpreters has been taken to be his final answer. I do not think it is. For if it were, it would rest on a calculation of pleasures and pains, the greatest good for the greatest number, all the niceties of "cost-benefit analysis"—in short, a mode of analysis that Mill in this work has advanced beyond. The ground of defense he arrives at instead is close to the idea of general utility we find in Hume and Burke. As Mill concludes, the reason for tolerating a foreign opinion and therefore, perhaps, *keeping an idea alive*, is the same when I think of its good to others as it is when I think of its good to myself. The reason has to do with the relations, first, between self-respect and the refusal to insulate oneself from disagreeable stimuli; and, second, between that principled refusal and the ideal of self-invention or the progress of a person.

When I forbid some expression or action as morally offensive to me, I act on an abiding impulse in human nature: the wish to believe that I have already come to a resting place. We may regard the impulse as coming from mere inertia, or we may regard it as the source of all stability. Mill only wants us to see that it is in our nature to resist change—not the shallow variations of manners or customs, which happen all the time and are themselves a great prompter of conformity, but the tremendous mutations of thought and feeling which alter permanently one's sense of oneself and the world. To keep myself in a state of rest, I will do anything to guard against this kind of disturbance, and intolerant laws can help by ridding my society of thoughts whose expression gives offense, or of persons whose way of life seems at odds with mine. In the face of every such fear, Mill seems to say to the liberal, you cannot stop the person or practice you detest from going its way as long as it allows you to go yours. The fear may well be justified. But the desire to act on it is a sick desire. Consequently, in the absence of a practical threat you must never reduce this fear to a practice of intolerance. For you agree to tolerance not out of kindness to the claims of the other person but from an irreducible respect for yourself.

A possible truth taken out of the world is a truth taken away from the world, and a stimulus to vivid thought removed for every single person in it. This includes apparently useless, or pernicious, ideas from the past, and aberrant views now in their first striving for recognition: "The peculiar evil of silencing the expression of an opinion is, that it is robbing the human race; posterity as well as the existing generation; those who dissent from the opinion, still more than those who hold it. If the opinion is right, they are deprived of the opportunity of exchanging error for truth: if wrong, they lose, what is almost as great a benefit, the clearer perception and livelier impression of truth, produced by its collision with error."[12] Toleration thus becomes a virtue whose total value can only be disclosed over time: it develops its results, both individually and socially, only by the collision of ideas.

A "merely social intolerance," Mill considers, may still be supposed a good for the sake of limited social ends. Its larger evil is the suppression of a virtue which Mill seems to think the species itself develops in the long labor of a tradition: "the price paid for this sort of intellectual pacification is the sacrifice of the entire moral courage of the human mind." Such moral courage is exhibited by every person who believes that "however true [one's opinion] may be, if it is not fully, frequently, and fearlessly discussed, it will be held as a dead dogma, not a living truth." For this reason Mill can claim a practical and not a mystical intent when he says, "Truth gains more even by the errors of one who, with due study and preparation, thinks for himself, than by the true opinions of those who only hold them because they do not suffer themselves to think." By silencing a line of thought, as much as by inhibiting the expression of an individual, I weaken the living truth that is in me and go some way to the hoarding of a dead dogma. And in doing so I kill what part I may have in keeping up the moral courage of the human mind.

The testimony from Mill, on the way self-respect must cooperate with a tolerance of diverse beliefs from the past and present, brings to a final focus the thought of reflection, morality, and tradition with which I have been concerned in this chapter. Self-respect, and a natural piety which consists in reverence for things that come to the world before me or apart from me, are the complementary virtues that the liberal idea of tradition works hard to keep together. The pressure to keep them together is as consistent from the side of Kant, Mill, and Rawls as it is from the side of Hume and Burke, even if the latter more steadily adopt the good of tradition as their starting point. The good of a thought that is mine, like the good of the monument or possession which represents that thought, is that it reflects feelingly my relation to persons not only whom I do not know but whom I cannot know. If liberal education adds up, it shows me a way to think for myself as if under their eyes, or at their half-acknowledged promptings. In doing so it suggests a way to act for something beyond myself.

PART THREE

5

THE CASE OF

LITERARY STUDY

These reflections on liberal learning began by attacking an ideology that promotes reverence for a few sacred texts and ideas; went on to raise parallel objections to an iconoclasm that supposes a new social system can be created by acts of textual solidarity; and have defended a view of tradition as reformable rather than inert—a way of thinking and feeling, and not merely an institutional fact. With this contest in the background, I now trace aspects of the recent evolution of literary study. The discussion calls for an extension of the analysis of institutional radicalism begun in chapter 3. For, in literary study above all, the idea that a cosmopolitan tradition must be fixed and therefore regressive has led to the encouragement of group cultures as a proper dissolvent of tradition. Granted, many of the cultures are only imaginable as responses to contemporary needs. Their utility for the rewriting of history, as for the unbuilding of tradition, remains no less potent for that. Yet regarding the group cultures as such, I have little to add here. I am interested rather in the theoretical movement that laid the groundwork for them.

The belief in culture-as-cure rests on a particular account of the history of literary study. It is a central feature of this account that, until the late seventies, when "important questions began to be asked," the only available idea of a literary tradition was the property of a moribund professional aristocracy. This may seem an odd establishment to have grown up when it is said to have done: just two generations after the canon of English poetry had been drastically revised under the influence of T. S. Eliot; and in the very generation when a challenge to the modernist canon itself was under way—with such conspicuous effects as a revival of interest in the poetry of Milton and Hardy. The tradition of English poetry as taught in the schools did not behave like a complacent and well-drilled entity. And with evidence as uncooperative as this, one may eventually have to face an awkward question. What if the received account of the history of literary study is false?

I think, in fact, that it is false, and part of my aim is to tell a truer version of a history with which I am acquainted. Yet the received version is so prevalent, and is now turned out to order for the sake of so many ad hoc *isms*, that I need to begin by saying what I take to be wrong with its broadest outlines. This is easily done for the story is simple. It says: a nostalgic, mindless, politically reactive idea of certain texts as the core of civilization, actually controlled the field of literary study in the 1940s, 1950s, and early 1960s. Thus the New Critics, among them William Empson, Kenneth Burke, Yvor Winters, John Crowe Ransom, R. P. Blackmur—who were called new because they worked at criticism rather than textual scholarship and promoted the study of poetry over prose—are pictured as early advocates of the Bennett-Will game of recovering civilization. Even, it is said, the New Critical terms of praise—words like *ambiguous, complex, difficult, subtle*—show that the game was closed to outsiders. That the works these critics admired could not be hitched to a short-term impulse of agitation only made their pedagogy a convenient tactic of repression. Now, as a reader and admirer of the critics I have just named (who, by the way, were sharply individuated as to taste and idiom), I do not begin to recognize them in the caricature that has lately achieved such currency. But here a confession may be in order.

I studied literature as an undergraduate and as a graduate student, not with any member of this critical school but under a diverse group of scholars, men and women of more than one generation who in some cases were themselves students of the New Critics. They had anyway been deeply, often tacitly, influenced by the writings of the New Critics. Yet from these teachers, I imbibed no doctrine concerning the defense of the West. I was not looking for that, but had I looked in earnest, I suspect my disappointment would have been very great. What stayed with me from courses on literature were some interesting (some unforgettable) critical *observations,* which carried conviction in themselves, and were perhaps more memorable as coming from persons of genuine learning. I also began to feel a sense of the possible connection between books and experience—emphatically including the experience of other books; together with a certain habit of attention, or patience; and, more slowly, I learned some clues to the difference between what I knew and what I did not know. As for imparting a coherent idea of civilization, the experience one could derive from good teaching in the years that I speak of—roughly the late sixties through the mid-seventies—was far too unorganized, too much a hodge-podge of affinities and enthusiasms, to accomplish any such result as a general rule. This may have been a loss. But the vindication of the imperial West was not an end compassed by the masters of orthodoxy: it hardly could have been, for no such effect was compatible with the mostly unmethodical practice which then prevailed.

My own view is that with the high commitment to intelligence and "close reading," something was gained which might not have come from another kind of regimen. Whatever stupor may have been induced by snobbery, or the rigging of social arrangements— however insipid, too, the avowed taste and prejudices of some academicians—a reactionary idea of tradition did not dominate literary study. To the extent that students felt oppressed by such a tradition twenty or thirty years ago, they were likely to have been colluders in their own oppression; their education came out flat because they lacked imagination, read the wrong books, or were without sufficient judgment of character to seek out the right teachers. There was not then and there is not now a mass salvation formula to guard against such an outcome. To the extent that a dull idea of tradition was invoked by some, a little ingenuity could show how to escape its clutch: you did it by reading your contemporaries, the live ones, in poetry and fiction and criticism; and you knew in what journals to find them. An escape was also possible within teaching, on the faculties of certain liberal arts colleges, as well as in select wings of the larger departments. The places for a free use of imagination were many, and they were widely scattered.

True, there was an "old-boy system" for promoting young scholars—favorite students, friends of friends of friends—just as there
is now a middle-aged boy and girl system which works in exactly
the same way. But criticism rather than genteel appreciation had
come to define the aims of literary study by the early sixties; and
the changes of taste or sensibility that it sometimes prompted could
seem giddy enough. Certain controversial and reflective essays of
the period—Lionel Trilling's "On the Teaching of Modern Literature," W. K. Wimsatt's "Horses of Wrath"—actually wondered if
the mood of *assumed* receptivity had not become unthinking. These
arguments by senior scholars would have been described by many
as conservative—a term that had not yet become a knock-down
argument against anything one did not like—but their tone of
reserved engagement marked a climate in which matters of tradition and reform could be openly debated. To speak for tradition
then was not a commitment to be undertaken without irony. Not,
anyway, among the better minds—and by whom else should an
age be judged?

In reporting these impressions, I go against a rumor concerning
the recent past: that a picked elite of stuffed shirts regulated every
aspect of literary study, and so far outlived their proper ascendancy
that it was natural for a change, when it did come, to be abrupt
and startling. This rumor goes hand in hand with an apparently
contradictory one: that the shift from criticism to theory in the
seventies and early eighties was only a repetition of similar changes
that have happened over the past two hundred years in American
education. The losers (this conciliatory story says) always complain,
the winners always announce that they are completely new, but
there is a flux and reflux in human affairs and the shifts we are
seeing now have happened many times before; it is all a matter of
generational rivalry, the natural succession of one behavior pattern
to another—a pathology that holds as true in intellectual life as it
does elsewhere. This normalizing, anti-catastrophic, thoroughly
Whiggish reading of the astonishing turn in the conduct of literary
studies seems to me a lie—in some cases a conscious lie, in others
a lie repeated unknowingly by the eager young who take their

gutless elders at their word. Those who were active in the profession in the sixties and seventies know that the work of the best teachers then had nothing to do with a hegemonic argument for the superior morality of the West. Teachers of literature did not think of themselves as moralists, certainly not as moral *forces;* the books they taught they did not refer to as a canon, nor was there any thought of *defending* a canon. They said what they pleased, and taught what they liked. That the results exhibited some degree of consensus should surprise no one.

According to the prevalent myth, the normal psychology of research in literary study changed drastically, after 1975, under the influence of two new waves called structuralism and post-structuralism. Both came from France, and concerning the former nothing much need be said, since it resembled a formalism already in place in North America. Sometimes, in more slapdash and journalistic accounts, these tendencies are combined and called for short *deconstruction.* The word is used imprecisely in such contexts. But in any case, the word has now been so devalued by polemical hype that it is likely to pass for almost anything: skeptical questioning, debunking, subtilizing, theorizing-in-general, legal or cultural or constitutional subversion; the intent to sap and impurify our precious bodily fluids. *Deconstruction* has an attractive-repulsive charm that will keep it in the language a few years more, and I leave it to its projects with one word of caution here. This critical school made its first impression as a school of reading. It had more in common with New Criticism than with any social ideology—though, in its dialectical atmosphere and habits of thought, it had most of all in common with existentialism.[1] It said that literary language must ground itself on a claim to permanence, just as epistemology must ground itself on a claim to natural truth; that, in working out their proper fates, the aspirations of language and epistemology irresistibly lean on each other; and that, since neither can make good its promise of stability, they are destined to fall rather than stand together. This negative truth is what we learn (a deconstructionist will say) once rhetoric and cognition are seen to be inseparably linked; and yet (an *and yet* the deconstructionist utters in tones that range from metaphysical pathos to clinical satisfaction), we cannot imagine living without the illusion of a more sustaining discovery. It is at this point that morality enters the picture; and at this point, deconstruction takes a quiet bow and leaves the room.

But deconstruction was not, and in its heyday did not pretend to be, a politics. Indeed, the lack of any such ambition is precisely what brought its advocates, once the climate in literary study shifted toward political things, to conjure left-wing credentials out of thin air: "Oh, yes, that's what we were always about." Neither the youthful history of their founder, Paul de Man, nor the polemical temper of the early manifestos from the school, lends the slightest credibility to this boast. Seen alongside the political or historicist or psychoanalytic schools of reading today, deconstruction appears as one tendency among others—neither separable from nor definitive of the others. But because it entered the scene in the middle of the historic transition I describe, it gave a name and a glamour to assumptions which have come to be widely shared, and which alone now unite the various schools that have followed. These assumptions are, first, the all-importance of the contemporary; second, the impossibility of distinguishing the literary from the nonliterary; and third, the epistemological irrelevance of knowing all, or most, of an author's work before one begins to write about it. Of these assumptions, only the third belongs properly to deconstruction and its theory of reading; the first two it came to share with the other schools, as tenets of obvious daily utility. Trotsky had beliefs like these in mind when he spoke with well-earned scorn of "intellectual labor-saving devices."

One may say that deconstruction was only the first of the theory camps. In that case one must add that it was far and away the least cynical, the most "idealist" and "high" in every sense of both words. One point, however, about its glamour is still worth noticing. The diabolic intent ascribed to deconstruction by its keenest detractors exactly corresponds to the apocalyptic virtue imputed to it by its warmest partisans. I take an example, not quite at random, from a recent book, *The Ethics of Reading* by J. Hillis Miller. The author is a past president of the Modern Language Association and a scholar renowned for his benignity and sanguineness of temper. It may have been these very traits, with something of the artless enthusiasm engendered by life in a sect, which led Miller to assert in that book: "The millennium would come if all men and women became good readers in de Man's sense."[2] He used the word *millennium* with its conventional meaning: *universal peace and justice.*

More modest results were prognosticated by the first crop of whole-length scholars of theory in the late seventies. In a few cases they could show by example, in more they were compelled to illustrate by precept, the worth of a new balance of reading among students at all levels. Where, in the preceding decade, one had read works of literature as distinct from theory in a proportion of, say, ten to one, the ratio was to be adjusted rapidly in the direction of one to one. The remote effects of this program can now be seen close up. Advanced students in the field are not becoming less literate, as is sometimes claimed. They are becoming more theory-literate—particularly, with the theories of the present day—and less well read in literature. Many of them admit this openly; they think it a sign of progress. The advent of theory has had its most pragmatic, non-millennial uses where it first emerged in force, in the discipline of comparative literature.

Comparative literature began by setting its standard almost unapproachably high. Indeed, it may be said that the field existed with perfect vividness only in the minds of the refugee scholars from Europe who were its guiding spirits: Erich Auerbach, Leo Spitzer, and a few others. Their demand of the second generation of comparatists included a sure knowledge of literature of a certain period (if possible, more than one period), with the mastery of two languages (if possible, three or more). The story a commentator told about certain texts might be thematic and generic (across periods). It might equally be historical and philological (within a single period). How many students in the postwar generations would rise to meet such a challenge? Theory shortened the discouragement of the answer. For one great discovery of the seventies was that theory itself could supply a universal language which lightened the burden of learning.

As a result of the same therapy, other branches of literary study have begun to feel the same interdisciplinary lift. Not to draw arbitrary limits around one's subject; not to define too narrowly the kind of texts one can study with real competence—these acts of common emancipation give an enormous freedom to scholarship. The fact remains that to do the work creditably requires greater discipline in two languages than it ever could in one. The universal language will not deceive those for whom the names it has lately supplied answer to things they have known long and intimately. But to register this warning is to miss a social premise of the new liberty. Under its dispensation, the ideal of a "fit audience" has dwindled to the vanishing point. A quite different audience, of a variable composition, now stands for the approval that the ambitious crave—an audience whose only shared sustenance comes from theory. It is understood that, having mastered that language, one will come off plausibly in the ranks of one's plausible contemporaries. To give a public lecture on a literary subject may now mean to address not an audience of peers, who are relied on to know the material as well as the lecturer, but an audience of fellow strivers eager to be entertained. In such company, works of the mind are viewed with something of the interest children bring to show-and-tell.

This is the big change in the institutional habits of literary study; and it has happened in less than a decade. There is, in consequence, a weakened sense of the honor of being admired by exacting equals, and a greatly heightened susceptibility to the applause of new appreciators, whoever they may be. A clue to the assurance with which the new habits have worked is the displacement of the word *interpretation* (in a number of contexts) by the word *negotiation*. In chapter 3, I noticed such other novelties in the slang of the literate as the Foucault-inspired vogue of *currency* and *circulation*. Mere intellectual fashion apart, a consistent motive for the charm of these words will now be evident. They flaunt a nonintellectual motive for scholarship. They refer our interest back—

endlessly, teasingly—to the status-hunger of the market expert. The enterprise is typically pursued with a facile cynicism ("We're all in this together, no?") which requires no comment.

Nevertheless, some part of the interdisciplinary move was inevitable, and it has already been a stimulus to original thought. A book like Lionel Gossman's *Between History and Literature*, an essay like Sabina Lovibond's "Feminism and Postmodernism," could, perhaps, have been conceived but might never have been ventured in a severer disciplinary climate than ours. And the result is a great gain, for us.[3] The announced widening of the range of objects is only a case of positive rules catching up with daily conduct—this, in a field where generic boundaries never marked out to anyone's satisfaction what counted as literature. If the subject appeared to include only poems, novels, and plays, its self-image was too narrow for writers like Carlyle or Harriet Martineau in much of their characteristic work. Theoretically, indeed, one can cite no reason why a generation of scholarship both intelligent and adventurous should not follow from a license to study anything in any way we choose. The trouble is that the disappearance of boundaries comes at a time when standards for judging the new work are nowhere near in place. It is clear already that a lot of interesting work on literature-*and* (and medicine, and economics, and politics, and gender) will come from the efforts of these years. A lot of fraudulent work on literature-*and* will also come; and the two will have this in common, that they both look unprecedented: so much so that within the discipline as it stands, they are hard to tell apart.

Our prospect therefore looks bright with an artificial brightness. The professional organizations and journals have done nothing to exemplify a standard of judgment which sorts out the legitimate from the false pretensions of the new work. They rely instead on ready markers of fashion, prestige, and political relevance. The fate of the English Institute—where a tiny fraction of the proceedings now are concerned with English literature, yet the speakers are picked and the sessions attended by literary scholars and no one else—can stand for many comparable institutional anomalies. The patient, in short, appears to be breathing, but his pulse is erratic;

and should he survive, the chances are appreciable that he will wake up tomorrow, look in the mirror, and ask to be told his name. If the answer is, "Professor of literature," he will be justified in saying: "Now, tell me what that is."

All this may suggest only a salutary uncertainty. But that is an evasive answer—the answer of those who do not like what they see but long since gave up fighting it. The worst of the new habits is that they are perfectly adapted to the creation of *as-if personalities*. The development is not confined to one profession, and its usual symptoms merge with a phenomenon of political life to which one became accustomed in the early eighties. As-if personalities scarcely know themselves except as a shuffle of possible roles. The marks of the type are that they will assent, in the right circumstances, to anything, and they cannot be relied on for anything. They have no consistency of opinion. What is remarkable is that an academic profession should have come to honor this type as its latest chosen model. If, in the coming years, people capable of a steady use of intelligence are to assert a larger control over literary study, they will have to do a great deal of work—much of it critical, some of it destructive. They have, at least, this hope. The current unjudging mood has settled not, as has sometimes been said, in the last twenty-five years but in the last eight or nine; if it has taken hold in many institutions and many careers, it is not the case that it has taken a deep hold everywhere. But where it does come in for good, the tenor of group conduct will alter ponderably even on the most formal occasions. Versions of the following incident have been reported to me by friends in several departments.

A scholar is brought up for review and possible promotion. The person may be a man or a woman; may be commonly seen as intelligent or plodding or somehow unratable; may be, in the light of "collegiality," pleasant or unpleasant to think of as company for future years. Anyway the scholar is doing the newer sort of work. What, precisely, that is, and what it should mean for promotion, remains unclear until the discussion has shaken itself into its usual shape. The candidate's manifest qualifications—published

work, teaching record, present and projected scholarly interests—
have been looked at for the department by an internal committee
that took first responsibility for reading and evaluation. One member of the committee is dimly qualified to judge the new work, by
being in a related area of study; another is wholly unqualified,
admits to feeling quite in the dark, but agrees to go through the
motions; a third comes forward as an intense advocate of the candidate. It is this third member of the committee who swings the
vote—by being young and well regarded, or old and poignantly
anxious on behalf of the young. The last member's words and
actions are informed by an energy of commitment the others do
not possess. With the sanction of the committee, a general discussion is now opened to the department.

Before we listen to the speeches and the chatter, let us add some
details to the case. The hypothetical candidate is a man named
Jonathan Craigie—married, as it happens, to a woman in the same
field, who teaches at a nearby school and is seldom missing from
his side at department functions (which both faithfully attend at
both institutions). The field for promotion has been "identified,"
with the approval of the college dean's office, as Postmodernism
and Cultural Studies. The author of two books and editor of three
collections of essays and interviews, the candidate in the last five
years has delivered thirty papers at professional conferences—
many of them deft and wide-ranging in the interdisciplinary way.
His undergraduate courses are popular. They deal entirely with
special subjects; for, armed with a counter-offer, Craigie negotiated
early to sever his obligation to teach the department's bread-and-
butter surveys. His graduate seminars have been almost as popular:
they are spoken of genially as creating an atmosphere in which
"you can say anything"; and the students who take them are rumored to have a surprising success ratio in finding their first jobs.
The only recorded exception to the consensus occurred a year ago,
when a pair of history students dropped the seminar at midterm—
because, they said, Craigie did not know the facts of the period
implied by his title, "Postmodern Politics and American Culture,
1945–1990."

This brings us to the article with which his senior colleagues will be concerned in their deliberations. It is far from his longest piece; but nobody has the time to read everything; and, for reasons of contingent laziness, one short publication came to be accepted as a fair sample. The article in question, which Craigie "got out of the seminar" and published in an avant-garde journal of American Studies (*American Cultural History*, lately renamed *Politics/Culture/ Critique*), treated the Hiss-Chambers case as a founding event of the Cold War. The point of view was sympathetic to both men, or, as Craigie called them, both players. It concentrated chiefly on their efforts of "storytelling" or "fictualization": Chambers, for his initial denial that Hiss was a spy and his subsequent claim that the case was intelligible only as part of his spiritual autobiography; and Hiss, more conspicuously, for the changing versions of an attempted denial that closed in his conviction for perjury. The case, it was here argued, could scarcely be understood by political analysis, any more than it could be digested as a moment in American history. It was, in fact, the first media event—*the* contemporary genre, before which the tools of criticism and of narrative history were alike impotent. Craigie's next book—now, as the committee reports, well on its way—is a double biography of Madonna and "a post-gendered novelist still to be named."

The members of the department were obliged to take the candidacy soberly; with results that could only have been predicted by the discerning. After all, their problem was complex. None had a language to describe or judge, let alone to praise or blame adequately, work that came in so curious a shape. But it was widely felt that the will to praise ought to be affirmed. The case, besides, on other grounds presented certain clear marks favoring tenure: a significant quantity of publications; an unexceptionable, perhaps even a noteworthy, record of teaching both undergraduates and graduates; and (what we have neglected so far), strong letters from referees, a few of them well-known persons in the field. Of course, the "field," as here defined, did not mean at all the area of the candidate's work. Of the six letters received, none came from a scholar who had done first-hand work on similar subjects; four, however, were written by eminences of theory, who could imply without quite asserting a meta-competence in several historical periods. (And, it was urged, what is postmodernism if not the theorist's topic par excellence?) All the referees claimed to have found profitable instruction in the writings, or, as a common locution had it, "the important new work" of Jonathan Craigie.

These carefully placed accolades were the fruit of assiduous networking: the cultivation, without ulterior intellectual aim, of influential cronies who are pledged to serve the advancement of one's career. Since Craigie had once devoted half a semester of a graduate seminar to the same subject of networking, it was natural for this to form the first topic of an unusually frank and speculative tenure review.

"Well, the network came through for him. I don't see that we have much choice. If we turn him down lots of people will be asking why."

"And there's plenty of writing. This is the amazing thing about Jonathan; *so* much. [A disarming laugh here.] Who can read it all!"

"I read the one on the Hiss case. It's clever—at least, if I may speak as someone who knows nothing about the Hiss case. . . . Now, as to Peter Jennings and Madonna, I don't know. But remember—the students like what he does. I mean not just any students, but some of the best, the most sensitive and knowledgeable."

"Really the best?"

"Absolutely."

"?"

"Granted his manner of argumentation isn't what we're used to."

"He doesn't argue at all. Point out an error and he backs off completely and just starts nibbling away at something else. Is this person capable of teaching our students to think about literature? Or even to think, period?"

"Literature, as he says in his new article ["Pornography in Quebec: Structure of a Decomposing Hegemony"], is itself under contestation now; when you use it as a value, you prejudice the outcome of any act of interpretation. Excuse me, I should have said negotiation."

"But we're a department of literature."

"Sorry, I wish the profession were different too, but we can't change that. We have to make room for other things."

"This thing doesn't even have much information; I don't see any evidence that he reads the works he cites. In the Hiss article, he bases the whole thesis of 'image-consolidation' on a single discredited work of cultural history. He doesn't seem to have read any political history. He didn't look at the transcript of the congressional hearings or the trial. He didn't read *Witness* or *In the Court of Public Opinion*—nothing!"

A brief silence falls. Then—quietly, significantly—are heard the following grave words from the front of the room. The speaker is a recent high-profile recruit to the department:

"A couple of you people talk as if you were opposed to anything new."

At which the meeting picks up a distinct second wind. The referees' letters are read aloud—"pathbreaking," "strange, perhaps brilliant," "as far as I can judge, a wholly adventurous mind," "important, new," "post-disciplinary," "brashness raised to the level of genius," "the sort of person we would welcome here as a colleague." The last of these phrases, coming, as it does, from Spenser Chase, a well-known translator of French theory and think-tank entrepreneur, carries special weight as emanating from the kind of expertise many in the department admire from a distance.

"That letter from Chase will be hard to go against."

"Look, Jonathan won't be here for long anyway. In a year or two, he'll have a great offer from Duke or Emory, and he'll leave. So what are we arguing about?"

These last considerations proved decisive. A strong, though not a unanimous vote, was achieved for the promotion of Jonathan Craigie. He was in due course approved by the university's senior appointments committee, of which one member chose to read a sample of his work, and pronounced it "refreshing, certainly." The chosen sample happened to be the same article we have discussed:

"Alger Hiss Remediated: America's Left/Right, Vertical/Horizontal Control"—which, since all this happened, has won the Freeform Prize awarded jointly each year by *Negotiator* and *Politics/Culture/ Critique*.

Several points are to be noticed about these deliberations—remote as they are from the common routines of professional judgment, as most people imagine those routines to be. First, with rare exceptions (which are easily exposed as eccentric), the voice in which the members speak is a group voice. The department itself is, in fact, a small group keenly apprehensive of the suffrage of a larger group outside which is felt to set the pace. The small group's opinions are replete with prophetic tremors concerning What They Will Think. And in this setting, it is almost impossible to get a discussion started on a proposition, an abstract idea, the semblance of a published argument that must be discussed. The atmosphere is closed and anxious; the verdict is always already in.

The respect for an unstated (and, perhaps, an as yet unformed) professional consensus, which puts every dissenter at fault, also detaches each member of the community from any responsibility to think about the issue at hand. Where explicit reference is made to published work, it can be outflanked by citing the unqualified opinion of a referee of high *general* prestige. Any attempt to begin a substantive inquiry is defeated by the sheer weight of possible replies that effectively change the subject: popularity with (what may be always asserted to be) a select portion of the student body; novelty of approach (you blink because it dazzles); and always, in however disguised a form, the belief that *in the exact degree that we cannot judge it, it is the very thing we want.* That programmatic evasion was first heard in the mid-seventies: it came with the rapidly induced need for every department to have a "theory manager." Some of the theorists who thereby advanced were first-rate minds; some were abject obscurantists who had never been caught (some will never be caught); but the way they made their mark began a process that has yet to reveal its outermost limit.

We need: the reader has heard the same phrase before, from the moral educators of the right in their search for civilization. Here it is again. We need, by definition, that which we do not have, that which will make us better by the infusion of a precious sedative or stimulant. Only, now, that which we do not have turns out to be that which we do not know. How then to purchase it? We will take the commodity on faith. From whom? From the opinion makers in the organized system of the profession. The system has always worked like this, of course; no one looks back to a gone era of rationality in the conduct of academic corporate bodies. But it once went at a slower pace, and the deliberation made a difference. It gave time for the review of a candidate's book to be as closely considered as the rumor of a successful conference paper. The *professed* desirability of criticism by one's peers is starting to seem a thing of the past: Craigie's story illustrates one consequence of the fact that many scholars no longer want to create an interest among readers or listeners with whom they share much common knowledge. They perform for those who have an altogether disparate competence. (In deference to this trend, veterans of the theory circuit sometimes speak of themselves as "the caravan.")

I have mentioned the emancipation that might come eventually from a climate as uninhibited as ours in literary study. The preceding anecdote suggests an opposite outcome. The work we foster will turn out to be surprisingly less varied than might be projected from a general order that has so few restrictions. This result, counter-intuitive as it is, becomes the more likely where tacit criteria for advancement have begun to be centered on social attitudes more than intellectual merit. For, beneath all the questions posed at the department meeting, the unspoken one that mattered was: "Will we get credit for taking this person as a colleague?" The referee who spoke of wanting to have Jonathan Craigie at his own school was touching the right nerve and he knew it. Meanwhile, the only speech of intimidation ("You talk as if you were opposed to anything new") was a lightly coded statement of political desiderata. As the decision wound up, it was a good thing for Craigie that he produced work which everyone could claim a serious incompetence in judging. If he merely did something familiar and did it well, his department would be back in the old game of trying to value his work by the things he said and did. They would then have to count carefully the positions open at senior rank to make sure that plenty of space was left for the important work they could not judge.

What I have been describing is not a system that incorporates some risk of error. It is a system moved, operated, and daily extended by error. And yet, though some of the voices we heard were weak, and some were unhappily far on the path to selling themselves out, they did not exhibit the brazen unconcern of people who know themselves to be acting in bad faith. They are trying to show a kind of good faith, perhaps. They go wrong because they have never disclosed to themselves the true object of the discussion. They call its defining trait its newness, and so have I in these pages, too hastily. But people do not accept what they fail to understand for that reason alone—novelty may be an attraction, but it cannot itself constitute a persuasive argument. What are these people afraid of? The answer, if I am right, goes a long way to explain the panic under which individual intelligence and good sense are surrendered on such occasions. For the answer is *science*. To be more particular, it is fear of science mixed with envy of science. And in the right setting, one hope is enough to crystallize both feelings. We hope that what evades a familiar standard of judgment—what presents itself as new and yet already bureaucratized—may turn out to have that character because it is science.

I explored this theme briefly in chapter 3. The payoff occurs at a scene of licensing such as the one we have just imagined. The talk about important work and unprecedented shapes of knowledge, which baffled the attempt to review Craigie's work, was a way of touching the key of "science" and hearing how many strings would vibrate. Just one tacit equation was needed to send almost all aquiver: science = new knowledge = new-looking possible knowledge = fashion. The study of literature, we have often been told, is "only" governed by considerations of taste. The scientific study of anything—or so many people remember having learned once—

is governed by considerations of hard knowledge. We understand that the shape in which hard knowledge first appears may suspend our reliance on good sense. Such, for a long time, has been the cause of the immobility with which the ordinary citizen regards the claims of technology. Why should a teacher of literature ever have supposed it was possible to feel differently?

In the presence of a new science, suspicions are put off in advance by the common fear of being judged a philistine. In the arts by contrast, it used to seem that an idea of taste—indistinguishable, at points, from an idea of good sense—could issue in a mode of answerable discussion that was critical without being philistine. However, let it once be supposed that the arts are manageable with equipment modeled on the ambitions of science, and all sense is at a loss. The new executants, aiming to be good scientists but still acting as what they are (aesthetes to the core), give an indefinite prorogation to their judgments and thereby assure that they will never be exposed as wanting in refinement. They decide, without being able to give an account of their decision. They know their choice was impersonal enough to have been the reverse of a matter of taste. It was the profession that made them do it. A profession acting impersonally, in the name of knowledge, seems to have in its charge all the usable traits of a science.

I want now to recount the passage of intellectual history that has helped to produce a consistent temperament among the visible leadership of academic literary study today. I have in mind the editors of some of the main journals, the heads of the larger professional organizations, the writers of advanced guides to the field and other textbooks of control. Their mood (relaxed, authoritative, susceptible on short notice to new *general* orientations) is not yet the usual mood among teachers, but it has the widest imaginable area of exercise; and it has met, thus far, not only no organized resistance but almost no conscious challenge within the profession. It would not be right to say that these persons have finished with the study of literature. They want to go on studying it, in the same sense that Jonathan Craigie does. It would be fair, and it puts the matter very much in their own terms, to say that they have suspended their interest in passing on to others an appreciation of great works of poetry and prose.

The history properly begins with a book in the philosophy of science that has had tremendous impact elsewhere, Thomas Kuhn's *Structure of Scientific Revolutions*. Kuhn argued that the usual Enlightenment story about the progress of science, which pictured a series of amalgamating discoveries that enlarged the domain of knowledge, could be recounted more accurately to show a sequence of discontinuous revolutions—each rejecting certain plausible discoveries for the sake of certain others along the path it happened to favor; and each sometimes valuing, as the case demanded, such pragmatic virtues as testability (with respect to a hypothesis) and conservatism (with respect to established evidence). Kuhn thus appeared to say that at moments of crisis the very shape of knowledge changed; and that, in a given revolution, the knowledge won or lost was decided by the interests of the discoverer.

This way of looking at science, in the light of the sociology of knowledge rather than the facts of the universe, was by some readers taken to imply that our most secure assumptions about the world were conditioned as much by consensus, or what Kuhn called "the psychology of research," as by a disinterested pursuit of truth apart from commonplace motives. Kuhn himself, it later became clear, actually thinks it is a fact that there are facts: he credits science with finding some of them, and agrees that much of the knowledge gained in this way will eventually be transformed without being destroyed. He is a believer in at least a version of scientific progress. But these elaborations of his view did not often survive a moral that many casual readers imputed to his story. As it came through to them, it sounded rather like this: "All knowledge, even the knowledge we once imagined to be 'hard,' is partly defined by context, including above all social context. Truth does not issue naturally in a right perspective on the subjects of learned inquiry. Truth itself is a product of someone's choice of a perspective. Further, since the dominant perspective may change quickly, and several often contend at once for preeminence, there is no idiom of justification that will assure the claims of one perspective over those of any other."

The scientist in this view began to look a good deal like the more adventurous sort of literary theorist. Did it follow that the literary theorist was a good deal like the more adventurous sort of scientist?

Even in a more scrupulous view of Kuhn's argument than I have just sketched, it could easily lead to two quite different thoughts about the relation between knowledge in the sciences and in the arts and letters. From his findings, one might come to see that the motives and conditions of scientific discovery were more similar than anybody had thought to the motives and conditions of, say, literary interpretation. Let us call this *leveling downward*—downward, I mean, only on a scale that runs from certainty to uncertainty. But one might also abstract from his general thesis a reassurance that the methods and procedures of humanistic scholarship were more rational than anybody had thought, because they looked more like the motives and procedures of natural scientists, once the ideal of "pure" truth had been eliminated. Let us call this *leveling upward*. Now a curious feature of the development of literary study in the 1980s was the way the self-image of scholars passed through both kinds of leveling at once. In departments of literature, there is a widespread sense today that the scholar-theorist is adding to hard knowledge: the vogue of such words as *tracking*, *rigor*, and *determination* testifies to this. Yet accompanying the same sense is a suspicion that the terms of discourse could change very quickly and leave stranded all one's previous interests, findings, rigors, and determinations. But then (goes the consoling thought) that is just what happens to all knowledge. The result of this new self-image among theorists and critics has been a weird combination of arrogance—*glib* adaptability—with a world-weary irony once confined to the sort of libertine who was played out before the age of thirty.

Some part of the recent change has been reflected in neighboring disciplines like history and philosophy; some—and yet, a smaller part than might be supposed from the subject matter of those disciplines. The reason for the slighter impact there is obvious and neglected, and it belongs so firmly to the professional development of the three fields that one almost takes it for granted. By the accident of institutional expediency that I described in chapter 3, departments of literature alone are now entrusted with the teaching of humane letters, of the great old books, of what has come to be called "the canon." At the same time, the desire to give up such an inherited trust has become a measure of advancement along a scientific path. It was natural for people in literature to envy the seriousness with which our prosperous neighbors added to their research while subtracting from their teaching along a whole range of possible encumbrances. What they did for themselves without ever invoking a philosophy of science, we should certainly be able to do for ourselves with the aid of one.

In chapter 3, I mentioned the debut of a broad scheme for the reorganization of literary study, which goes under the name "teach-the-conflicts." Since those pages were written the idea has been widely publicized as a conciliatory solution. After all, its attractions are great. It wears a look of reasonableness, even as it embraces the inevitability of progress; its message is, "Let us keep on talking to each other (by talking about each other)." Plainly, teach-the-conflicts is ideal propaganda for our moment of advanced professional self-regard. The model has now been proposed for adoption even by faculties where a conflict hardly yet exists. Teach, it says to them, *what your conflicts will have become*, once you have recognized the state of advanced knowledge about literature. Here we find again the unstated premise that a sociology of knowledge (a situation shared by knowers) is by definition a teachable science (the subject in which they ought to instruct others). Suppose that Spenser Chase and I both teach poetry. We have, however, certain differences of emphasis. Why should our differences not be made a leading, a "foregrounded," element in the composition of a new curriculum? It can easily be done: Spenser Chase and I are equally willing; our own views seem to us as teachable as the poems we used to teach. The suggestion, then, is practicable, and will seem

inviting to teachers whose ascetic posture may always have beto-
kened a suppressed narcissism. But the worth of adopting such a
change does not follow from any of these conveniences.

Only in the entertainable field of literary study could much credit
have gone to a proposal that derives its whole authority from a
sense of public relations. Given what we have, this is the way to
sell it now. And yet, one need merely reframe the proposal as an
argument for "teaching the debates" to realize that it has long been
the dominant curricular model in philosophy. It is the reason why
that field can seem to an outsider so fantastically overprofession-
alized: to study "the mind-body problem," you must first suppose
that the problem has always presented itself in much the same
way; then sample the contributions to the problem of Plato, Des-
cartes, Hume, and a half-dozen academic philosophers of the present day; and conclude by taking a position yourself. In this system,
the old books are taught as a grid of abstracts in the service of
obsessions that are peculiarly contemporary. The system was well
described by a living philosopher (who had the slogan printed on
his office door): "Just say *No* to the history of philosophy." This
kind of abstinence becomes conventional as soon as teaching-the-
conflicts has entered standard practice; and it marks the discipline
that fosters and rewards the practice as deeply anti-historical. Still,
to invoke some such view as central to the discipline may compro-
mise the ideals of philosophy less than it would the ideals of
literature. Dialectical habits, a certain regimen of argumentative
moves—these have always been a large component of the learning
required among philosophers. If advanced students are now asked
to exhibit these strengths at the sacrifice of all others, the tact of
historical imagination will suffer greatly, but some sense of common purpose may survive.

To contemplate the study of literature without historical imagination seems a very different matter. I stress both words, *historical*
and *imagination*, because they have a meaning together that neither
can have apart. Language changes over time: if I impute my meanings to a work of another time, I am only using the work as a
background against which to imagine myself again. But imagina-

tion is also an individual and irreducible fact: if I impute to a work of another time features which it is supposed to share with many other phenomena of the time, what need was there for the work itself? There are strengths of attention to a distant object that can be learned only by experience; and nothing is more distant than an object made from language by someone who died long ago. The reading of a great book can partly create the skill for such attention—a thing the reading of new tracts of theory cannot do, for reasons that must remain as inscrutable as any appeal to experience. "One may learn to read," says Oakeshott, "only by reading with care, and only from writing which stands well off from our immediate concerns: it is almost impossible to *learn* to read from contemporary writings."[4] Evidently, "reading" here is another name for imagining anything outside the bounds of cliché. This has long been the name of a value to which literary scholars felt committed, if they were committed to anything; and it meant that their work served a motive which was bound to be, in part, anti-contemporary. So long as this remained a sufficient defense of the teaching of literature, its aim was to resist a leveling idiom which other disciplines could not afford to resist—because they had modeled themselves on the natural sciences; or because they were committed to an idea of progress which must always be unreal to someone who knows the unequaled power of works of art from earlier ages.

A feeling persists among many who care for old books that a similar professionalism, if it took hold in literary study, would make for shallower conversations between teachers and students. The psychological probabilities seem to me strong in favor of this supposition. But to explain those probabilities is an intricate or anyway an unscientific affair. One's defense of interpretative critics (who want to read all of an author before they say anything) against contemporary-conflict negotiators (who want to triangulate a sample of an author with the relevant theories) may come to little more than the defense of one temperament over another. It is, perhaps, a different way of saying: "I want literary scholars to be more like Protestant commentators on the Bible, and less like corporate lawyers." Asked for a reason, one can reply that it is the commentators who are not yet redundant—an unsatisfactory answer to those who find no real incompatibility between the two callings. And yet the negative response by some teachers, and more students and observers, to the recent massive innovations in literary study, does presume some such sense of incompatibility. What these people are seeing now, and not always liking, is the fast disappearance of the scholastic temperament.

In *Professing Literature* Gerald Graff firmly dismisses the fear of rapid professionalization. "Such a complaint," says Graff, "leads nowhere, for it envisages no role for the professional interests of the scholar except to extinguish themselves." But Graff's dismissal of the complaint requires that we accept a stark alternative: either to preserve certain habits of teaching and learning or to permit the advent of new professional interests. As a matter of record, professional interests have often found their way into teaching without always, or at every point, or with a mandatory emphasis, determining the content of a curriculum. Professional and pedagogic interests have often been mutually influential. The doubts about "teaching the conflicts" come from people who accept this fact, and hardly suppose that teachers will extinguish their professional interests. They say instead that with such a curriculum, we would risk forgetting the separate worth of teaching; the worth, that is, of talking and thinking about books which are bound to relate to our interests, but which may relate to our published researches only indirectly.

The view that professionalization is one good, and teaching quite another, and that it is the former now that must chiefly be looked to, conceals an important premise. It is a premise we have noticed before in the remarkable sentence I quoted from the pamphlet *Speaking for the Humanities:* "Professionalization makes thought possible." Graff believes this, too. Indeed, the remark is easy to credit if one takes it to mean, "Professional circumstances help thought to assume an intelligible shape." It becomes quite another matter if one takes it to mean, "Professionalism alone shapes thought—it is the same thing as originality." In a tract written by a committee, there would have been a natural tendency to split the difference: "What we call a thought is also what I call a thought." With the reduction of Kuhn on science as part of the background, the reader is now in a position to notice the suppressed steps of a syllogism: *All thought is scientific; professionalization alone suffices to turn an art into a science;* therefore, for us, *professionalization makes thought possible.*

It would seem to follow that in earlier times, the talk that went on in courses on literature was, strictly speaking, *thoughtless.* Most likely this belief explains the alarm of those who deplore any infringement of professional interests by the lower-order demands of the classroom. But a less exclusive view has often been held of these interests and these demands. The novice literature instructor was never expected to contribute to the higher learning from a freshman class on *Hamlet* or Augustine's *Confessions.* It was merely assumed that what the instructor had to say would add to the student's sense of taking part in a conversation larger and other than that supplied by the daily surroundings. This understanding had to do with an acknowledgment of great writing not as familiar and acceptable but as unfamiliar, and worthwhile under a description one can only make for oneself. The tradition that a teacher thought of evoking was an awareness of the impalpable links that bind one person to others remote in time or space, the recognition Burke thought more vital to humanity than any social contract, and which he called "a partnership in all science; a partnership in all art."

This is the idea of tradition which a self-conscious literary professional is now most apt to reject. For the sake of what? Again, we may take instruction from *Speaking for the Humanities* and its examples of the way professional thought can serve the ends of teaching. Scottish history (the spoken-for profession tells the teacher to say) matters to the reader of *Macbeth,* Shylock's religion to the reader of *The Merchant of Venice,* and so on, through Caliban's racial affiliations and Milton's sexism. These are all interesting, and familiar, topics: indeed their familiarity proves too much. All of the data mentioned in *Speaking for the Humanities* were standard class-

room fare even in the dark days of paleo-professional consciousness. For other reasons too, the examples are beside the point.
What troubles many people today is whether—given the professional drift away from the classics in favor of television and mass
culture—writers like Shakespeare and Milton will continue to be
required reading at all.

To judge by illustrations like these, the ritual invocation of science as an earnest of professional concerns may safely be classed
as a protective illusion, and dispatched to the limbo of vanity. But
here as elsewhere the scientific promise is likely to outlast an exposure of the results. Besides, if science is nothing but the sociology
of knowledge among a corporate body of interpreters, who will
deny that literary theorists have their own sociology? And what,
alongside that, can be the claim of a tradition whose greatest representatives are dead, a tradition whose interests are correspondingly dead to *us*? It only adds up to a story, after all, and a story
difficult to believe: our story we know better; we see our own
reality confirmed every day. It is at this point that the mystifying
power of a canon is likely to be adduced to clinch the argument.
The word *canon* is, of course, misleading. In the sense in which the
Hebrew Bible was canonized, made permanently meaningful and
put forever in place, by the Christians who renamed it the Old
Testament, there have been few canonical texts in secular literature.
In the history of English criticism, Shakespeare is the only author
whose reputation has held steady for more than forty years at a
stretch. There have, however, been reading lists that plenty of
people deferred to for a long time. The controversy now in departments of literature has to do with how much continuity such
lists ought to show from generation to generation; and the professional position seems to have become that there need be no continuity at all, except what is warranted by the demands of a given
mode of teaching or advocacy.

Even when the scientific motive is weak, an inducement remains
to throw in one's lot with the professional, the "progressive," view.
Somewhere in the background, for all literary scholars but acutely
for those just setting out on their careers, are feelings of inadequacy

regarding the great books that are held in suspicion. How can I say anything true about them without reading the secondary literature? And with a text far out of my field, what reward is there in that? This motive is assisted by the supposed menace of the great-books priesthood that controls the antique pedagogy. Few such priests can be found in literary study now; but their presence in any number makes a start for an otherwise self-serving apology: it is natural to want to announce in triumph, "Well, we've come a way since *that*." I dealt in chapter 2 with the small, but significant, reactionary priesthood which exists in civilian life, among the opinion-makers of the mass media. Their therapy for civilization does not include thinking about books, or interpreting them, or arguing about them in a spirit of self-trust. Rather, one is supposed to come to the right books with a received image of one's culture; the books are then used as primary documents to confirm that image: as if, only after having read them all could one say, "Yes, I found it there." For books to work in this way, one must have been finding in them only what one was expected to find. A curriculum used like this becomes a machine for coming of age in a culture.

Newly seasoned literary scholars have no trouble disposing of this vitamin-injection theory of culture—which, they pretend, still exerts a dangerous force in their field of study. But their own ideas are no better. A conceit of much modernist writing after *Peer Gynt* likens human character to the skins of an onion; and the negative therapy of the new professionals seems to derive from an onion-skin theory of many things. Peel away the layers, says the *Peer Gynt* allegory, and you will go on peeling until you arrive at nothing. It follows that there is no deep or shallow in matters of character. The professionalists of literary study draw one further moral: there is no deep or shallow in matters of education. Once we have seen that any consensus is founded on nothing stable—nothing, anyway, more stable than social coherence, political agreement, personal and moral belief—we can take pleasure in finding that all education has become a scene of *dissensus* (a barbarous coinage of American Studies that nicely suits the current mood). The onion-skin theory of education, which is also a theory of cultural liberation, would be credible if we could be sure of one thing. For it assumes that in unmasking layer after layer of meaning, to expose the context, grounding, and presuppositions in which all meaning is embedded, the reader will learn something that has not been planted already. But the means employed here defeat the ends. This more-or-less historicist therapy of unloading meanings is, like the anti-historicist therapy of loading them, a Socratic game which only one can play, and in the classroom that one is the teacher. It would be hard to show that either technique is congenial to thinking.

Thinking I take to be the process of creating, through reflection and judgment and, when necessary, invention rather than mere acceptance, a relation true for oneself between certain parts of one's experience and certain parts of the world. "True for oneself" because thinking goes on in a single mind. It cannot be done, though it may be helped or hindered, by a school, a network, a profession, a learned society or corporate body of any imaginable kind. Many of the heroes of American intellect—Emerson, Thoreau, Whitman, Dickinson, William James, Gertrude Stein, Marianne Moore, to come no closer to the present—took for themselves a similar premise. Yet it is a premise that both of the theories I have named agree in despising. For them, thinking is always subordinate to the larger purposes of a culture—purposes, for the command of which individual thought and language are supposed to be ordered by a discourse already in place. Beside this point of general concurrence, their dispute about whether the ends of Western civilization are beneficent or the reverse is a comparatively trivial affair.

As an argument against fast professionalization, or against the idea of institutional knowledge which is the literary scholar's best notion of a science, these last admonitions may sound far-fetched. But the applications are not at all obscure. As with the conformists of the civilization, so with the conformists of the profession, the voice to distrust is the "we"-voice of collective judgment. "One of our best recent studies of X," "A perspective that will help us inestimably in the advanced discussions of Y," "Clearly a Z that we will be learning from for a long time to come." Conformity needs this voice—will never go without it for long—because the solitude in which a great book is written is something it wants to forget. Recall the professionalist maxim: "We need to teach not the texts themselves but how we situate ourselves in reference to those texts." How many *we*'s are here! In a mood of such bureaucratized narcissism, it has become necessary to assert the obvious: we do not even know who we are, except in the long run. Certainly we, who read, and some other earlier we, give a context to every word that has a meaning for us. But the imperative of thinking comes back however we try to avoid it, from certain passages in the work of a great writer. It touches any reader of the phrase, in Words-worth's ode on childhood, which speaks of "the faith which looks through death," where no religious consolation is in view. It is there, too, in Swift's remark that climbing is done in the same posture as creeping. We do always situate ourselves with respect to texts. And yet powerful words also, perhaps otherwise, situate themselves in a mind that thinks.

A significant part of the new-modeled science of literary study is founded on two dogmas—received ideas so poorly forged that they are easily exploded. The first concerns the suppression of knowledge in the past. The second concerns the sort of knowledge that is supposed to arrive when all of the dead weight of the past is removed. These dogmas, as the reader will sense, are corollaries of the myth of generational exclusion which I mentioned at the start of the chapter. In a story in the *New York Times Magazine* (June 5, 1988) about the Department of English at Duke University, James Atlas told how a short version of the first dogma had been offered by several sympathetic professors. Atlas reports their view as follows: "Occasional disputes broke out, reputations flourished and declined. T. S. Eliot smuggled in the seventeenth-century meta-physical poets. Malcolm Cowley promoted Faulkner, there was a Henry James revival. For the most part, though, the canon was closed. You were either on the syllabus or off the syllabus." This jaunty summary covers, it would seem, the suppression of the past two to four centuries, in contrast with the liberation of the past five to ten years.

A noteworthy detail is the word *syllabus*. Appearance on a syllabus is here taken to decide membership in a canon: an equivalence that would have been strikingly unfamiliar to Eliot and the other inventors of a new way of thinking and feeling about the arts, who in this story are grouped under the catch-all rubric of "occasional disputes." But that is a small confusion, or anachronism. Pass over it and you come to a pretty steady assumption. History can be divided into two parts: first, the way they used to do things (*they:* Pope, Emerson, the Brontë sisters, people like that); and second, the way we do things now, in the classrooms and the color supplements. The caption here ought to read: *We're so smart today because they were so dumb yesterday.* Scholars who believe this will often believe more. They recite the fable with their own careers as evidence, and show how wise they are this evening by proving how silly they were this morning. But how far is the historical claim borne out by historical evidence?

We may confine ourselves to the cases mentioned, starting with the seventeenth-century metaphysical poets, whom Eliot is supposed to have "smuggled in" to the canon. Donne was the most controversial of them; and it is easy to learn something about him. You can find a sentence of qualified praise for his originality in Samuel Johnson's *Life of Cowley.* Coleridge admired his poems, spoke of them warmly and often, and wrote an imitation of them. Yeats knew a good deal about Donne without any help from Eliot. So it begins to look as if this were not quite a matter of smuggling, after all. What Eliot actually did was to convince a lot of readers that Donne ought to be valued in the special way of a poet who still matters to living poets. Eliot gave reasons, and wrote poems of his own, and he changed people's minds; in this, he did what persuasive readers have often done, throughout the history of literature and criticism. Indeed, so far was the canon from being "for the most part closed" that it takes an act of recovery to see how the great reputations came to be what they are today.

Consider the fortunes of Wordsworth. For the first two decades of his career, he was appreciated by a small circle and heartily despised by the established reviewers. He climbed, slowly, to a safe esteem, and clinched his public respectability by accepting the poet laureateship a few years before his death. By then, however, he had lost the respect of his poetic successors—one of whom buried him five years before his death in a poem called "The Lost Leader." His work stayed alive partly because a good anthologist, Palgrave, and critics like Matthew Arnold and A. C. Bradley, wanted to hold on to certain poems and passages. Their kind of approval seems to have lasted well into this century, in the text-books at least; meanwhile, it was already under siege in the anti-Romantic manifestos of Pound, Eliot, and their modernist school; so that, for the New Critics, the rare defense of a poem by Words-worth could seem a test of mastery on a par with the more intricate moves in chess. The large-scale revival of Wordsworth, which the current anti-canonical wisdom holds to be a thing of timeless prove-nance, was (it is no exaggeration to say) the effect of advocacy by readers, critics, and scholars working separately or in concert over the past thirty years. At present, the severer sort of academic republicans have come to dislike his moralism again, and are there-fore trying to supplant him with the always popular, continental and ingratiating Byron.

In short, the academic consensus in 1988 (a year of romanticism-and-revolution centenaries) approached a point the argument had reached around 1818, which did not prove to be the end of any-thing. Here Wordsworth is a representative and not an exceptional case. Why, then, do scholars come to picture the literary tradition in English as wholly exclusionist? They do it to impress themselves. For if the story were true, they would stand out as courageous rebels. Still, how can they credit a story so *evidently* shallow? For Atlas's report suggests that the scholars before deceiving others have been at pains to deceive themselves. He recounts an interview with Stanley Fish, then chair of the English department at Duke; after some extensive descriptions of clothes and furniture, we come to Fish's opinions: "He's never been comfortable with the T. S. Eliot tradition, he says, though he's one of the leading Milton scholars in America." This is a remarkable judgment—exactly as cogent as: "I have never been comfortable with the Jeremiah tradition, though I am one of the leading scholars of the Gospel of John." Milton simply was not part of "the T. S. Eliot tradition." He was at the center of a Protestant tradition Eliot wanted to displace; and Eliot attacked it (and Milton above all) with scorn, snobbery, and a fine selective connoisseurship; but anyway he did his work consistently. The truth is that Eliot and Milton have little in common—apart from the fact that they were white males. If that is enough to constitute them as a tradition, and even the sole "great" tradition (to be reviled the more fiercely on that account), then we are all in trouble—the people who believe the story, as much as those who, knowing better, would rather not be drawn to take note of irrelevant complexities.

What should we conclude from the ease with which errors like these are propagated?—errors which concur in the treatment of several centuries as a solid block of opinion, and the treatment of the present age as a finely differentiated scene of conflict, to which the most significant attention is owed. Morals, said William Carlos Williams, are the memory of success that no longer succeeds. Institutional radicals say that great work in the arts, too, is a matter only of provisional success, and they want to see it become an indistinct memory. With journalism now ready to flatter this claim, they are in a position to evangelize more thoroughly than ever before. But they argue better than they read, and their arguments all have the same first step: a confusion of mass culture with democracy. This error is so deeply entwined in an ascendant logic of theory that it may be worth unraveling the beliefs that make its work executable. All the beliefs fall into the category of the *sociological reduction;* but in some ingenious instances, sociology is nicknamed history so that the reduction becomes "historicism"; while in others it is nicknamed culture so that the reduction becomes "cultural materialism."

Before we number these new axioms, which license the second dogma concerning the liberation of new knowledge, it is worth rehearsing the different axioms that once disposed teachers of literature not to concentrate their efforts on work that was contemporary, or popular, or clear-cut in its didacticism. The work might be any of those things, but it had to justify itself on other grounds as well; and the following other grounds were supposed to possess some utility in constituting the readings for a course: the assigned work should be something that students would not routinely find for themselves; and the work should meet the teacher's highest standard of what is worth reading and worth talking about. Notice that both criteria refer to the quality of the work, and not just the interest of a possible approach to it. This is the initial judgment that must be made: those, it was said, who cannot make the judgment have not begun to know their own minds, and ought not to be instructing others. Neither criterion, however, refers to the age or medium of the work. In a class on modernism in the visual arts, Cocteau's *Blood of a Poet* might well pass both tests. In a class on narratives of the frontier, "The Beverly Hillbillies" would not pass either test. To the extent that the age of the work makes for distance from what a student routinely finds, that fact recommends it. To the extent that the medium of the work makes for such distance, that fact also recommends it.

If these premises are now far on the way to being reversed, we should, on the argument I have advanced, expect to find that the new axioms explicitly favor the reversal. They will be so formed as to reflect not a common sense about the education of aesthetic judgment but a research program in which the arts and letters imitate the social sciences imitating the natural sciences. This, I think, is what one does see in some main assumptions of professionalist literary scholarship in the year 1992:

1. All writing has an influence on the lives and opinions of its readers; and, since writing always contains doctrine of some sort, to understand the doctrine is to understand the character of the influence.
2. In a given period, the most popular works have the largest influence.

3. Writing that in its time belonged to polite or respectable or "high" culture will be seen to have worked on contemporary readers so as to confirm their acceptance of the political status quo.

These points are restated often, and casually, and as having the quality of established facts, in a vast quantity of the emergent commentary on English and American literature. They are taken to be simple deductions from the idea that art cannot save the world and that "men make their own history, but they do not make it just as they please." We are dealing therefore with what now qualifies as tacit knowledge. An unargued acceptance of the third assumption often leads theorists to assert that popular texts subvert the established order while classic texts by definition cannot do so. An unargued acceptance of the second assumption leads the same theorists to assert that in a mind free of the prejudices of high culture, elite and popular texts cohabit undiscriminatingly and are felt by the reader to share an equal status. Together, these beliefs compose the dogma of liberation. Once the new science is seen to have established them as facts, it will have proved itself to be emancipatory.

The unsettling fact remains that the axioms have never been properly established; and yet, unless they are taken as proved, a great deal of current writing on literature is exposed as empty posturing; and worse, a continuous waste of time for the student who has to memorize the results because they have entered the curriculum. I believe the results not only are not proved but are susceptible of historical refutation of a sort the contemporary theorist is bound to respect. The refutation when it comes—well begun in Jonathan Rose's 1992 *JHI* article "Rereading the English Common Reader"—may be expected to have the following shape. It will review the primary testimony of readers who were of humble rather than elite status, at formative times of their moral and political development—taking, for example, as a possible archive the memoirs or autobiographies of working-class men and women in the last half of the nineteenth century and the first half of the twentieth.

Such a review of the historical evidence will establish certain facts about those readers and their reading: first, that self-educated persons were capable of reading many books without much effect; second, that they by no means held popular books of the day in high esteem, though often enough they read them; and third, that they could experience as a personal discovery, or as a stimulus to radical thought, the reading of books that have come to be considered part of high culture.

At the point when such an account emerges, the whole populist theory of reader-response ought to collapse under the weight of popular revolt against it. Even where the protest is from voices a hundred years old, they call out against a lie that cancels the very tone and shading of their experience. Of course, there would still remain a way to prop up the dominance of mass culture over the mind of the mass reader. For the bad historical theory can be salvaged by an untestable cultural theory: a comprehensive thesis concerning the prevalence of "false consciousness"; according to which it is inevitable for people lacking the right weapons of analysis to submit to a wrong understanding of their own experience, and equally inevitable for the theorist who has such weapons to supply a right understanding. Versions of this account have been promoted at various times by Jonathan Culler in his discussions of reader-competence. Like other publicists of theory, Culler points out that a lay reader can hardly understand literary conventions *as such* in the way an academic theorist can. Doubtless this is true, and confirmable in a great many contexts. But a puzzle here may be remarked. For the drift of the argument is far more elitist than the most fastidious specimen of the traditional judgment it wants to supplant. And clearly, if there is such a thing as competence in mastering a background of narrative devices, rhetorical schemes, and so on, there may also be such a thing as competence in understanding a background of human emotions or human experiences. Can the theorist also claim an advantage here? The response of Jonathan Culler to a complex allegorical text like *Pilgrim's Progress* is bound to be edifying. A response to the same text by a lay reader like Martin Luther King, Jr., might possibly be edifying as well.

Theory has reached a point, however, where it has no choice but to send the second sort of reader to school with the first. It is a school that teaches not only the conventions that go with reader-competence but the delicate doctrine of the uselessness of experience.

So far, I have only touched on a staring fact about those who embrace the new axioms. In the name of a democratic attack on high culture, they launch a profoundly anti-democratic attack on the powers of judgment of the lay reader. The assumption seems to be that "the people" believe everything they read. The theorist is then in a position to rescue any member of the people with a consolation. On the one hand (this is said to placate), anything you read is as good as anything else. On the other hand (this is said to admonish), you are apt to be deceived by the hidden ideology of anything you read, and by the approved texts rather more than by the unapproved. My generous endorsement of all your present habits is thus matched by my unselfish willingness to tell you which of those habits are depraved.

These tactics mix presumption and contempt in about equal parts. And it is certainly odd, for so important a hypothesis, that from the historical record thus far not one instance of the imputed state of mind has emerged. The theory literature is full of talk about "the reader" being worked on by a deceitful text; you would think at least one document from a formerly misled but now repentant lay reader might be produced; and yet, we still await "The Empire of Human Nature: How I Was Steered Wrong by the *Essay on Man,*" or any confession in a similar mode from any period whatever. The propagandized reader surely exists in reality. It is an anomaly of literary study that observers so fully acquainted with that reader's thoughts should have preferred to leave his or her identity merely ideal.

Wrote Burke of the eighteenth-century theorists who invented the mass culture of political morality: "Hypocrisy, of course, delights in the most sublime speculations; for, never intending to go beyond speculation, it costs nothing to have it magnificent." In the selfless enterprise that literary theorists have chosen—the work of divining, for other people's sake, the deep truth of other people's lives—it has cost them nothing to have it magnificent.

The refined speculator comes to embrace the principle of mass suffrage in the arts by reasoning as follows: "The more we show a distaste for everything, the better we guard ourselves against possibly wrong sensations. And what but a distaste for works of art could support our claim to have acquired a taste for unclassified works of the present?" This is defensive logic and bad psychology; and, as a matter of experience, almost the opposite is true. Genuine critics build on what they love. They do not extrapolate their admirations by simply inverting the values they condemn. Besides, the gift for writing well about popular works is not given to critics who ask in advance: by how many people is this liked, and by what sort of people? George Orwell's essay on "The Art of Donald McGill," for example, shows no trace of the prophylactic tone that is now preferred. Rather, Orwell took McGill and his comic postcards, with their "utter lowness of mental atmosphere," as a clue to a forgotten sympathy—"something as traditional as Greek tragedy, a sort of sub-world of smacked bottoms and scrawny mothers-in-law which is part of Western European consciousness." The unscandalized description does not affect to be an act of homage, and does not require the critic to praise the work for being what it is not. This freedom of inclination allows the essay to end with a small discovery: "A dirty joke is not, of course, a serious attack upon morality, but it is a sort of mental rebellion, a momentary wish that things were otherwise." The effect is to humanize a partly unpleasant subject, rather than to anatomize it, further alienate it from one's sympathies, and pretend that the result of this process has been to render the thing more pleasant.

One of the great appreciators of the blues, Albert Murray, still works in the Orwell tradition, and two aspects of his criticism are worth noting: an intense dislike of social science, and a wish to honor, rather than to discredit, the domain of high art. Murray declines to say, "If Count Basie is great, Mann and Malraux must be less great." He says, instead, "They matter, as he matters, too; let's talk about why." In his polemics, Murray has brought to light, as well as any living writer, the cold enthusiasm of those who praise both esoteric and popular artists because something-of-the-kind is wanted. The pacesetters of the academic avant-garde seem to him always a little behind the pace. For the arts draw their impulse from singular persons, whose minds are on their work, and who have no time for the obedient question: how many people will like this, and what sort of people will they be? In *The Omni-Americans*, Murray writes of "the serious novelist's complex aware-ness of the burdensome but sobering fact that there is some good-ness in bad people however bad they are, and some badness or at least some flaw in good people however dear. In fact, sometimes the artist comes pretty close to being politically suspect; because on the one hand he is always proclaiming his love for mankind and on the other he is forever giving the devil his due." The credo seems as appropriate to an ancient dramatist as it does to a modern novelist or to a singer of the blues. Works that gain a wide audience do not differ from those with a small audience by reducing this complex awareness to something more digestible. They differ only by offering it in an idiom that many rather than a few embrace. There is nothing superior in being one of the many, and nothing superior in being one of the few.

For the social construction of literature to go forward, credence in the new research is less important than rejection of the aesthetic confidence that sanctioned the old. Aesthetic criticism took for granted the worth of distance and the belief that art can be a non-utilitarian good. That belief, that sense of worth, and the judgments they together yield have been classed since the eighteenth century in the difficult category of *taste*. The past few years have therefore witnessed some energetic attempts to overturn the traditional idea of taste: I want to discuss here a representative work of this kind, Barbara Herrnstein Smith's *Contingencies of Value*.[5] Because I confine the discussion to Smith's central argument and her general, though tacit, moralizing drift, I need to make one warning at the outset. Her work is vulnerable largely owing to one of its less fashionable traits: the lack of any declared political commitment. For such a commitment can be persuasive, and it can preempt criticism, in the following way: it sets the (admitted) good of art against the (admitted) good of political progress, and suggests that one good drives out the other. This is always true in an obvious sense: time that we give to reading may be time that we subtract from a canvass of voters in an electoral district. If the second kind of good were recognized as somehow having a commanding claim, we might well be obliged to let it decide the rules for teaching. This in the end is a civic argument against spending time on teaching literature at all. It can draw support from Plato and Rousseau, both of whom cherish a republican, and iconoclastic, distrust of art which is associated with a distrust of spectatorship in general. But Barbara Herrnstein Smith, another former president of the Modern Language Association, has no real interest in such a conclusion. Rather, she hopes to prove that there are equally good arguments for any literature we choose to teach.

I will be paying close attention to what Smith has to say about the "contingencies" that "relativize" our choices in teaching. But it seems to me that the strongest justification for the teaching of literature is not embodied in the older defenses of taste, even though those defenses are a great deal subtler than Smith has understood. A personally credible reason for coming to know a book that has "pleased many and pleased long" will always be intuitive; for it relates to the conviction that books are part of a larger discipline of humanity which the knowledge of the past may serve: one thing we know about a book that has survived for a generation is that someone has found it useful. The study of literature is therefore defensible as an act of recovery that connects us with the persistence of human nature over time. To the extent that one is behaviorist or resolutely determinist in one's beliefs about human nature (supposing, for example, that all the productions of art are controlled by laws of stimulus and response, or by the exchange of social power and knowledge), such an argument for the uses of art will carry no weight. The same will be true of all other arguments: whatever their temporary intellectual authority, they will lack emotional conviction. Still, bearing in mind the limited authority of any result from abstract disputation, let us look at Smith's attempt to prove that every canon of taste is built on shifting sands.

Though Smith describes herself as a relativist, the tag is imprecise and brings with it a number of empty, quasi-moral, puzzles. She is in fact a hard-line utilitarian who happens to be uncertain, as yet, just how to quantify the utility she is prepared to measure in works of art. But the view she proposes of art, as of all other human activities, comes from a belief in its functional service to a society, to a group that may constitute a society-in-small, or to a person who may be understood as a social unit by having his or her choices redescribed as behaviors. The verdict on art at which she aims is, in her own words, that "there is no *bottom* bottom line anywhere." Every judgment we produce is contingent—that is to say, dependent on other factors than the apparent subject matter of the judgment itself. By showing how aesthetic judgments in particular are conditioned by prejudice, vanity, and interest (above all, something at once pervasive and indefinable which she calls "cognitive interest"), Smith aims to divest high culture of the prestige it enjoys as a somehow autonomous realm. This would free the genetic and environmental cultures, some of which we have sampled in chapter 1, to pursue and enforce new rules of interest in keeping with what Smith thinks is a general human "will to epistemic self-maintenance—a *conservatism* that may be even deeper than that of politics." It speaks for her candor that she does not affect to challenge, or decompose, the sources of this conservatism. She simply wants to spread its gifts to a greater number of self-maintenance groups than have thus far been able to use it.

Smith launches her defense of contingency in a disarming way. The first pages of her book tell how, for a great many years, she taught Shakespeare's sonnets continuously—all the while pursuing scholarly work with the same texts as an editor, annotator, and critic. Looking back at her record of response to the poems, she is struck by the enormous variability that it exhibits over time and the intense conviction it nevertheless carried at certain moments. She went back and forth in her feelings about lots of poems: one temporarily convincing reading ("a lovely reading . . . when I believe it") might rescue a poem she had formerly disdained, another might spoil a poem she had long admired and cherished. She came to know, in a hallucinatory fashion, poems that were not in fact in the text, and accidentally blotted from her memory poems that were in fact in the text. Anyone who has ever read, and reconsidered, a single work a half-dozen times will have shared something of Smith's acquaintance with these phenomena, though it is fair to add that hers does seem to have been an extreme case. But the point about her confession is that it strengthens the general argument for contingency. How true, she implies, must contingency-of-value be for an entire culture, if it has this kind of grip on the life of an individual reader. Where a larger number of variables exist, we may expect still more variability.

One cannot help feeling that Smith's memories typify the experience only of a small subset of the impassioned and inquisitive readers alive today. Many of the symptoms she describes are related to the peculiarly rewarding, but also peculiarly repetitious, work of the modern professional exegete. There is something unnaturally depressive about the routines of teaching the same poem year after year (Smith calls this "professing" the poem), without any letup for two decades or more. In the circumstances, an occasional manic interpretation may have a rousing effect. But that is not the only way out. Much healthier was Nietzsche's decision, after years of professing Wagner, to turn from the subject entirely and celebrate *Carmen* for its cheerfulness, its dumb vitality as an antidote to Wagner. Anyway, given the predicament of the academic specialist, it seems wrong to draw a general inference about the reading of intelligent people who do not happen to teach what they read. And yet, from the company and conversation of such people, Smith has been so long shut out that she now inclines to doubt their existence.

Her book owes much of its confidence to the knowledge that such doubts will be widely shared by academic readers. In consequence, Smith allows herself few Nietzschean "antidotes." *Contingencies of Value* is written from the classroom and the think tank;

its characters are teachers, students, and more teachers: from them, the theorist extrapolates a culture. And it is clearly felt to be, on self-evident merits, a culture of considerable variety and texture— one whose contingencies will show as much as is needed about the fluctuations of taste over long tracts of time and space. Yet as a historical account of contingency, the book has no pretensions. After the sonnet-reading anecdote, Smith offers not a single story of the reception of a poem, a novel, or a work of any kind by a sequence of readers who took for granted disparate values—just the sort of demonstration that the argument seems to require, if it means to be taken historically and not metaphysically. In Los Angeles, there is a radio station that is "all news, all the time." Smith's book is all theory, all the time.

I explored in chapter 3 what "theory" may imply, in this sense of the word. It is a way of talking about meaning or the possibility of meaning in the moral sciences, to a mixed audience of readers across the disciplines of literature, anthropology, politics, philosophy, and the law. The strength of the theory community lies in the scope and generosity of its interests. The weakness lies in the questionable capacity of any member to understand what is at stake in the vocabulary, the history, all the tacit conventions of argument that another member, who lives and thinks some distance away, may take as a thing that goes without saying. Given these limitations, not only a universal language but a universal topic is needed to join the competence-sensations of people so diverse in their starting points. That topic has in recent years fixed itself firmly, and it is called epistemology: the study—as the theorist understands it—of how our manner of coming to know a thing may affect what comes to be known. In the understanding of the topic shared by this community, the first step in any discussion is a rehearsal of the "irremediable gap" between ourselves and the "Other" whom we try to know. The foregoing reminder will prove to have been necessary as soon as one looks at a passage of any length from Smith.

The personal vignette about teaching Shakespeare's sonnets may have seemed non-institutional to the point of anarchism. The next stage of her argument settles quickly on familiar terrain:

> The epistemological conundrum, however (that is, the puzzle of how to find out how the Other's meat tastes to *him*), remains uncrackable, and other questions are raised for normative cultural criticism and its associated pedagogic and missionary imperatives, including whether the quality of other people's lives or cultures is appropriately or usefully measured by the extent to which either the objects of their experience duplicate our own or their articulation of those experiences are [*sic*] produced in the idioms of our own cultural discourses.[6]

In its ponderousness the style adequately represents the current idiom of the readers to whom it is addressed. The point is not made more subtle by the blend of cliché ("the Other's meat"), moralism very faintly disguised ("pedagogic and missionary imperatives"), and a passive bureaucratic abstractedness ("articulation of those experiences are produced"). To restate the matter in plainer words: you can never know why some people like some things, but since you want to respect those people anyway, you might as well give up trying to judge their different taste in your own language of taste.

The sociological emphasis of the argument will now be clear. The utilitarian aim comes out in another characteristic passage: "Since there are no functions performed by artworks that may be specified as generically unique and also no way to distinguish 'rewards' provided by art-related experiences or behavior from those provided by innumerable other kinds of experience and behavior, any distinctions drawn between 'aesthetic' and 'nonaesthetic' (or 'extra-aesthetic') value must be regarded as fundamentally problematic."[7] Smith's doctrine here turns out to be as much behaviorist as it is utilitarian; an understandable convergence, given the similarity between the two standpoints on art. But again in this slow sentence, the intended meaning is very simple, and Jeremy Bentham said it faster: "prejudice apart, the game of push-pin is of equal value with the arts and sciences of music and poetry."

Throughout *Contingencies of Value*, Smith has taken over from Bentham the metaphor of cost-benefit analysis; like him, she uses it to discredit the idea that aesthetic judgment can be distinct from moral or political calculations. The affinity is less odd than it looks. It was Bentham and James Mill, long before Marx and Engels, who first exposed the liberal assumption of disinterestedness as a mask for class interest. Smith wants to show that the aesthetic pleasure of the connoisseur is in no way superior to the sensational or torpid pleasure of the philistine. When we exalt the first kind of pleasure over the second, we only show our unwillingness to countenance "the Other" whose interests are foreign to our own.

Her real target of course is the belief in general standards. Hume wrote an important essay "Of the Standard of Taste," and Smith takes several, unsatisfactory, passing shots at his argument without quite giving the sustained demolition that she promises. But Hume was offering a skeptical *defense* of such a standard: though founded on nothing outside human nature, it might be worth preserving for its contribution to "general utility"—which, in the Humean argument I sketched in chapter 4, is not a utilitarian concept at all. Rather, he takes it to be a point of reference for whatever may assist the survival and improvement of a given society, and of the human species over time. One reason the difference makes no impression on Smith is that she has no interest in a defense either of taste or of judgment. She proposes instead a skeptical refutation along the following lines:

A. There is no such thing as an impersonal, or unsituated, judgment, any more than there is a view from nowhere. Every judgment comes from a person in a situation.

B. With persons and situations come interests. Every settled evaluation of a work of art flows from particular interests, and it serves ends of some importance to those interests. This is emphatically true of the "permanent" value that is associated with canonical works.

C. Having felt the weight of these observations, one will want to detach oneself from all persuasive assertions of the form "X is better than Y." For, in seeking to inculcate a belief about value, one appeals to nothing beyond habit and the usual tacit supports of value, the authority of which is always relative to our own time, place, and situation.

It can be said for Smith's theoretical resolve that what she proposes is not an easy way to live. Even in the classroom, a tolerance like hers runs the risk of uprooting complacent belief only to supplant it with complacent unbelief. But considered strictly as a piece of theory, the argument leaves two questions standing. It is not clear how we get from *A* to *B*, and it is not clear how we get from *B* to *C*.

Thus, from the fact that every work and every judgment—the reader's and the writer's alike—*emerge from* certain interests, it does not follow that a given work or judgment must *serve* the same interests. That Ur-canonical text, the Sermon on the Mount, emerged from the lives of the early Christians. It can now serve the utterly opposite interests of Cardinal O'Connor and the Liberation Theologians. Still, says Smith, no canonical work will remain canonical for long, unless it is found to answer the demands of some "establishment." Notice how implausible this claim becomes in the light of the present example. We have here to project a meta-establishment, comprising all North American and Latin American humanity, which unites at a higher level the demands of both far-right and hard-left interpreters. Such a solution is certainly possible and just as certainly vacuous. But let us follow a little the clue of religious commentary, since it promises to illustrate, a fortiori, anything that can be said of a secular canon. What do we make of an atheist like Shaw, who wrote: "There has really never been a more monstrous imposition perpetrated than the imposition of the limitation of Paul's soul upon the soul of Jesus." Shaw had found something in the utterances of Jesus that made a moral claim even on him; and something in the utterances of Paul that violated the spirit of everything Jesus said and did. We may suppose if we like that Shaw was a Protestant of some sort. How much help is that?

Before Smith can be credited on the question of interest generally, she will have to say what establishment a judgment like his emerges from, and what establishment it serves.

Yet suppose that we do admit the interest-serving character of all judgments of value. It does not follow that we have only an arbitrary authority for saying of two poems, "P_1 is better than P_2." Two readers, each confronting the other for the first time, may do well to adopt an unassuming tone. But their politeness has no implications whatever for the trust we can still choose to place in a qualified judge. Such a judge is distinguished by a knowledge of the goods internal to a practice—those goods that do not make a novel's worth exactly correspond to its sales, or an article's worth exactly correspond to the journal in which it was published. The judgments that flow from a person thus qualified will only count if one believes that there *are* goods independent of money and prestige; independent, too, of the claims of universal rights and equal representation in a culture. Smith, from the tenor of her book, must want to deny that there are such internal goods anywhere, but she does not address the question directly.

Hume did. Because he also shares some premises with Barbara Herrnstein Smith, it is worth saying a few more words for his conception of taste. Hume thought there were conventions of seeing, and understanding, a work of art, on which so general an agreement could be obtained that the resulting judgments would seem "natural." Appreciation was therefore an art that could be taught. That much, Smith in a charitable mood can allow. But she thinks that where the arts are concerned, the whole logic of appreciation has been mystified by the long renown a canonical work by definition has already enjoyed. To give a fair hearing to both critics, we ought to look at a pursuit less easily mystified: say, the taste for croquet. There are things a good fan knows to watch out for, that the casual tea-sipping onlooker can scarcely perceive: why, for instance, it is sometimes advisable to blast through a wicket your different-colored rival, even though that may seem on the face of it a rather tediously gentle tactic. Now Hume believed the standard of the seasoned fan, or of the experienced reader, was decisive for the pursuits to which they respectively belong. Smith's reply is a rhetorical question. Who are *we*, after all (since our nature is only convention, our pleasure a conditioned and not a timeless custom, our viewpoint specific and non-transcendental)—who are we to dismiss the person who judges either the game or the work quite differently?

Hume's implicit answer comes not only in his essay "Of the Standard of Taste" but in the companion essay "Of Delicacy of Taste and Passion," and more generally in his *Enquiry concerning the Principles of Morals*. A standard of taste, which Hume calls "a standard of sentiment," is a convention that a society observes and agrees to enforce for the sake of general utility. Though artificial, because man-made (a fact we have no trouble keeping in view), it is also necessarily natural, being suited to the ways of human nature as they are modified by a given society. What Hume calls "a standard of judgment" is natural in quite another sense, being built up from our discoveries about natural laws in the physical universe. The standard of taste alone corresponds to inward feeling; the standard of judgment corresponds to matters susceptible of deduction or proof. It is with this in mind that Hume can say, "Truth is disputable; not taste." The conventions of taste are more subtle, or implicit, but not therefore more chaotic than those of judgment. Who then sets the standard? A general culture such as the Enlightenment imagined to be possible and desirable—a culture, that is, defined by its cosmopolitanism, its practice of toleration, and its respect for the achievement of different talents in different walks of life. These talents we may think of broadly as "callings"—though the religious shading of that word would have been repugnant to Hume.

And yet his are, to repeat, only arguments for the depth of certain habits that seem by long use and assimilation to have joined our nature itself. *Outside* the dense medium of social legitimation— from a point of view antagonistic to a whole given complex of arts and habits—there is no Humean answer to Smith's question "Who are we?" He did not anticipate a culture so divided against itself that anybody would even want to ask it. Within such a culture, it will seem highly significant "that there are many people in the world who are not—or are not yet, or choose not to be—among the orthodoxly educated population of the West: people who do not encounter Western classics at all or who encounter them under cultural and institutional conditions very different from those of American and European college professors and their students." Yet by itself this fact does not point a moral. It would begin to do so only if good evidence were available that the reputation of certain Western books is a substantial cause of the economic misery and political oppression in the world today. Smith stops far short of this. To the Western "orthodoxly educated" academic reader whom she addresses, careering from proprietary regard to a proprietary disdain for high culture, her sole message seems to be: distrust yourself.

Contingency then—epistemological contingency which may have its source in a more immediate social anxiety—has become the watchword of a professional class unsettled in its beliefs; and unsettled, perhaps, in other ways as well: there are some who pass from school to school as often as Smith, in her first chapter, appeared to pass from reading to reading. What are they in flight from? Partly, from the ideals one might espouse if one could consider the work of aesthetic judgment a calling and not just a profession. Smith's book, I think, says about as much as the profession now can say for itself in the line of theory I described as a historicist unloading of meanings. To complete the picture I have aimed at from the start of this book, I want to close by looking at a critic who seems to write as Smith's antithesis; who, with an emphasis that has become rare inside the academy, speaks in favor of an anti-historicist loading of meanings. The critic is Allan Bloom, and the book is *Giants and Dwarfs*—a collection of essays written over the past thirty years, which gives a fairer representation of his thinking than *The Closing of the American Mind*.

The comparison makes a very unequal contest in one respect. In point of critical interest, Bloom has a continuous advantage over

Smith, for he is still interested in interpreting works of literature and philosophy. Not "how we situate ourselves with reference to texts" but the texts themselves are capable of holding his attention. But the symmetry between the two camps persists. Where the left-wing theorist finds a typical work of art convincing in no way at all—for it can only be the symptomatic expression of an "epistemic self-maintenance" already in place—the right-wing interpreter finds a typical work of art convincing in exactly one way. These are aspects of a single error about art, the error that Sir Philip Sidney had in view in his *Apologie for Poetry* when he said that the poet "nothing affirms, and therefore never lieth." The sentiment has been kept memorable, closer to our time, by D. H. Lawrence's remark "Never trust the artist. Trust the tale." However, our theorists consent to no such trust. Barbara Herrnstein Smith shows us tales that are compelled to be, in the nature of the attention we can bring to them, confirmations of a social identity that we already hold. Allan Bloom shows us tellers who unerringly guide the moral of their tales to assist a civilization.

Bloom has long been known as a translator and interpreter of Plato and Rousseau. I find him more instructive as a reader of Shakespeare, and am concerned here with the three essays on Shakespeare in *Giants and Dwarfs*.[8] In all these his critical practice becomes more interesting than his premises. Still, something should be said of the premises. "Poetry," writes Bloom, "is the most powerful form of rhetoric"—a controversial claim since it implies that poetry is *only* a form of rhetoric. Yet from Bloom's perspective, this general belief is consistent with the way Shakespeare conceived of his characters: "A man is known, not simply by his existence, but by the character of his actions—liberal or greedy, courageous or cowardly, frank or sly, moderate or profligate. Since these qualities produce happiness or misery, they are the specific subject matter of poetry. Passions, feelings, the whole realm of the psychological are secondary." From this extraordinary judgment, one might project the whole plot and treatment of Addison's *Cato* and many another neoclassical exercise in controlled morality; but not *Othello*, not *Measure for Measure*, nor any of the two dozen other plays in which Shakespeare's psychological knowledge is part of his interest in humanity.

To judge by an allusion elsewhere in his book, Bloom thinks of *Hamlet* as the story of a fight between two politicians, Claudius and Fortinbras, in which certain disruptions appear from an unauthorized quarter. If some such reading held our attention, then we could agree that psychology is secondary and settle for a view of poetry as one more form of rhetoric. Few readers, however, will want to confine themselves like this in the presence of *Hamlet*. Curiously, Bloom, in portraying an original work of drama as a timeless digest of morals, has chosen to invoke the authority of Schiller: the great defender of the moral *and* psychological groundwork of the aesthetic ideal. Bloom associates with Schiller the hope that by "living awhile" with Shakespeare, "perhaps we can recapture the fullness of life and rediscover the way to its lost unity." But it is doubtful that Shakespeare believed he was in possession of any such unity; and as for Schiller, he suspected that a distrust of enlightenment was at the bottom of every nostalgia. That is why he argued, in the essay *On Naive and Sentimental Poetry*, that the lost unity of culture belongs to the domain of human fantasy and not to history or experience. We shall see presently the importance of a "lost unity" to the modern whole-length apologist for civilization.

Bloom's interpretations of *The Merchant of Venice* and *Richard II* are impressive pieces of criticism. They offer concentrated readings of the dramatic action of the plays—the sort of guided summary that can sometimes follow from scrupulous thought. And as they move forward to the mark, one notices that the flow of weighty talk about the value of "permanent questions" (familiar to readers of Bloom on education) has almost all dried up. In discussing *The Merchant of Venice*, he is content to show the impossibility of embracing, in a single society, the Christian charity of Antonio and the Jewish honor of Shylock. He avoids taking sides on the justice of religious persecution, as against the justice of legal revenge, and does not try to guess the degree of sympathy we are expected to feel for Shylock. The play is said to exhibit the fallenness of the City of Man—in the comic frame of Portia's Venice, though it is a condition that might lend itself to tragic reflections. Maybe because *Richard II* is close to tragedy throughout, one comes there to recognize the allegory that Bloom's method of reading is bound to find in any text. This is an allegory in which all of Renaissance culture can be identified with a single name, betokening a single idea, with a fixed meaning in one view of political theory. The name is Machiavelli. The meaning is the crisis of modernity. And the salient features of the crisis are that all our beliefs lack ultimate grounds, and that their ungroundedness is a secret known only to the few. The work of an interpreter is to show how a great work at once discloses the secret to these few and keeps it systematically concealed from the many. In this way, political dramas like *Richard II* and, to a lesser extent, *The Merchant of Venice*, become apologies for the necessity of concealment.

His full commentary on *Richard II* interprets the legitimate king, Richard, as an object of sympathy but not respect. The usurper, Henry, does command respect but with a loss of sacred reverence. Thus, Richard "never succeeds in finding himself, but we see the articulation of his soul as he gropes toward his goal. We do not find that Richard is ever good, but we do find him touching." Henry, by contrast,

is split. He cannot bear to face the possibility that the sin of Cain, as Machiavelli teaches, may play a role in the establishment of earthly justice. In deposing Richard he was halfway to the realization that he was committing a crime but that such crimes are sometimes necessary for the common good. . . . His son returns to his father's original impulse and with healthy self-assurance abandons crusades in favor of unjust wars with France which serve the evident interests of England instead of serving his conscience, using the priests as his political ministers rather than as the masters of his beliefs. He thus unifies England and himself. The Henriad as a whole shows the limits of conscience. Henry V provides a contrast to his predecessors not unlike the contrast between Hamlet and Fortinbras in a play that seems to bear a similar message. The exquisitely refined souls do not belong to the best political men. Knowledge of political things brings with it the awareness that in order for the sacred to become sacred terrible deeds must be done. Because God does not evidently rule, the founder of justice cannot himself be just. He cannot be distinguished from the criminal by his justice or anything else accessible to earthly eyes.[9]

This is a deeply felt analysis and an acute description of the morality of Shakespeare's histories. At the same time, there is something queer about the passage—a hesitation it forces on the reader, from a tacit suggestion that the critic endorses every particle of the morality he is describing.

Conscience, says Bloom, is out of place in the politics of this story, and in any other politics. In the City of Man, it is right to want a leader like Henry V. For there are two elites that matter on earth: the nobility of mind and the nobility of action. That of action is the more important. But to that of mind alone belong the exquisite souls. Fortified by such a soul, a moral philosopher's aim will be to induce a healthy lawlessness in the young blond jungle animal of politics, whose only earlier impulse was a brainless quest for approval from his elders. Bloom has always been kindly disposed to the aristocratic skepticism of Nietzsche, and here one starts to see the reason. Apart from the ruler whose every prayer is a command, there is one social type worth considering, and that is the philosopher. And yet the philosopher, who sees things unknown to others, is by comparison morbid, inward, "secondary." There is, however, one way for him to rise above the mere irony of his situation. He can do it by backing the edicts and the performances of the king himself.

"You are different," says the philosopher and defender of the West to the aspiring politician. "You are a doer, as I am a knower, of 'political things.' The terrible deeds that you do, I will strive to make sacred." These words were not written by Bloom, of course.

They are nothing but a direct inference from his engaging summary of a work of fiction. Yet the words he writes as a commentator on a text recall other words he has written in his own voice. By the acts of a king like Henry V, or, perhaps, a kinglike executive who seizes control of a decaying republic, the lost unity of a nation may become historical reality with a vengeance. The great-souled interpreter is he who does not shrink from this great spectacle; who knows that the very idea of the sacred is a noble lie, and a lie that must be told; who is not thrown back on his conscience by the mention of a higher law, for "God does not evidently rule."

The atheism of Allan Bloom is not the most surprising thing about him. It says more about public opinion in America than about the character of one man, that Bloom should have written a popular book, *The Closing of the American Mind*, which became more popular in proportion as its message was taken to be: a return to the old pieties. Bloom does cherish select monuments, practices, even persons. But his pieties are not America's. They are not like what ours ever have been, or could have been. By two great movements of thought, in particular, which have affected the lives and feelings of most people today, he shows no sign of having ever been touched in the slightest degree. The movements are Romanticism and Christianity, and they have more than one thing in common. They say that all men and women are equal in the eye of a power that surpasses every worldly authority. This truth, they say, is a spiritual law beyond the reach of any vicissitude of fortune. And so it must remain—whether one commits terrible deeds, or apologizes for the deeds of others, or does neither. One comes to know this authority not by schooling, however methodical, but by consulting the evidence of the soul—or, as it is also called, the mind or self or spirit.

Broad as these conceptions are, they have much to do with the reasons for the founding of the United States. That they have had absolutely no influence on Bloom (who speaks for what he takes to be the culture of the West), any more than on Barbara Herrnstein Smith (who speaks against what she takes to be the culture of the West), suggests the terminus at which the advocates of the argu-

ment on culture have left us. The mistake, I have been suggesting
all along, comes partly from the flat choice of loyalties that has
been pressed on us in the past few years of the debate about higher
education. But there is as great an error in our assumption that
these choices match up with an allegiance to "larger values"; for,
as it happens, Smith and Bloom alike grow carefully dull when the
applications of their views are about to materialize: they agree, at
least, that such matters are rightly kept from vulgar eyes. One
reads in the company of the licensed thousands of a professional
association, or in the company of a few close friends. The wider
social world is still there in the books; otherwise it is out of the
picture—and a good thing, too. Those others would hardly understand what one had to say.

The sensation of easy or uneasy height that comes from keeping
a distance from the world: we are back in the story that began with
an account of the new fundamentalists on campus. The subject, on
its academic as on its social side, may finally be inseparable from
a generation's sense of despair. Much of the apparent boldness,
the real timidity and euphoric bad faith, with which departments
of literature now conduct themselves is owing to the ambiguous
middle status of the graduates of the sixties. Here my plot starts
to look like Roger Kimball's in *Tenured Radicals;* but my reading of
the new mood differs from his. Not even the youngest of these
persons, who were old enough to witness a last afterglow of the
sixties, are now so youthful as to be confused with the really young.
Besides, a more important fact about them than their former political opinions, if they had any, is that they came for the first time
then to think of their intellectual and moral relations to their elders.
"Bliss was it in that dawn to be alive, / But to be young was very
heaven!"—and to be old, something less than heaven. As the generation of the sixties matures in the academy and grows more
magisterial, we have begun to see evolved a new kind of compliment. This is the act of inverted patronage in which a well-known
younger scholar says something nice about a well-known elder. It
is carried off in a tone that is quite new. For the praise is delivered

on the score of the senior personage's having become, at however advanced an age, wise enough to care to follow the junior personage. My mentor is given a lift for having retooled most marvelously to adapt himself to the new thinking which I represent.

Such adaptations, of course, do happen. New thinking does come to scholarship, sometimes with such authority that it matters to everyone. And senior scholars formed in a different mode of thought are among those who feel the change most sharply. To the extent that their nerve and intelligence, rather than their fashion sense, is the true object of praise, it may even be right to hold this among the late-coming and secondary reasons for admiring them. But in a walk of life that has much decency, these matters will not be talked of much. More particularly, the generational compliment will not be spoken by younger scholars who in delivering it are only flattering themselves. The act of inverted patronage is not so much presumptuous as it is simply out of place, considering from whom it comes. To a teacher who has mattered (as to parents and to certain friends), one has, by definition, a kind of debt that can never be paid back. The consolation is that the teacher has his or her debts, too; and so the source of the debt recedes, back to the beginning of time. As Kierkegaard pointed out in *The Case of the Contemporary Disciple*, the only way to achieve the illusion of escape from such a debt, without falling into vain pretense or despair, is so to intensify the aspect of the teacher which has mattered most that student and teacher come to seem identical for moments at a time. One then thinks of each as a transparent medium for the other. This is not accurate, of course—not how things could ever look to an intelligent and properly detached observer. It is merely the inward—the psychological, rather than the socialized—way for the disciple to unload the weight of a debt.

We have lately seen some awful scenes of unloading. The author of a catalogue in a recent museum show praises his patron and collaborator, an elder who happens to be the museum's director as well, for the proofs he continues to give of being *an incomparable learner*. A Renaissance scholar in a book review embraces his mentor for having adjusted to a trend with which the student's name is

identified. The author of a first book of criticism gives his dissertation supervisor high marks for *the consistent high quality of the
attention she gave to my work*. What do these reversals of piety, in
which by paying tribute to my teacher I pay a deeper tribute to
myself, have to do with the sixties in American culture? Nothing;
and everything. Nothing, because that was not a time when one
could praise a new friend, or a converted enemy, for seeing the
light that one carried on behalf of a collective *us*: you were not
good for being like me, no matter how many like-me's there were.
An ego trip at group rates was still an ego trip. Even to think
otherwise was considered noxious and cowardly—and so it is, and
so much the better for the sixties.

And yet it was also in the sixties that many young persons grew
used to hearing themselves flattered as a group, simply for being
young, for being a generation. "You're wonderful people"—how
many rock concerts began or ended with those words! This was
both a comfortable and a foolproof method of enhancement; who
that saw its uses would be so priggish as to refuse the offer? But
here we meet a puzzle. How was the same generation to keep its
hold on the collective praise which, by definition, it need have
done nothing to earn, but which like other forms of gratuitous
reward is hard to give up? Part of the solution we have seen in the
anecdotes of a paternalistic filial piety. The reward is not to be
given up by any means. The elders are to be kept distinctly as
elders; they make an incomparable foil. Meanwhile, the youngers
have the unique credit for good will, and the infallible self-justifi-
cation, which come from being recognized as worldly, authoritative, and uncorrupt all at once. The child of the sixties is still young;
and the child is father of the man.

Young, I said. Younger than whom? The author of this book is
forty. Most of the persons described here, for whom self-patronage
has become a way of life, are in their forties. Those who "came
over" early enough to get away with it are now in their fifties and
still getting younger. We will soon run out of elders to patronize.
A pity: for, up to now anyway, the game has held up well. We,
young boys and girls, are those who could never become old boys.

And we still complain of the old boys ("tweed-jacketed, pipe-smoking, clubby, anglophile") in a language pathetically outdated: it is the memory of a memory of somebody else's memory. (The authors of *Speaking for the Humanities* actually speak of the present "middle ground" in the humanities as committed to the transmission of a "gentlemanly ideal." Nobody has seen that ideal around the house for years.) The truth is that the old boy of today wears a leather jacket, or, with homage to *Miami Vice*, an imported linen jacket. The old girl wears monklike left-bank black on black. The forces that might once have concerted against such people getting promoted, and their habits and their costumes alike canonized, have now for some time ceased to exist. Even so, the tone of generational self-pity can be augmented, when suitable, by all the shades of generational bullying. It is an unpleasant mixture anywhere.

I have mentioned often in these pages the sixties-trained view that the university is a microcosm of society; and have noticed how easily the view can slip into the public language of administrators. It is a highly convenient notion because it cooperates with an older functional idea of education, a kind of anti-intellectualism that is never far from resurgence in this country. The idea of the university-as-microcosm also gives a symbolic focus to the moral-minded scholar who in actual politics is doing very little. The ad hoc curriculum reformer (the effect of whose efforts may include being able to teach directly some specialist topics of research) thus becomes one of society's unacknowledged legislators. The self-exalting tenor of such action-proof engagements may be delusive, but, by itself, it would be essentially harmless. Yet hand in hand with this belief has come a maxim of quietism which is destructive of all the impulses of reform. The maxim says that *one need do nothing but be oneself, nothing outside one's personal and professional routine, in order to conduct politics of the most effectual and admirable kind.* The trick of social-constructionist theory in literature has been to bring "local sites of resistance" into the professionalist routine. You can now get both moral and capital credit for pursuing a single piece of business.

Do nothing but what you do anyway. Teach your class just as

you would teach it anyway. As Fredric Jameson told an activist skeptic in an interview, Who knows but that all this may pan out some day?[10] And here is where the ideology of the eighties chimes in. What we in the academy tell ourselves about accomplishing a social good without a social effort, is exactly what the most popular instructor of that time, Ronald Reagan, was busy telling the nation as a whole. That you can get something for nothing *and get moral credit*, was the great teaching of his eight-year seminar. It bears its fruit each day in slogans like the one that recently helped defeat a school budget in the town where I live. Municipal employees had been laid off in considerable numbers, the reeducated citizens who had lately experienced some inconvenience were now being told that they should pay taxes for schools, and the slogan said: "Cut taxes, not jobs." It was magical thinking. How many of us now believe something like this magic? If the academic theorists I have been describing could have a slogan, it would surely be: "Do not distract me from the politics of theory by talking of mere politics. By engaging in one, I engage in the other as well, and besides I see no epistemological difference between them."

Of course, much of the influence of national quietism on institutional radicalism must have been unconscious, and it is hardly avoidable in the youngest grown-up generation, whose whole political experience has been circumscribed by Ronald Reagan. They have come of age in a political culture dominated by a man whose every unprompted utterance was a testimony to the amiability of thoughtlessness, and who, at the end of two terms characterized by immense popularity and an abuse of constitutional power, narrowly averted impeachment by a profession of total incompetence and memory loss. This man, before the last days in office when he spoke frankly of having "no recollection" of his mind, was, in fact, the most successful front-man of all time. Never would it be said of him: "Deep on his front engraven / Deliberation sat and public care." No. The enchantment he gave the American people was a message we have heard before in another connection. "You're wonderful people," he said, "like me; you don't have to do anything to prove it—perform any duty, test any virtue. Just being who we are in the system we have makes us as good as we can be. And the world is a better place for our being in it."

It would be a mistake to regard President Reagan's great work—the education of a whole society down to his level—as having affected the mind and habits of just one class or one political side. Outwardly hostile to everything he stood for, the academic culture of the left did not fail to extract every possible comfort from his message. That man, whose years in office will be marked by historians as a faultline in the passage of the American mind, on the other side of which everything had to begin again at a lower level—that weak and unattentive man, with his strong attitudes and stronger feel for the miraculous, taught the very rich that they could benefit society by benefiting themselves; while, with no less effect, he taught the middle classes that they could retain their prosperity and all the regalia of culture without renewing one particle of their former interest in education. The welfare of education, like the welfare of society, could be left to the experts. All this he taught by precept, but he also taught by example, simply by being who he was; day after day without blame, a president who had at his command not a fact of history more than two weeks old. The theorists of literature who suppose that today is the first day of the year zero are among his most faithful disciples.

These chapters have been concerned throughout with two, partly separable, subjects: the meaning of a tradition for society, in the performance of a citizen's duties; and the meaning of a tradition for learning, in the exercise of a teacher's judgment and imagination. The two activities touch only at points. The mind of someone engaged with an ideal object like a painting, a poem, or a play will not see the object consistently against a background of a tradition. Or rather, the tradition may define much about the interest the object claims, but it neither exhausts nor more than slenderly supplies its meaning. To suppose otherwise is to commit the fallacy of connecting every work of art, every possible use of the power of imagination, with a given framework of thought or practice. As a teacher interested in the tradition that has helped to form me, I will, to the extent that I am faithful to the works I am given to interpret, also be interested in knowing their tradition well. But I must not confuse this with knowing their reason for being. To make such a claim for tradition is to credit one more version of the argument I have disputed throughout: that culture—a genetic or communitarian or political or general "civilizing" culture—can be the all-important determinant of judgment for a person who thinks.

This leaves, of course, a puzzle for the teacher of literature. It would seem implausible, and perhaps, in some hard-to-capture moral sense, wrong also, to teach books in no order at all. Accordingly, if one prefers not to teach literature as a social science, one is apt to teach books in an order largely given by tradition. This means talking about them as if certain connections between them actually existed. Yet in the very degree that the connections are made to seem real, the work of teaching departs from the work of imagination and enters into an oppressive contract with culture. Anyone who has ever taught a book that mattered to himself or to herself—for as long as he or she was attentive to the book—cannot have felt that an idea of culture was at stake. It hardly comes into the matter. One's relation to a book is personal: it is mediated by experience and thought, which may themselves be "formed"; but concerning the laws of their formation, no one has said anything approaching the intelligence of the artists one is impelled to teach.

In civic or cultural terms, this places the person who teaches a book in an ironic position. One's views are not anti-cultural, in this light, so much as they are non-cultural. Doubtless a culture has its deep life somewhere—in museums, or on library shelves, in the rituals of a group saying a prayer, chanting a slogan, or lobbying for a new footnote style. All this is not what concerns the interpreter of a book. Still, the idea that the various works one explores are "all of a piece" makes a good story and gives a motive for a student's initial commitment of interest. It is success here that may draw a teacher closer to the belief that tradition is something substantial: as if an artistic tradition could imply acts of citizenship comparable in their solidity to the acts that may be required in social life. Books are not like that; they never could be. Every community of art is a community of one that wants to be two (not more). Its only criterion of truth is "I see it that way, too." Its only obligation is fixed by elective affinity. If I were asked to describe the teaching of literature as an activity that may be compatible, though it can hardly be congruent, with the activity of membership in a liberal society, I would say that its possible worth comes from considerations like the following.

Literature is an affair of books and authors; of books, more than of authors. Its value lies in the power of writing to communicate a human experience. This need not imply a description of something that has been "lived," or conceivably could have been lived, by a person in daily life, since there are experiences of the mind as of the body. In fact it is easier to say what writing accomplishes than what it describes. The aim is to create a mood of attention. The mood impresses us with a sensation that has the force of an imperative—the command to *Stop; Stand back; Respect,* which Kant associated with moral freedom and with aesthetic judgment. Moral and aesthetic thought thus share the task of inculcating a duty to treat persons as ends. Persons, and one category of objects which, it follows, must have a peculiar power to represent the dignity of persons. We honor in works of art as we do in persons the mere fact of their autonomy. Unexpectedly, this sense grows stronger and not weaker when we attend to books rather than to authors.

Literature may want to convert or persuade its readers to something besides a mood of attention: the preference for a certain way of life; a habit of valuing choice sensations; the strengthening of solidarity within a given social group. This persuasive aspect is useful to study but it is not itself what defines literature. When taken to explain comprehensively the motives of a writer's work, biography and history and sociology are likely to have the effect of making readers impatient, that is to say, unattentive to the words on a page. Wordsworth said in his Preface to *Lyrical Ballads* that just one "restriction" stood between the poet and his interpretation of the image of things. That restriction was the reader—in particular, the requirement of the poet that he give pleasure to the reader. Wordsworth guessed that the reader ideally could be imagined as an accidental listener to the dialogue of the poet's mind with itself. By contrast, the pragmatic bond between poet and reader, the limited contract of the poet's somehow having to give pleasure, might be regarded as an unhappy necessity or as a preservative of sanity for the otherwise solitary poet. Anyway the pleasure in question is not to be confused with a pleasing feeling. It can be any reminder of the "blind love" by which we are attached to life itself.

Literature is an abstraction part way down a chain of similar mental entities that begin as serviceable fictions and end as institutional lies. More vivid than "literature" are such ideas as the individual mind or the sense of a possible relationship between me and someone else. Less vivid is the idea of culture, and much less vivid are hegemonic structure, dominant ideology, discursive network. But the idea of culture is already close to a lie. We use it to suggest that works of art come to us grouped together, as if there subsisted among them, over time, a set of internal relations on which some elusive larger good depended. A debate about culture therefore is always a debate about lists of books. It deals with authors as a lump sum, and with readers in the mass. Once we suppose literature is nothing but authors conciliating the aggregate purposes of readers, the way lies open to the demand that authors conform to the social aims of a group. These come to us predigested, as the aims of a person do not. Yet if literature has held, in many times and places, a single common end it is that of breaking up every such group image by showing that the same words can matter immensely and matter differently to different persons. Only to a small extent can this lesson ever be taught. It would be better not to teach literature than to teach it as one among the many available techniques of mass persuasion.

No one can tell what literary study will become. I close therefore with some qualifications which may add up to a hope. The two sorts of group that have figured in this discussion—the ethnic community bound by an extracurricular identity, and the professional community bound by a shared psychology of research—are altogether discrete phenomena. The alliances of the moment may have made them appear for a moment the same, but in the long run, they operate from different imperatives and that fact is bound to be decisive. Within the profession alone, one must not forget the sheer range of scholars who have been drawn by the unlimited scope that the subject affords today. The gradual labor of treating, with sympathy and accuracy, an author to whom modern commentary offers scarcely a clue, will make for a discipline and a style of irony whose effects have just begun to be felt.

A fair survey now would have to proceed not place by place but person by person. For there is a risk in taking, as I have done, statements of high exposure as sentiments of high standing. If one credits the evidence of conversation and casual debate, views of an opposite kind seem to be widely entertained. That they are less widely articulated remains unfortunate but not baffling: positions until lately taken for granted do not lend themselves to quotable formulation. The uneasy institutionism of the present oddly resembles the principled anarchism to which it might one day yield. Generosity apart, most of the ingredients are there. Meanwhile the audience on all sides is full of questions that nobody planted—a condition to make the corporate body of text negotiators hum their tune more softly.

During the months that I spent completing this book, public interest in the subject of campus politics grew at an extraordinary clip. There were cover stories or feature stories in *Newsweek, Time, New York, Atlantic Monthly, Harper's;* a special issue of the *New Republic;* a long review with a protracted correspondence in the *New York Review of Books;* special coverage on TV news programs like *Nightline* and the *MacNeil-Lehrer Newshour.* The issue quickly became so current that George Bush, the most important conformist in America, whose forty years of public service are a standing discouragement to the very idea of self-trust, himself felt irresistibly drawn to claim the issue and put in a word for political nonconformity. This seemed to me a sign that the subject was close to being trashed beyond a hope of intelligent debate. Nevertheless, I have written the book; and a question now naturally arises: what accounts for the stir of interest outside the academy? There is a parallel and less obvious question to ask of persons inside. In a climate where the inquiries had been agitating for two or three years—though, until 1990, confined to the lower-circulation media—why had there not already emerged within the academy a substantial voice either of self-defense or self-criticism? Where the party that lacks information wants to hear so very much, why has the party in possession of the facts found so astonishingly little to say?

One reason for the clamor is that the public mind has long been deprived of any political issue. One reason for the silence is that the academic mind has grown unused to anything approaching democratic give and take. By the meager standards of today's politics, these doings have real interest, and the following particular topics have quickly come to prominence: multiculturalism; the threat to free speech; and a less easily framed supposition that the minds of students are now being subordinated to a new dogmatism. These issues may be linked by a single suspicion: that students are not learning things either useful or lasting enough; that the place of something central in education has been usurped by a lot of special interests. The something central may have been chiefly an ideal, but that need not void the suspicion of its force. It can be awful to realize that an ideal has been definitively lost. A well-remembered hope of American higher education was to leave a place for thinking, which did not attach thought, in any immediate way, to the pursuit of short-term rewards. It could always be replied that this was an elite ideal, possible for those to whom questions of status had been, up to a point anyway, agreeably settled. Others, now in the game for the first time, should not be expected to relax their pursuit of social gain even at the scene of education. This is a consistent reply but not therefore a settler of the argument.

All these doubts lead back to an intimation that learning itself may have become nothing but a pursuit of political power by other means; a conceit (for those who think this a *good* outcome) which often yields the following polemical deduction: "Since nothing we teach can be altogether isolated from the moral and political views we hold, let us, as efficiently as possible, adopt our own morality and politics as the self-conscious message of everything we teach." Since we can never be free of an interest and a signature, we are bound to make sure that every bit of canvas we fill gets daubed over with our most conspicuous trademarks. This curious argument many academics have broached to each other in school over the past few years. They have been reluctant to say it out of school because it could only excite the fears they seek to calm. Here, evidently, is a good tactical reason for the silence. Again: though public-minded academics feign a more than average disgust at the "sensationalism" of the journalistic treatment, they are inhibited from taking the objection far, because many of their own have theoretically established that there is no difference between sensation and thought, just as there is no difference between politics and education. Besides, it looks wrong to hold oneself above the battle: that would be elitism, and one is bound to reject elitism. Finally we are kept from disdaining the controversy as merely popular and therefore mindless, so many of us having so visibly embraced the popular and denounced the intellectual. In the new field of cultural studies, the derisive use of the term *intellectual* shows the easy absorption of an old populist bigotry into the academy itself. In short, the academics whose interests may lie in a strong reply are trapped. When somebody's inside statement is quoted suddenly before a larger audience—the klatch-opinion being taken as a genuine credo (which, of course, it was) and therefore as worthy of public scrutiny (which was not what it aimed at)—then the author of the statement feels at once trapped and outmaneuvered.

We have not yet witnessed the final scene of a drama in which there is now a heaped portion of resentment on both sides. The old defense of standards might have been the one clear protective gesture open to the academics under siege. But where standards have been decomposed into utility and interest by the leading theorists and association-leaders of the day, this proves to be another way out that has been closed from within. We have, or so our institutionist leaders tell us, no separable standard in the confused flux of American culture at large. We have, at most, separate rituals. Might we now claim therefore that we have our own culture ("academic culture"), which deserves as much respect as, say, a native culture under threat from a colonial power? This would be, anyway, a novel argument—hints of it have already appeared, and the full-blown thesis awaits only an institutional anthropologist both skillful and innocent of irony. To see ourselves as *natives under siege* would lend credibility as well to the poignant evocations of "community" from university presidents and other incapacitated local chieftains. The perspective of colonial victims could be, if not the light at the end of the tunnel, certainly an apt and acceptable light in the tunnel itself.

There remains a problem even with this elegant solution. After all, it is still a version of the ivory tower. In the last generation, we have executed a series of ever more intricate turns and dialectical involutions to prove to ourselves that we do not work in an ivory tower: that knowledge and interest go together in all-too-human ways, in every conceivable enterprise; that it is wrong to distinguish the knowledge of means from the knowledge of ends, as it is wrong to divide the pettiest from the most exalted interest; that every act of useless deference to an admired object probably serves the protective instinct of a still-to-be-exposed caste of ethical sages. We have become so clever that we have now proved to ourselves that no action on reflection, and no reflection on action, is possible. Scholars are not permitted even the illusion of sublime ends which common citizens do allow themselves to believe that they serve from time to time. What an odd outcome this is—and how consistent with the steps we took on the way. To guard against appearing precious, or anyhow remote from daily concerns, we conceded the very reverse of a disinterested explanation of all that we were doing. Yet the reverse of disinterested, in American culture, turns out to be not "engaged, passionate, socially committed," but rather "functional, corporate, scientifically cashable."

The scholar's old exemption from the claims of utility had never been more than partial, but it was founded on an interesting possibility: that the good of study, while not directly translatable into a social good, might always serve some distant and less measurable good. The commercial spirit of American society never had much time for this justification; it was always ready to pick up a more serviceable rationale, as soon as scholars would declare themselves willing. "If it doesn't lead to hard knowledge, useful knowledge, what's the good of it?" There is a true answer we have almost stopped giving: "The imaginative and interpretative part of education is a learned art, it is a moral habit, and it leads to people who can think. Do you see the good of that?" It has been said that the genius differs from the plodder in art only by virtue of taking certain options at a higher level. The old reasons for a liberal education depended on a generous idea of what might happen if enough citizens learned the arts and habits in question; the reasons may have carried extra weight from the hope that the same arts and habits could help a society to take *its* options at a higher level.

To the extent that the universities have junked this idea, they are now left to compete in the production of short-term goods.

Our arguments for doing what we do have grown so weak that one can understand those who would rather say nothing than rehearse these arguments in the wrong company. So much for the silence; what, then, of the scandalized mood of inquisition in the mass media? That too calls for explanation. The abuses by the new fundamentalists have been real; I have documented some of them; and a reader who has followed the magazines will know of many more. Yet, to a degree that surprises me, it has remained a scandal without suppression, an atrocity without victims, a protracted and grievous litigation without plaintiffs. Some commentators say that there is a silent majority of victims: today's students en masse. But it is remarkable how few students have come forward with complaints to match the jeremiads that are uttered on their behalf. The truth is that this seems to have become a subject on which the mood of many people veers regularly from calm to panic and then back. In writing this book I have become familiar with these alternations, and have done what I could to bring the two moods into contact.

The issue on which a steady alarm seems to me warranted is free speech. The harm that any dogmatic pedagogy, or that any number of exclusionist cultural ideals can do, is strictly limited so long as this freedom remains. Here we are likely to be saved by civil libertarians rather than by the academic left, which has talked itself out of an understanding of a principle. It has taken as an unquestioned maxim that the speech of historically disfranchised or "unempowered" groups holds priority over the speech of persons who are not thus defined. A natural corollary of this maxim—namely, that insults to the members of such groups are more grave than insults to persons already "empowered"—was all that anyone needed to produce the sensitive speech codes. The saddest fact of the controversy is that so many scholars have come to feel baffled at this point, uncertain what they ought to say or think about the principle of free speech. This is doubtless the central issue. But if it were the great issue in the public view, one would expect most of the fire of the press to be concentrated here. As far as I can judge, it has been treated only as one curiosity among many.

What most appeals to both the writers and the readers of these accounts seems to be the idea that the academy now is a hotbed for every exotic variety of dissent. Americans are taken up with this idea because it serves our appetite for politics. At present, it is almost the only thing that serves that function. And it is now for most of us a *vicarious* function. While the professor reforms the world in the classroom, the lazy world peers in—to be reminded or half-reminded what the thought of reform may look like. The world is right to complain about the quality of the instruction. The inhabitants of the classroom, if they could speak for themselves and did not depend for their lines on salaried demagogues, habitués of the think tank, and artists of the perpetual leave, might well complain that the product is dismal indeed but at least they make the pretense of an effort. Plainly, anyway, we are all in the same boat. We have no politics in America.

There is a terrible chance that can befall a society when too wide a distance opens between the use of power and the use of intellect. We expect some lag-time for the actions of one to catch up with the thoughts of the other. When the lag comes close to the length of a generation, a poison of inertia and bad faith sets in everywhere. For we do anticipate—it is an undeclared truth about a democratic society that we have a right to anticipate—the side that wins a battle of educated opinion to make some impression on the shape of subsequent policy. This holds acutely for a policy that has been a cause of much suffering. The drawing out of the Vietnam War was a critical instance of the defeat of such anticipations—the policy of one president having been exploded a full six years before another decided to end the war. Less than a decade later, a policy no less disastrous was pursued in fact after being exposed in public debate—a policy whose effects will reverberate far into the next century. This was the innovation which determined that prosperous citizens ought to pay as little as possible for the welfare of the society in which they prospered. The self-respect of a people can survive occasional massive errors like these; but the errors must eventually be faced; and they ought not to be too many, or too close together. At a time when the defeat of thought has become usual, a new class of alternative politicians will flourish. Those who have "nothing of politics but the passions they excite" will be drawn to displays of resistance as shocking as they are empty.

Our recent displays on campus are just one aspect of a general crisis in America. On one side, we have a place for practical politics without any contest of ideas or even, as it now seems, any contest of wills. On the other side is a mimic politics, haunted by the memory of something better, but paralyzed from venturing again on that doubtful terrain. The moral of the episode is the good of a liberal politics, and not the good of a liberal learning under per-petual and restless challenge. The experiment of allowing politi-cians to educate us down to their level has been tried. On the whole, it has worked out badly. The experiment of allowing edu-cators to politicize us down to their level may now have reached a temporary halt. But it, too, by its nature cannot work out well. We ought to recite these discoveries without regret, but not without a sense of the future to which they equally point. There will be no end of the unreal politics of the academy until we have again a real politics outside the academy. It cannot come too soon.

Chapter 1. The New Fundamentalists

1. Harold Rosenberg, "The Herd of Independent Minds" (1948), in *Discovering the Present* (Chicago, 1972). This essay is also remarkable for the following prophecy: "The mass-culture maker, who takes his start from the experience of others, is essentially a reflector of myths, and lacks concrete experiences to communicate. To him man is an object seen from the outside. Indeed it could be demonstrated that the modern mass-culture elite, even when it trots around the globe in search of historical hotspots every six months where the destiny of man is decided, actually has less experience than the rest of humanity, less even than the consumers of its products. To the professional of mass culture, knowledge is the knowledge of what is going on in other people; he trades his own experience for an experience of experience." For Rosenberg, mass culture in intellectual life as in the arts is defined by just this "trading" of experience.

2. August Wilson, "I Want a Black Director," *New York Times*, September 26, 1990.

3. On the uses of the sentiment *it takes one to know one*, I borrow a train of thought from Henry Levinson. The analysis of suffering and pride was suggested by a passage in Judith Shklar, *Ordinary Vices* (Cambridge, Mass., 1984): "It is . . . not only undignified to idealize political victims; it is also very dangerous. One of our political actualities is that the victims of political torture and injustice are often no better than their tormentors. They are only waiting to change places with the latter. . . . Even at the cost of misanthropy, one cannot afford to pretend that victimhood improves anyone in any way" (pp. 18–19).

4. Ralph Waldo Emerson, "Self-Reliance," in *Selections from Ralph Waldo Emerson*, ed. Stephen E. Whicher (Boston, 1957). The best modern gloss of the essay is that of T. W. Adorno in *Minima Moralia:* "To say 'we' and mean 'I' is one of the most recondite insults." He did not foresee the condition of a later human type who might say "we" and be capable of meaning only "we."

5. In a review of a recent anthology, *The New American History*, George M. Fredrickson notices the weight of "accentuation of the negative" by left-wing historians who work from an activist impulse. They run a risk of

blotting out all hope for the present—if the present is assumed in any way to follow the past. "One suspects," writes Fredrickson, "that historians who identify strongly with struggles for black, women's, or working-class liberation fear that celebration of past accomplishments will decrease the pressure for further changes. Paradoxically, the lack of a progressive past is seen as the spur to a progressive future." See George M. Fredrickson, "What Is the New History," *Dissent*, Summer 1991.

6. The emerging left consensus in reply to charges of "McCarthyism of the left" is to say that no one has lost an academic job in response to the conformist pressure of today. It is a clever answer, and exactly half true. Very likely the pressure is weaker now than it was in the 1950s when it came from the other side: many sectors of society were mobilized then; now it is only several powerful branches of a single profession. On the other hand, most of the people who would be likely to suffer loss of employment are too old now and too full of tenure for that to happen to them. At the earlier stages of recruitment, many jobs are lost before they are found from a gross or subtle failure of political decorum. See, in the present chapter, my account of the experiences of Professors Wallen and Holland at Hampshire College. So far as principle is concerned, the left academy is poorly armed to stop this sort of thing from happening again, more quickly when it can be managed, and of course with less publicity.

7. This view of the universities as a compensatory culture is seldom brought forward explicitly. It was, however, formulated with candor by Professor Gail Shepherd of Carnegie-Mellon University, in a letter to the *New Republic* responding to that journal's "Race on Campus" issue ("Your Turn," *New Republic*, April 15, 1991). "The truth," observed Shepherd, "is that the urban culture of poverty, the shocking rate of infant and adult mortality among populations wracked with AIDS, drug use, and myriad related social ills are precisely those issues now being debated in college classrooms. Indeed, *neither our government nor our media have the honesty to address them. Only our campuses have the courage to voice critiques*" (emphasis added). I agree with every point of the analysis. I differ from Shepherd in doubting that the universities can long support the moral burden with which they are loading themselves. Also, in taking this as their primary function, I suspect they may lose the competence and habits for performing other kinds of work to which their resources are better adapted.

8. Essays in social criticism as diverse as C. Wright Mills's causerie *The Power Elite*, Paul Goodman's *Growing Up Absurd*, and Richard Hofstadter's *Anti-Intellectualism in American Life*, concur on the significance of this change.

9. Lionel Trilling, "The Two Environments," in *Beyond Culture* (New York, 1965), p. 226.

10. Starting in the mid-seventies, when humanities enrollments went into decline, business schools and law schools saw a tremendous surge of new applicants. This is now in its third wave. The shift has been blamed by shallow observers on a falling off in the quality of teaching such subjects as history and literature. I see no evidence that this was true, and besides, it is not maintained by the same observers that for the period in question, the quality of teaching in business schools and law schools suddenly improved. Economic anxiety will account for most of what happened: the search for life-security, which used to be deferred for the length of a college career, began to haunt the prudent young as early as high school. The pattern unquestionably had the effect of shrinking the numbers of students with good preparation who went on to graduate study in the "second environment."

11. Trilling, "Two Environments," pp. 227–28.

12. On the growing intimacy of these connections, see Russell Jacoby, "The Greening of the University," *Dissent*, Spring 1991.

13. The lecture was given on November 7, 1990, and has not yet been published. I was an invited respondent, together with Professor Theodore De Bary of Columbia.

14. As near as I can estimate, fifteen students, over the past six years, talked to me of their sense of an unspoken limit on allowable opinions in class. It does not suggest a panic—but a teacher who claims *never* to have heard such a confidence is living under a stone. All of these conversations preceded the mass discussions of campus politics that began in mid-1990. I never brought up the topic and in each case was surprised by its grip on the student. The undergraduates were baffled or amused: they did not like what they saw but supposed that it need not affect them essentially. Often, too, they blamed other students rather than teachers for setting a restrictive tone. With graduate students the matter was more serious: they had relevant anecdotes from the job market.

15. On the French academy, see Thomas Crow, *Painters and Public Life in Eighteenth-Century Paris* (New Haven, 1985); on the Soviet academy, see *The Glasnost Papers*, a selection of articles translated by Barry Rubin and reprinted in the *New Republic*, February 20, 1989, including V. Chubinsky on *Darkness at Noon*, Dmitri S. Likhachov on *Dr. Zhivago*, Mikhail Polivanov on Nadezhda Mandelstam's memoirs, and Y. Kovalenko and E. Polianovsky on the career of Joseph Brodsky.

16. Michael Oakeshott, *The Voice of Liberal Learning*, ed. Timothy Fuller

(New Haven, 1989), pp. 23, 39, 49. My criticism here of "the reflection theory of education" is indebted to Oakeshott.

Chapter 2. Moral Education in the Age of Reagan

1. John Crowe Ransom, "Empirics in Politics," in *Poems and Essays,* Vintage edition (New York, 1955), p. 137.

2. Edmund Burke, *Works,* 12 vols. (Boston, 1869), 10:450–51.

3. Marcuse in "Repressive Tolerance," the essay that formed his contribution to the *Critique,* asserted that the range of opinions aired and admitted as serious by the American establishment, was narrow by comparison with the range of opinions worth hearing in politics. The liberal theory of tolerance thereby, in practice, assisted the de facto regulation of political expression. The same observation had earlier been made by C. Wright Mills, who pointed out that the Cold War slogans of the West, which never failed to mention speech as a primary liberty, concealed from the sloganeers themselves the timidity with which the right of speech was *used.* But Marcuse's argument had a second stage. Given the repressive ends to which the practice of a well-mannered tolerance was directed, the morality of a revolutionary vanguard today might oblige its members to enforce a compensatory intolerance. This could be seen as an inevitable consequence of the revolt against liberalism—a counter-practice which required no apology from people who knew beyond question that certain opinions were intolerable (for example, those that denied the humanity of whole classes or races).

In the early nineties, George Will became a strong critic of the "sensitive speech" codes I discussed in chapter 1, which aim, for the sake of a higher morality, to restrict first-amendment rights in educational communities. Will's recent objections have been framed in the language of liberal tolerance; yet his previous writings would seem to allow him no recourse to that language. Tolerance, he thinks, is a merely negative practice which in a genuine civil society must yield to the claims of a positive morality. There is thus no difference of principle between Will and the police of the left academy. They differ only in the choice of sensitivities in whose name they would enforce a selective intolerance.

4. Keats's phrase occurs in a journal letter to his brother and sister-in-law (April 21, 1819): "The common cognomen of this world among the misguided and superstitious is 'a vale of tears' from which we are to be redeemed by certain arbitrary interposition of God and taken to Heaven— What a little circumscribed straitened notion! Call the world if you please 'The vale of Soul-making.' Then you will find out the use of the world."

Keats explains the notion of soul-making by the supposition that "there may be intelligences or sparks of the divinity in millions—but they are not Souls till they acquire identities, till each one is personally itself." How then do souls acquire their individual existence? "How, but by the medium of a world like this?" In an earlier letter, he has said that he cherishes no other idea of Heaven than that of "having what we called happiness on Earth repeated in a finer tone and so repeated." See *The Letters of John Keats*, ed. Hyder E. Rollins, 2 vols. (Cambridge, Mass., 1958), 2:101–2, 1:185.

5. George Kateb, "Nuclear Weapons and Individual Rights," *Dissent*, Spring 1986, p. 172.

6. Writing in 1986, I had in mind a speech lately given by President Reagan in which he had said that the Contra army, then committing acts of systematic terror in Nicaragua, and supported in secret by money from the sale of arms to Iran, ought to be admired by all Americans because its gunmen were the "moral equivalent" of the Founding Fathers. Not long before, he had answered a question about the lot of the unemployed by alluding to the perfectly good jobs he himself had seen advertised in a newspaper.

The lies were acknowledged at the time, though they have since been covered by euphemisms—"laid-back management style" being only the most transparent. That phrase, the coinage of a 1986 presidential commission which palliated crimes of state as warmly as if it had been paid to do so, referred, as we now know, to a presidential "finding" of December 5, 1985, which authorized the illegal shipment of arms to Iran. Ronald Reagan saved himself from prosecution for this impeachable offense by claiming a special exemption that amounted to a plea of mental incompetence. In a review of Reagan's memoir *An American Life* (*New Republic*, September 9, 1991), Hendrik Hertzberg summarizes a view of his character which was familiar to the advisers and publicists who saw him from day to day. He is, by his own account, "a childlike and sometimes childish man. His head is full of stories. He is unable to think analytically. He is ignorant. He has notions about the way things work, but he doesn't notice when these notions contradict each other. He has difficulty distinguishing between fantasy and reality. He believes fervently in happy endings. He is passive and fatalistic. He cannot admit error." Not one element of this portrait was unknown to George Will. And yet, this man of mind imagined that such a president could, perhaps not govern, but somehow lead without governing, and do it without injuring the mind of the country.

7. George F. Will, *Statecraft as Soulcraft* (New York, 1983), p. 50.

8. William Hazlitt in *A Letter to William Gifford* first described the char-

acter of the government critic—"the invisible link, that connects literature with the police."

9. Will, *Statecraft as Soulcraft*, pp. 71–72.

10. David Bromwich, "Solzhenitsyn and Freedom of the Press," *Dissent*, Fall 1978, pp. 377–78.

11. Will, *Statecraft as Soulcraft*, pp. 145–46.

12. *The Correspondence of Edmund Burke*, ed. Thomas Copeland, 10 vols. (Chicago, 1958–78), 9:373.

13. In the regime of George Bush he has become more of a critic again. Starting with his description of Bush as a two-hundred-pound lapdog, it has been clear that Will finds this president easy to despise. By contrast, he cherished Reagan to the end as a man who had preserved an aura of personal amiability, notwithstanding everything that came to be known of his public dishonor. An honest social critic—particularly when, like Will, he writes as an advocate of "public life"—owes his readers a less capricious sorting out of private affection and public judgment.

14. In a very thorough response to the published version of this chapter, Neal Kozodoy, speaking for the Committee for the Free World (*Contentions*, November 1986), pointed out that the phrase "flesh of the flesh, blood of the blood" as used here by Bennett was an echo of a speech by Lincoln of July 10, 1858: "Mr. Bromwich may be allergic to religion, but his allergy has not caught up with his ignorance." I am twice grateful to Kozodoy for correcting my ignorance and for drawing to my attention a great specimen of American oratory.

The language and argument of Lincoln's speech reflect curiously on the quality of Bennett's echo. Lincoln is considering those Americans who are descended from the signers of the Declaration, in contrast with those who, though they trace no such descent, still feel a powerful adherence to an idea of American liberty.

We have besides these men—descended by blood from our ancestors— among us perhaps half our people who are not descended at all of these men, they are men who have come from Europe—German, Irish, and Scandinavian men that have come from Europe themselves, or whose ancestors have come hither and settled here, finding themselves our equals in all things. If they look back through this history to their connection with those days by blood, they find they have none, they cannot carry themselves back into that glorious epoch and make themselves feel that they are part of us, but when they look through that old Declaration of Independence they find that those old men say that "we hold these truths to be self-evident, that all men are created equal," and then they feel that that moral sentiment taught in that day evidences their relation to those men, that it is the father of all moral principle in them, and that they have a right to claim it as though they were blood of the blood, flesh of the flesh of the men who wrote that Declaration, and so they are. That is the electric cord in that Declaration that links the hearts of patriotic and liberty-loving men together, that will link these patriotic hearts as long as the love of freedom exists in the minds of men throughout the world.

The full context may be found in Abraham Lincoln, *Speeches and Writings 1832–1858*, ed. Don E. Fehrenbacher, Library of America edition (New York, 1989), pp. 455–56. All told, the speech is far from being an appeal to religious unity as a proper foundation of patriotism.

Lincoln, in fact, is particularly concerned to throw off the cloak of religious sanctity by which Stephen Douglas, in an earlier exchange, had seemed to cover the iniquity of the Dred Scott decision: "The sacredness that Judge Douglas throws around this decision, is a degree of sacredness that has never been before thrown around any other decision." As the passage above shows, Lincoln's use of "blood of the blood, flesh of the flesh" has a distinct prosaic intent; referring to the idea of association by lineage or inherited blood, his sense is as simple and unmysterious as Bennett's is trite and sacramental. The trouble with Bennett remains that though he may have known where the phrase came from, he did not know how to adapt it truly because he did not care what Lincoln meant. Bennett insinuates that belief in the Constitution *depends on a prior faith* in a religious doctrine of some sort (the doctrine that he calls "the Judeo-Christian ethic"—a phrase scarcely to be found in the works of nineteenth-century moralists or statesmen). Lincoln suggests that belief in the Constitution *involves a commitment as intense as faith* in religious doctrine. He makes this clear by speaking not of a heavenly father but a "father of all moral principle" in us—a particular depth of conviction, in describing which the secular phrase, "moral sentiment," says all that Lincoln wants to say.

15. Text courtesy of the U.S. Department of Education, 1986. Bennett chose to omit the speech from his collection of similar addresses, *Our Children and Our Country* (New York, 1988). That book covers the entire period during which William Bennett served as secretary of education—a time of the dismantling of the national program of university scholarships, reduced federal support for secondary schools, and falling academic performance on national examinations. As his preface attests, Bennett's speeches accounted for a large share of his activity in office.

16. These habits have held steady. In a column for *Newsweek*, April 21, 1991, Will explicitly offered the argument for great books as a key ingredient of national defense. Lynne Cheney, director of the National Endowment for the Humanities, was, he said, America's "secretary of domestic defense. The foreign adversaries her husband, Dick, must keep at bay are less dangerous, in the long run, than the domestic forces with which she must deal. Those forces are fighting against the conservation of the common culture that is the nation's social cement." If he really believes this, what stops Will from saying we should spend more money on education than on defense?

Chapter 3. The Limits of Institutional Radicalism

1. Quoted by Robert Detlefsen, "White Like Me," *New Republic*, April 10, 1989.

2. John Stuart Mill, "Bentham," in *The Philosophy of John Stuart Mill: Ethical, Political, and Religious*, ed. Marshall Cohen (New York, 1961), p. 30. The context is an enumeration of the aspects of life either insufficiently noticed or entirely neglected by the utilitarianism of Bentham: "There is no need to expatiate on the deficiencies of a system of ethics which does not pretend to aid individuals in the formation of their own character; which recognizes no such wish as that of self-culture, we may even say, no such power, as existing in human nature." Mill associates the want of provision for individuality with what might be supposed an opposite deficiency—namely, the indifference of Bentham's method to the culture of other or earlier selves. "Bentham," he says, "failed in deriving light from other minds."

3. This pattern of apology commonly goes with a story that the present discontents of the schools are just the usual tremors at the changing of a guard. The guard here is defined in generational terms; and thus the apology begs two questions at once. How long is a generation? Gertrude Stein in "Portraits and Repetition" remarked that "a generation can be anywhere from two years to a hundred years." This, she thought, was bound to be true for Americans above all, who measure existence itself by the mere fact of movement. A genuine movement of thought and feeling adds up to a generation; an irritant, whether acute or chronic, does not.

Besides, it remains unclear how far any generation, within which a good many beliefs may be shared, is obliged to acquiesce in its own extinction. Doubt on this score will grow more acute where the change in question implies the termination of those beliefs. The judgment from which a thinking person anyway has no power to abstain, is, whether a given transition is likely to produce effects for good or for ill. The fascist revolution in Europe brought, to the culture of several countries, a great shift of customs and habits, and not least in education. It was also indisputably a generational changing of the guard.

4. The anti-communist hunt of the fifties had just such an impact on American education; the adjustments of policy to fit the national mood appear a disgrace in retrospect. With the passing of William Bennett from the Department of Education and the apparent revival of libertarian principles among conservatives in education, the main threat of loyalty tests now seems to come from the left.

5. Quoted in Gerald Graff, *Professing Literature: An Institutional History* (Chicago, 1987), p. 262. The words are James Kincaid's, but similar formulations can be heard, these days, at almost any session of a professional colloquium on literature.

6. William James, "The Social Value of the College-Bred," in *Writings, 1902–1910,* ed. Bruce Kuklick, Library of America edition (New York, 1987), p. 1243.

7. Quoted by Michael Oakeshott, "The Voice of Poetry in the Conversation of Mankind," in *Rationalism in Politics,* Liberty Press expanded edition (Indianapolis, 1991), pp. 491–92.

8. David Norbrook, "Life and Death of Renaissance Man," *Raritan* 8 (Spring 1989): 101–2. In the eighties, the word *subversion* was widely adopted by critics of this school as a term of broad though unspecified approval; it could be applied to any cultural practice that was seen as daring and possibly dangerous. The corresponding term of reproach was *containment.* It is remarkable that neither sense held the slightest currency in the English Renaissance. Half consciously, the words were lifted from the lexicon of American Cold-War security, but with the values inverted.

"'Subversion,'" concludes Norbrook, "seems to imply the primacy of total destruction over any utopian possibility of building new moods of thinking and feeling" (p. 107); this matters less than may appear, for "the picture currently being constructed of Renaissance writers as timorously submissive to a vast machine of control goes far beyond the available evidence" (p. 103).

9. George Levine et al., *Speaking for the Humanities,* ACLS Occasional Paper no. 7, p. 8.

10. See Jeffrey Stout, *Ethics after Babel* (Boston, 1988), pp. 272–76, 285–86. Both here and in chapter 5, I am indebted to Stout's treatment of the distinction between internal and external goods.

11. Since these pages were written, Bork has emerged in his second career as a hero, martyr, and bearer-of-witness for the reactionary opinion-

makers I describe in chapter 2. His ideas are the same as theirs. He believes the right understanding of the Constitution can be derived from original "materials" embedded in the text. Even though we ask the Constitution to solve problems the Founding Fathers never saw—and therefore ask questions its framers could not anticipate—by a proper use of materials we can come to know which judgments the text favors and which judgments it frowns upon. Nor is such reconstruction a matter of fidelity to the *historical* usage of the late eighteenth century. Libertarian scholars have advocated a severe accuracy here; but Bork is not a libertarian. As much as Will and Bennett, he is a paternalist. The wisdom of the great document must be made to show that no social practice not explicitly licensed by the framers is consistent with the vision of the work they created; and this, in spite of the avowed belief of the framers themselves that manners and morals do not stand still forever.

Bork considers the function of a constitutional jurist to be supremely impersonal—sharing, in fact, attributes both of scientific reasoning and of priestly divination. It is an irony the jurist must live with that his or her acts occasionally will be subject to a personal gloss. When Bork was asked, by Senator Howell Heflin at the confirmation hearings, how, on becoming the acting attorney general in the last months of the Nixon White House, he had found the stamina to execute the president's first command and fire the Watergate special prosecutor, he replied that he knew the job would be intricate but, fortunately, the constitutional materials were there.

12. In "Teaching Like It Matters" (*Lingua Franca*, August 1991), Jane Tompkins defends an innovation in teaching that may satisfy both an interdisciplinary ambition and the program of "teaching the conflicts." Her argument, as will be seen, is anomalous in some respects, but from the point of view of traditional competence it is representative.

Early, says Tompkins, in a recent fall semester, she came to know far in advance that "I wouldn't have time to prepare my classes in the usual way." She was therefore impelled to borrow "a new teaching method from a colleague"; and in doing so, she discovered "a way to make teaching more enjoyable and less anxiety-producing." The method was to construct the syllabus herself but then let the students run the class. It worked, she felt, better than similar courses she had run in the past.

The following spring she taught another course, "in a subject I had been wanting to explore but knew little about." Tompkins does not name the subject in a single phrase; it appears to have been the relation between emotion, the history of sexual stereotypes, and epistemology: "I decided we would look at the way emotion had been dealt with in the West—in philosophy, psychology, anthropology, literature and literary criticism, and religious studies (this was an interdisciplinary course both in subject matter and in enrollment). We ended by looking at examples of feminist writing that integrated emotion and ideation both in substance and in form." As a literary scholar, Tompkins's field had been nineteenth-century American writing.

"Since I had no expertise," she continues, "in any of the areas we were dealing with except the literary, there was no way I could be responsible for presenting the material every time. So . . . I distributed responsibility for class presentations." A different small group of students took control of each class; but one aim throughout was "to break down the barrier between public discourse and private feeling." For, writes Tompkins, "I wanted never to lose sight of the fleshly, desiring selves who were engaged in discussing hegemony or ideology or whatever it happened to be." She got what she had looked for in breaking down more than one sort of boundary.

On some days, "people went at each other so destructively that students cried after class or got migraine headaches (I started getting migraine headaches after every class before long). There were huge misunderstandings, factions, discussions at cross purposes, floundering, a sense of incoherence"—in short, it was "in some respects a nightmare." But it was a good nightmare: "I never knew what was going to happen. Apart from a series of stunning self-revelations, wonderful readings added to the reading list by the students, and reports whose trajectory came as a total surprise, we were led, as a class, by the various reporting groups into role-playing, picture drawing, and even on one occasion into participating in a religious ceremony." The result for Tompkins has been that she "can never teach in the old way again"—as regards both the definition of a subject and the definition of teaching. "I know now that each student is a walking field of energy teeming with agendas. Knowing this, I can conduct my classes so as to tap into that energy field and elicit some of the agendas." The discovery is made to confirm a general aim she has declared at the start of the essay: that students and teachers should come to see *the classroom as a microcosm of society.*

Consider, in this frank narrative, two particulars that stand out vividly. First, a single teacher was supervising an interdisciplinary curriculum, a small part of which she admits to having mastered. The students did the rest, but it made a kind of sense: they, after all, came from various disciplines, even if the course was breaking such new ground that none of their equipment was any help. And second: conflicts were indeed taught here, "emotional" conflicts it is true—but that word, as the course proved, is the basis of a distinction without a meaning. It also happened that the conflicts had to be created in order to be taught. In this way preeminently, they may have forged a path for still newer innovations.

13. Friedrich Nietzsche, *The Gay Science*, trans. Walter Kaufmann (New York, 1974), sec. 50, pp. 114–15.

14. The best known academic uses of these corporate tactics have been the fast rebuilding of Duke's English department and the full-scale transfer of Johns Hopkins's French department to Emory University.

15. My position is closest to that of Collingwood, in *The Idea of History* (Oxford, 1946), who argues that the knowledge of history comes from a dialogue between historian and subject, and is always mediated by memory and self-knowledge, "the gap between present and past being bridged not only by the power of present thought to think of the past, but also by the power of past thought to reawaken itself in the present" (p. 294). Thus "the mere fact that someone has expressed his thoughts in writing, and that we possess his works, does not enable us to understand his thoughts. In order that we may be able to do so, we must come to the reading of them prepared with an experience sufficiently like his own to make those thoughts organic to it" (p. 300).

See Rorty, *Philosophy and the Mirror of Nature*, part 3, where the definition of "edifying philosophy" depends on an idea of conversation; and Oakeshott, "The Voice of Poetry in the Conversation of Mankind," in *Rationalism in Politics*, esp. pp. 488–95.

16. James, *Writings, 1902–1910*, pp. 1243–44.

Chapter 4. Reflection, Morality, and Tradition

1. Edmund Burke, *Reflections on the Revolution in France*, ed. Conor Cruise O'Brien, Penguin edition (Harmondsworth, 1969), pp. 192–93.

2. Ibid., pp. 176–77.

3. Ibid., p. 183. The comparable phrase in Butler comes from *The Analogy of Religion* (New York, 1961), chap. 5, p. 80.

4. David Hume, *Enquiry concerning the Principles of Morals*, in *Enquiries*, ed. L. A. Selby-Bigge, 2d ed. (Oxford, 1902), sec. I, p. 172.

5. Ibid., app. I, pp. 290–91.

6. Ibid., sec. I, p. 173. This is also a premise of Hume's essay "Of the Standard of Taste," which I defend in chapter 5 from some recent criticisms. The connection between taste and morality often eludes those who read the essay without knowledge of the *Enquiry concerning Morals*, of book III of the *Treatise of Human Nature*, or of the essay "Of Delicacy of Taste and Passion."

7. Hume, *Enquiry concerning Morals*, sec. III, pt. II, p. 199.

8. Annette Baier, "Secular Faith," in *Postures of the Mind* (Minneapolis, 1985), p. 304.

9. Ibid., p. 305. Baier's thought on the asymmetry of care is developed in chapter 9 of the same book ("Frankena and Hume on Points of View").

10. Immanuel Kant, *Idea for a Universal History,* in *The Philosophy of Kant,* ed. Carl J. Friedrich (New York, 1949), pp. 119–20.

11. John Rawls, *A Theory of Justice* (Cambridge, 1973), p. 289.

12. Mill, *On Liberty,* in *The Philosophy of John Stuart Mill: Ethical, Political, and Religious,* ed. Marshall Cohen (New York, 1961), p. 205. The nearest precedent for Mill's concern with the "lively impression" of personal thought comes from Mary Wollstonecraft's *Vindication of the Rights of Men* and her *Vindication of the Rights of Woman:* tracts composed, with a revisionist intent, entirely in the idiom of Hume and Burke. The strongest contemporary opponent of this view, James Fitzjames Stephen in *Liberty, Equality, Fraternity* (1874; reprint ed., Cambridge, 1967), replied that Mill had steadily confused the proposition "goodness is various" with the proposition "variety is good." If I believe that I hold the right view of conduct, and if I further suppose that all morality is founded on consensus, the benefit I gain in sustaining my view will more than offset the loss I suffer from prohibiting certain kinds of expression and action.

Stephen faces directly the question of the survival of early Christianity on such stringent terms—that is, at a time when the faith was militant and proscribed, and seemed to be chiefly a force for disorder. "Was Pilate right in crucifying Christ? I reply, Pilate's paramount duty was to preserve the peace in Palestine, to form the best judgment he could as to the means required for that purpose, and to act upon it when it was formed. Therefore, if and in so far as he believed, in good faith and on reasonable grounds, that what he did was necessary for the preservation of the peace of Palestine, he was right" (p. 110). He then imagines the analogous position of a modern Pilate, "an English Lieutenant-Governor of the Punjab," who receives from the established priesthood "complaints against the new religious reformer curiously like those which orthodox Mahommedans make against Wahabee preachers, or orthodox Sikhs against Kookas" (p. 114). The analogy gives added weight to Stephen's conviction that a man so placed may be bound by the duty of his office to act as Pilate acted. The proper criticism of the Roman system thus is not that it persecuted Christianity, but that Pilate and his successors did so in a "brutal and clumsy" way, "just enough to irritate their antagonists, to give them a series of moral victories, and not enough to crush and exterminate" (p. 116). Had the persecution been at once severer and more consistent, the contest of beliefs might have worked to the mutual improvement of Roman and Christian morality: "If they had met as enemies in spirit, would they not have been generous enemies? If there had been strife, would it not have been noble strife?" (pp. 118–19). Stephen makes it plain that he regards such a contest of force as cleaner and ultimately less destructive than an unrestricted clash of opinions—the Mill-like outcome which, in fact, the Roman empire got from its indulgence of a wavering policy toward the insurgent faith, "a touching though slightly hysterical victim mauled from time to time by a sleepy tyrant in his intervals of fury" (p. 118).

Stephen rather than Mill is the ancestor of the modern adepts of moral education whom I canvass in chapter 2, and the theorists of education as a fight for institutional power, whom I consider in chapter 3 as well as in chapter 5, below. Like the radical institutionists in particular, he admits no distinction between persuasion and force: "Persuasion, indeed, is a kind of force. It consists in showing a person the consequences of his actions. It is, in a word, force applied through the mind. Force, on the other hand, is a kind of persuasion" (pp. 129–30). The idea of progress with which he is able to incorporate such views is progress solely with reference to society. The progress of a person drops out of the picture—and is, it would seem on his view, always a fantasy anyway. For Stephen and his successors, what becomes of "the entire moral courage of the human mind"? Perhaps it is fair to say that with them the individual may claim a share in the *self-confidence* of a society. But self-respect no more belongs to a society than charity belongs to a building; and there is no place in this account for the singular liberal and modern virtue of self-respect.

Chapter 5. The Case of Literary Study

1. A distinction remains important. Existentialism was in its way a heroic creed; deconstruction aimed to be a non-infectant therapy. The difference springs in part from the pressure under which an idea of the self develops. In existentialism, that pressure is enormous: the self is cut loose from moorings in the object-world as in the world of other people; nothing sustains it, moves it forward, apart from the energy of choice and the proof of choice in action. In deconstruction, all the pressure has let up and the self has vanished. The questioning may continue but the object-world has absorbed any voice that might offer response—the world being defined of course as a text, just as the self is now a text. Hence the dogma that *language speaks me.*

2. Quoted in Richard Rorty, *Essays on Heidegger and Others* (Cambridge, Mass., 1991), p. 129.

3. Lionel Gossman, *Between History and Literature* (Cambridge, Mass.,

1990), aims to preserve an idea of imaginative accuracy from the rival claims of memory and social myth; Sabina Lovibond, "Feminism and Postmodernism," *New Left Review* 178 (1989): 5–28, treats feminism as part of the Enlightenment project of human autonomy that is not yet finished.

4. Oakeshott, *The Voice of Liberal Learning*, ed. Timothy Fuller (New Haven, 1989), p. 69. The point about "distance" applies, as I notice elsewhere, to distance in space and not only in time. Doubtless the latter appeals more vividly to a scholar of literature because it includes an idea of the depth and resonance that grow over time within a single language. The question is likely to appear in a different light to a scholar of religion or anthropology, for whom testimony that is contemporary, and comes from persons divided from oneself by the strangeness of their beliefs, may be a comparable source of wonder. The two sorts of evidence in any case engage the same faculty of imagination.

5. Barbara Herrnstein Smith, *Contingencies of Value: Alternative Perspectives for Critical Theory* (Cambridge, Mass., 1988).

6. Ibid., p. 84.

7. Ibid., p. 34.

8. Allan Bloom, *Giants and Dwarfs: Essays, 1960–1990* (New York, 1990).

9. Ibid., p. 93.

10. My paraphrase covers a passage from an interview of Jameson that has achieved wide currency: "As far as 'the political' is concerned, any single-slot, single-function definition of it is worse than misleading, it is paralyzing. We are, after all, fragmented beings, living in a host of separate reality-compartments simultaneously; in *each one of those* a certain kind of politics is possible, and if we have enough energy, it would be desirable to conduct all the forms of political activity simultaneously." I take the quotation from Jonathan Arac, *Critical Genealogies* (New York, 1987), p. 306.

Jameson goes on to warn of a possible misunderstanding, "the misconception that when one modestly outlines a certain form of political activity—such as that which intellectuals in the university can engage in—this 'program' is meant to suggest that this is the *only* kind of politics one should do." But it is too late for regrets like these: he has promoted this very misunderstanding among his academic followers by describing the accidents of their daily life as "a kind of politics" on an equal footing with any other; indeed, a kind of political *activity*; and even in the reserve-clause, he speaks of it as advancing nothing less than a *program*. True, he places *program* in inverted commas; but then, *politics* gets inverted commas, too.

Let us descend from these heights. *Every thing is what it is and not another thing.* There are contexts in which saying so may bring discussion prematurely to a close; others, in which it is the only certain charm against imposture. I am for a "single-slot, single function" idea of politics, when I see what the opposite looks like. Politics means thought and action respecting our relations with one another as members of a society. That is, members of a given rather than a chosen community; a community with which we cannot negotiate terms quite at pleasure; a group we are bound to, even if bound by voluntary loyalty; a place we more than visit, and not a chamber we enter and pass from periodically. A community is real enough and demanding enough and just because it is we do not ask that it be other things. Nor do we honor other things by pretending that they are it.

Schiller, Friedrich, 216
Schmidt, Benno C., 35
Shakespeare, William: low regard for
ethnic central casting, 12–13; and
for lost unity of civilization, 216;
poetry v. rhetoric, 216
WORKS
The Merchant of Venice, 216–17;
Richard II, 217–19
Shaw, George Bernard, 156, 211
Shepherd, Gail, 238n7
Shklar, Judith, 237n3
Sidney, Sir Philip, 215
Smith, Barbara Herrnstein: anti-
aesthetic theorist of taste, 204,
212–14; curricular implications of
theory, 205; behaviorist and utilitarian, 206; invokes epistemology,
206, 208–9; idea of contingency in
person, 206–7; and in culture, 207–
11
Smith, Robert C., 23–26
Solzhenitsyn, Alexander, 76
Sommers, Christina Hoff, 26–29
Speaking for the Humanities, 115, 190–
92, 223
Speech: sensitivity codes devised to
regulate, 8–9; academic politics
presumed to determine in Wallen
and Holland case, 9–10; construed
as action to prosecute Hann case,
30–33; Mill's defense reviewed,
161–63; importance of freedom asserted, 234–35; how far con-
strained in classroom, 239n14
Stein, Gertrude, 244n3
Stephen, James Fitzjames, 249n12
Stout, Jeffrey, 245n10
Strauss, Leo, 60

Theory, interdisciplinary: used as scientific legitimating device, 106–7;
as expedient in comparatist training, 173–74; sources in perspec-
tivist thought, 185–87, 210–11;
confidence of adepts, 201–3; and

speculative purity, 202–3; and inhibition, 203–4
Theory, social constructionist: rise in
literary study, 191–92; varieties of,
198; some common axioms, 198–
202
Tompkins, Jane, 246n12
Trilling, Lionel: "The Two Environments," 36–38; "On the Teaching
of Modern Literature," 170

University: sees itself as compensatory culture, 32, 44, 47–49, 238n8;
may reflect what society already is,
42–43; sees itself as microcosm, 43–
44, 116, 119–20, 223, 235, 246n12;
may teach possibility of self-culture, 102–3
Utilitarianism: contrasted with idea
of general utility, 149–50, 160–61;
and behaviorist theory of value,
204–6, 209; cost-benefit analysis of
poetry, 210; failure to draw light
from other minds, 244n2

Wallen, Jeffrey, 9–10
Will, George F.: platitudes we live
by, 56; culture as redemption, 57,
65–66, 83; public apologist for Reagan, 57–58, 242n13; reaction
against sixties, 58; secular morals
not enough, 58–59, 63–65, 73–75,
95–96; zeal for civic virtue, 58–60,
80–82; distrust of liberal tolerance,
59–60, 63–70; compared with Marcuse, 60, 242n3; a corrective to errors of Founding Fathers, 63; core
consensus of West, 63–64; soulcraft
defined, 64; supervision of inner
lives, 68–70; soulcraft deficiencies
of modernism, 71–72; and of
American novels, 72–73; legacy of
soulcraft, 77–78; private friend of
Reagan, 80–82; culture as immune
system, 95–96, 244n16. *See also* Paternalism